Isle of Rum

*Havana Club, Cultural Mediation, and the
Fight for Cuban Authenticity*

Christopher Chávez

RUTGERS UNIVERSITY PRESS
NEW BRUNSWICK, CAMDEN, AND NEWARK, NEW JERSEY
LONDON AND OXFORD

Rutgers University Press is a department of Rutgers, The State University of New Jersey, one of the leading public research universities in the nation. By publishing worldwide, it furthers the University's mission of dedication to excellence in teaching, scholarship, research, and clinical care.

Library of Congress Cataloging-in-Publication Data

Names: Chávez, Christopher, author.
Title: Isle of rum : Havana Club, cultural mediation, and the fight for Cuban authenticity / Christopher Chávez.
Description: New Brunswick : Rutgers University Press, [2024] | Includes bibliographical references and index.
Identifiers: LCCN 2023051481 | ISBN 9781978838840 (hardcover) | ISBN 9781978838833 (paperback) | ISBN 9781978838857 (epub) | ISBN 9781978838864 (pdf)
Subjects: LCSH: Advertising—Rum—Cuba. | Rum industry—Cuba. | Nationalism in advertising—Cuba. | Government business enterprises—Cuba. | Cultural diplomacy—Cuba.
Classification: LCC HF6161.L46 C43 2024 | DDC 659.19/66359097291—dc23/eng/20240506
LC record available at https://lccn.loc.gov/2023051481

A British Cataloging-in-Publication record for this book is available from the British Library.

Copyright © 2024 by Christopher Chávez

All rights reserved

No part of this book may be reproduced or utilized in any form or by any means, electronic or mechanical, or by any information storage and retrieval system, without written permission from the publisher. Please contact Rutgers University Press, 106 Somerset Street, New Brunswick, NJ 08901. The only exception to this prohibition is "fair use" as defined by U.S. copyright law.

References to internet websites (URLs) were accurate at the time of writing. Neither the author nor Rutgers University Press is responsible for URLs that may have expired or changed since the manuscript was prepared.

⊚ The paper used in this publication meets the requirements of the American National Standard for Information Sciences—Permanence of Paper for Printed Library Materials, ANSI Z39.48-1992.

rutgersuniversitypress.org

For Judy, Alexandra, and Daniela. And for my mother.

Contents

    Introduction   1

1 Advertising and Authenticity   24

2 Selling Cuban Culture   47

3 Long-Distance Nationalism and the Logic of Capitalism   69

4 Museums and Memory   92

5 Rum, Race, and Representation   113

6 The Losing Game of Authenticity   135

    Acknowledgments   157
    Notes   159
    References   161
    Index   173

Isle of Rum

Introduction

But we are not capitalists, Mario. We know nothing about capitalism. We are socialists. And we are participating in this adventure to come into contact with capitalist economies from all over the world, in the midst of the US blockade. Conditions are special here, and we are learning. We have been resorting to our common sense, to our rationale, and to our criteria.
—Fidel Castro, interview with Mexico's director general, Mario Vázquez Raña,1995

On November 3, 2014, a crowd of young, attractive, British tastemakers gathered at the Lighthouse Bar and Club in East London's arts district of Shoreditch. They were there to celebrate the launch of *Havana Cultura Mix—The SoundClash!*, a musical collaboration between British deejay Gilles Peterson and Havana Club International, the producers of Cuba's state brand of rum. As part of the album, ten amateur deejays from around the world were selected by Peterson to travel to Havana, work closely with Cuban musicians, and create new interpretations of original music. The product of this effort is a compilation that includes an eclectic mix of hip-hop, R&B, and Afro-Cuban jazz.

The participating deejays came from all over the globe, including Germany, Chile, South Africa, and Russia. A short film documenting the making of the album (Havana Club International 2014) depicts the project as a sort of foreign expedition, in which the artists traveled to an unexplored land with the purpose of "discovering" and then developing untapped Cuban talent. Peterson, in turn, serves as the viewer's tour guide to the Cuban music scene. There is footage of the group evaluating local Cuban musicians. Other scenes depict the deejays wandering through downtown Havana and interacting with local artists and musicians.

A highlight of the film features a recording session in Hávana's famous Abdala Studios, in which the deejays are working directly with Cuban musicians to develop music for the album. During an interview, Hungarian deejay Géza Szekeres, who goes by the name of Chillum Trio, describes the opportunity to record at Abdala Studios as a purer, more authentic creative experience: "It's an amazing place. The architecture is so perfect. The technic [sic] is so great. The guys are amazing. It's a great thing to be here, you know. Because we all work in digital environments. All digital. All in bits. Then we traveled back in time here, to the age of the analog. It's so real, so human" (Havana Club International 2014).

Szekeres's characterization of the experience as "traveling back in time" connects to ongoing discourses about Havana itself. As James Clifford Kent (2019) argues, Havana has long been perceived in Western imagination as a city that has been frozen in time, as if life on the island had simply ceased to evolve in 1959. This characterization of Cuba's capital also connects to a general dissatisfaction with modernity, in which individuals seek genuine experiences and emotions by consuming products and experiences associated with historical periods and other cultures (MacCannell 2013).

Szekeres also taps into a second preconception, which is that Cuba is a repository of untapped resources, open to foreign development. Despite the labor of local musicians, actual Cubans play only a peripheral role in the video. The focus is squarely on the foreign producers. Given the commercial nature of the enterprise, the filmmakers made sure to convey a sense of transnational solidarity. Deejay Noi5er, from Chile, described the project as a form of musical exchange: "Being here in Cuba, getting to know so many new people. Sharing with the others from Russia, South Africa, Switzerland, Holland . . . and with people that live on the island. It's a fantastic experience" (Havana Club International 2014).

This feeling of transnational solidarity was incorporated into the launch party itself, which was intended for British tastemakers but which showcased Cuban culture. Peterson served as host, while East London's Rukaiya, one of the album's featured deejays, performed at the event. Yet the party had a distinct Caribbean theme. Guests were treated to Cuban food, cocktails, and music, and the highlight of the evening was a live performance from Afro-Cuban musician Daymé Arocena, who was a rising star at the time. Described by NPR's Felix Contreras as "a magical mash up of The Queen of Latin Music, Celia Cruz, and The Queen of Soul, Aretha Franklin" (Contreras 2017), Arocena has become a featured artist for Peterson's record label, Brownswood Recordings.

Ultimately, however, the film, the album, and its launch party were designed to facilitate the sale of Havana Club rum to international markets. It is no accident that the album's deejays hail from markets that have strategic importance for Havana Club. A video crew shot footage of the party, which was later edited into short videos and then uploaded onto YouTube for marketing purposes. These videos connect the brand to images of beautiful, young, diverse bodies, engaging the viewer in a sort of postracial fantasy. Furthermore, the Havana Club logo was ubiquitous. Depictions of young Britons, wearing Panama hats with Havana Club branding, were spliced together with images of bartenders mixing Cuban cocktails.

Havana Cultura Mix—The SoundClash! is the fifth album that was produced as part of Havana Cultura, an effort to promote Cuba's state brand of rum while serving as a global platform for the promotion of Cuban culture in multiple forms, including music, visual arts, film, and design. Launched in 2007, Havana Cultura was conceived by global advertising agency M&C Saatchi, which was tasked with establishing product superiority against other rum brands, several of which also have ties to the Caribbean. To distinguish the brand in a crowded spirits marketplace, the agency decided to leverage Cuban culture as a point of differentiation. According to the agency, "We wanted to embody Cuban culture and become the reference. We designed a communication program on three dimensions that we called Havanización: (1) Sharing Cuban culture, (2) promoting contemporary Cuban culture, and (3) making people experience Cuban culture" (Cannes 2013).

Havana Club's goal of leveraging the state's proprietary relationship with Cuban artists has been a measurable success. Since the Cuban State entered into its partnership with Pernod Ricard, Havana Club has grown into one of the largest rum brands in the world, and it has become competitive in the United Kingdom, Germany, France, Italy, and Spain. The success of Havana Club makes apparent that just two decades after Castro declared Cuba's Special Period in a Time of Peace, the Cuban State had become quite proficient in the practices of capitalism.

Havana Club International may be viewed as the product of the larger process of economic reform, which was meant to reintegrate Cuba into global markets. To achieve this objective, the Cuban State recognized that Cuban culture could help differentiate the Havana Club brand in the global marketplace. Over time, the Cuban government has proven to be effective at employing cultural products (dance, music, and film) and commodities (cigars, rum, and technology) to support diverse political, diplomatic, and economic goals (Bustamante and Sweig 2008). Therefore, Havana Club's efforts can also be seen as a form of cultural diplomacy (L'Etang 2009) in which soft power is directed toward developing emotional bonds with overseas domestic publics.

Whether or not these efforts adhere to the principles of the state, as Castro claimed in 1995, is uncertain. Cuba's economic and political goals are largely accomplished with the help of creative partners, who are based primarily in the West, and who are quite adept in marketing practices. These kinds of partnerships have become more common in Cuba's post–Special Period. As Sujatha Fernandes (2006) notes, the Cuban State has increasingly capitalized on Cuban culture through the foreign licensing of Cuban records, joint film productions with overseas companies, and the sale of Cuban art to foreign buyers. These activities have enabled the Cuban government to generate much-needed revenue.

Let us consider the various players who are involved in the *SoundClash!* project. First, there is Havana Club International, which is a joint venture between Pernod Ricard, a global spirits marketer based in Paris, and Corporación Cuba Ron, the state's producer of rum. Pernod Ricard, in turn, hired M&C Saatchi, a global advertising agency based in London but with satellite offices all over the world, including Paris, which runs the Havana Club campaign. To help execute the music component of the effort, the agency recruited a British deejay to produce the album and host its launch.

The launch party itself was an exercise in event marketing. The celebration was organized by London-based Mistral Productions, an experiential marketing company that specializes in courting influencers. In their words, they specialize in producing "content which appeals to taste-making, forward-facing audiences around the world" (Mistral Productions 2022). However, the true purpose was to use the event to produce a set of videos that would showcase the product to viewers all over the world. The careful orchestration between the brand, the agency, the record label, and the event marketing firm involved a set of players who are extremely proficient in navigating the marketplace.

Focusing on Havana Club as a case study, I examine the ways in which various cultural producers, based primarily in Western Europe and the United States, have assumed responsibility for representing Cuba to the outside world. I focus specifically on the role of corporate executives, working in collaboration with advertising practitioners, music producers, filmmakers, and art curators, who collectively broker between the Cuban State and Western consumers, who desperately crave authentic experiences that exist outside the purview of the marketplace.

But what, exactly, is an authentic Cuba? As Anna Cristina Pertierra (2011) points out, Cuba is a complicated concept that will shift depending on one's point of view. For some, Cuba has come to signify repression and poverty. For Cubans living in the diaspora, the island can represent displacement and the loss of private property. For would-be tourists, Cuba is the embodiment of rich cultural expression. And for many across the Spanish-speaking world, Cuba remains a symbol of resistance to U.S. hegemony.

In this book, I argue that Western representations of Cuba are, to varying degrees, filtered through the logic of capitalism. However, Havana Club raises unique considerations. Most forms of commercial discourses are designed to benefit private enterprises, yet Havana Club is also a product of the state, which means that it generates revenue while simultaneously advancing Cuba's political interests. In the process of selling rum, Havana Club uniquely promotes musicians, artists, and filmmakers, thereby serving as a kind of cultural diplomacy (L'Etang 2009), aimed at developing emotional bonds with overseas domestic publics to gain their identification and sympathy. Havana Club's marketing efforts, therefore, can translate into the flow of economic resources into the island, while also promoting Cuba's influence in the geopolitical landscape.

Western cultural producers themselves stand to profit by advancing various iterations of Cuba to the world. Here I am interested in the ways in which cultural producers, working on behalf of the Cuban State, negotiate competing, and sometimes contradictory, goals. After all, leveraging Cuban culture to sell rum necessarily requires a rearticulation of an entire political ideology, which has the dual effect of selling a global commodity while simultaneously advancing socialist ideals. The presence of Western brokers who profit from the sale of Cuban commodities and culture is not new, but rather links to an ongoing history of exploitation on the island.

Sugar Island: The Politics of Sugarcane and Rum

In 2019, the Museo Nacional de Bellas Artes de La Habana held an exhibit titled *Isla de Azúcar* (Sugar Island), as part of the XIII Havana Biennial, one of the largest visual arts events in Cuba. The event itself is a contradiction. On one hand, the Biennial promotes tourism and facilitates the sale of Cuban art to international buyers. On the other hand, the event provides a highly public platform for Cuban artists to critique the state's ambivalent relationship with capitalism.

Isla de Azúcar delivered on the museum's larger theme "La Posibilidad Infinita: Pensar la Nación," a suite of five shows exploring Cuban history, identity, and ideas of nationhood. Artists, working across mediums, explored the ways in which the rise of the sugar industry and its by-products have profoundly shaped Cuban politics and culture. In her description of the exhibition, the museum's curator, Carina Matamoros, wrote, "Not only art, but the whole national culture is illuminated by sugar. The sugar industry penetrated life in almost all areas: technology, social thought, popular culture or the collective imaginary" (*Cuban Art News* 2019). Matamoros later added that "sugarcane carries both sweetness and thought. An industry associated by history to the ignominy of slavery and its aftermath. A monoculture that raised us to the world's leading producer of both sweetness and devastating decay. Cuban artistic production has explored our famous manufacturing through diverse perspectives for four centuries."

Some of the art was ethnographic in nature, including nineteenth-century illustrations by French lithographer Eduardo Laplante, whose series *Los Ingenios de Cuba* documents the architecture, layout, and social conditions of the island's prominent sugar mills during the mid-nineteenth century. The paintings are notable for not only their depiction of the distilleries but also the slave labor involved in its production. Others were more critical, highlighting the connections between the sugar industry, capitalism, and the transatlantic slave trade.

For example, the exhibit featured a painting by Pedro Álvarez Castelló, an artist who rose to prominence under Castro's Special Period in a Time of Peace.

Much of Álvarez's work juxtaposes Western popular culture with traditional Cuban images, such as nineteenth-century peasants and troubadours (Álvarez 2008). The painting that was included in this exhibition is titled *La Canción del Amor* (1995) and has anachronistic figures set against a colonial background. Álvarez foregrounds two kinds of sugar-based drinks that exemplify foreign domination and racial inequity in Cuba. In the foreground, a Coca-Cola delivery man, painted in the style of a 1950s-era advertisement, is carrying a palette of the product. He gives a welcoming gesture to a young, white Cuban boy driving a toy car of the same era. In the background is a colonial-era Afro-Cuban couple, looking distressed and holding an empty, unbranded bottle of rum. By juxtaposing Coca-Cola and rum, Álvarez draws attention to how the marketplace has become the new site of domination. Power, once exercised through colonial force, is now accomplished through the benign face of consumerism.

Sugarcane and rum have followed different paths to economic importance for Cuba, yet their histories are inextricably linked. Sugar was always intended as an export product, whereas rum became an unexpected by-product of sugar production (Smith 2005). Rum is made from molasses, collected during the boiling, refining, and packing processes. Using molasses to make rum originally added value to the sugarcane crop by making practical use of something that would otherwise be discarded as waste or fed to animals (Gust and Matthews 2020). Both products, however, share a common history of intervention, oppression, and exploitation. More than other commodities in the Americas, sugarcane and rum were inextricably linked to the transatlantic slave trade.

Both sugar and rum have also been subject to the exploitation by foreign actors: first by the Spanish, who over the course of 400 years of colonial rule extracted profits through sugar production, all but ensuring Cuba's reliance on Madrid. After Cuba gained its independence from Spain, the United States maintained a significant military and political presence on this island, on and off, for almost twelve years. During their occupation of the island, the United States imposed economic policies, which affixed Cuba's position as a monocrop economy. Cuba's subordinate role to the United States had become so firmly entrenched that *National Geographic* casually labeled the country "America's Sugar Bowl" (Grosvenor 1947). The 1959 Cuban Revolution was meant to free Cuba from foreign influence, but for decades the island depended heavily on the Soviet Union for basic everyday commodities related to food, hygiene, transportation. Today the island relies heavily on its partnerships with transnational corporations to provide much needed revenue.

A Brief History of Cuban Rum

Sugarcane was first carried to the Caribbean by Christopher Columbus, who during his second voyage in 1493 brought with him several hundred sugarcane shoots from the Canary Islands, as well as experts on sugarcane cultivation (Barty-King 1983). From that point, a burgeoning sugar industry emerged expeditiously. Cuba's reliance on sugarcane came from the simple reason that it was one of the few crops that would grow in the area. The unique climate and soil, combined with a forced workforce provided the conditions necessary to produce sugar on a mass scale.

In Cuba, the goal was always to find ways to convert sugarcane into an export commodity that would benefit Spain. Shortly after the first *ingenio* was established in 1516, the Spanish government invested heavily in the establishment of a thriving sugar industry, which involved a network of planters, refiners, bankers, shippers, and government officials (Mintz 1985). As Fernando Ortiz points out in *Cuban Counterpoint* (1995), if a colonial entrepreneur wanted to cultivate sugar, the Spanish monarchy would readily provide the land grants for plantations, subsidies for bringing in expert workmen, and tax exemptions that would incentivize production. If financial difficulties were encountered, the entrepreneur could lobby for the cancellation of debts.

The profitability of Cuba's sugar production would not have been possible if not for the use of forced labor. The Siboneys and the Taínos were wiped out by enslavement, massacre, and disease, prompting the Spanish monarchy to sanction the importing of slave labor from West Africa. This practice increased exponentially during the brief period of British occupation from 1762 to 1763, during which, thousands of enlsaved persons were brought in to boost Cuba's burgeoning sugar industry. Thus, Cuba's sugar trade was essential to the "Triangle Trade," whereby New England merchants shipped their rum to West Africa, where it was traded for slaves. Those slaves were then taken to Cuba to work on sugar plantations, or exchanged in Havana or Santiago for Cuban molasses, which was shipped to New England and distilled into rum (Gjelten 2009).

Although sugar was, from the outset, intended to be an export commodity, Spain's economic interest in rum was less direct. The initial prevalence of rum on the island simply began with an innate desire to make alcohol from the materials that were available locally. The Spanish who colonized the island came from a country with its own traditions of alcohol use (Smith 2005), and when they arrived in the Caribbean, they concocted a variety of spirits from a variety of ingredients, including red potato, pineapple, and sugarcane. These crudely distilled spirits were largely referred to as aguardiente, combining the Spanish words *agua* and *ardiente*, or burning water.

In his history of Cuban rum, Miguel Bonera (2000) characterizes early rum consumption as a possible coping mechanism for the brutal project of colonialism. "The European had to drink to fraternize with those around him, and sometimes we suspect, to lose sight of them for a while," Bonera writes in *Oro Blanco: Una Historia Empresarial del Ron Cubano*. "Maybe even to stop seeing himself. To forget his daily work and the horrors that he will have to face and commit" (2000, 7).

For much of colonial rule, rum production was an artisanal enterprise, and at first, most Cuban rum never left the island, thereby limiting its value as an export commodity. Distance, shipping costs, and the demand for other necessary provisions placed imported alcohol beyond the reach of most early colonists. That said, those living on the island consumed spirits for a variety of practical purposes. In some cases, rum added flavor to a bland diet which included cassava, maize, salted pork, and fish (Smith 2005). For slaveowners, rum was seen as a cheap alternative to food, and was used to the supplemented diets of those who were enslaved. Rum was also seen as medicinal. Spirits were also a way to counter various ailments on the island. Furthermore, concerns about tainted water encouraged colonists to consume alcoholic beverages.

Any attempts to cultivate a large-scale rum industry, however, were hampered by Spain, which feared that the rum industry would threaten its wine and brandy trade, which had become important to the Spanish economy. However, a combination of poor administration, high taxes, and lack of political representation contributed to a growing resentment toward Spain, culminating in Cuba's war for independence. To express their dissatisfaction with Spanish domination, many Cubans began to reject Spanish wine.

Toward the end of Cuba's fight for independence, the U.S. military intervened, securing a victory for Cuba. But when the Spanish finally surrendered, it was the American flag that was raised over Havana (Rathbone 2010). And so began a new period of occupation. As Ada Ferrer (2021) notes, the U.S. intervention was motivated more by securing America's financial interests on the island than by any genuine desire to empower the Cuban citizens. During U.S. occupation, Cuban land was sold to North American investors who expanded and modernized the sugar industry.

Cuba's rum industry flourished during Cuba's Republican era. American troops stationed in the country began to acquire a taste for the spirit, which had become an essential ingredient in newly created cocktails, including the Cuba Libre, the mojito, and the daiquiri. These preferences were brought back to the United States, which opened up a lucrative export market abroad. Later, the sale of rum benefited from an increase in tourism. During World War I, Cuba became a natural alternative destination for tourists seeking an alternative to Europe. Travel to the island flourished again during the 1920s and 1930s, as Americans sought alternative access to alcohol during U.S. Prohibition. During the 1950s, dictator Fulgencio Batista transformed Havana into a lucrative destination for wealthy businessmen, tourists, and celebrities.

The sale of Cuban rum had become so successful that on the eve of the 1959 revolution, the Cuban rum industry was dominated by two large family-run companies: Bacardí y Compañia and José Arechabala S.A. (Sociedad Anónima), the producers of Havana Club. Advertising was essential to ensuring their success in both domestic and foreign markets, and both families had access to marketing and distribution networks in the United States and Cuba. According to Emilio Morales and Joseph Scarpaci (2012), by the end of World War I, Cuba had clearly entered the sales-marketing era, making prolific use of trade journals, direct mail advertising, newspapers, motion pictures, streetcar advertising, and billboards. The 1959 revolution would interrupt Cuba's political economy in profound ways.

The Invention and Reinvention of Havana Club

Havana Club, in many ways, embodies the cultural, social, and economic disruptions that have occurred in Cuba over the past 150 years. What started out as a family-run business that emerged during Spanish rule became a thriving corporation under U.S. intervention, only to be reinvented as a state-run enterprise after the 1959 revolution. Havana Club's current iteration as a transnational partnership reflects the ethos of globalization, in which networks replace traditional geographical spaces as the major frames of affiliation.

By the time the Havana Club brand officially launched in 1934, it was just the latest commodity produced by José Arechabala S.A., one of the largest rum manufacturers in Cuba. The company's founder, José Arechabala y Aldama, was born in 1847 in Gordejuéxa, a small town in Vizcaya, the Basque region of Spain.[1] But it is not entirely accurate to describe Arechabala as a Spanish émigré. Basque country was, and continues to be, a region that has its own distinct identity, customs, and language. This sense of regional affiliation would shape how Arechabala imagined his company.

At the age of fifteen, Arechabala set sail for Cuba on board the three-mast frigate *Hermosa de Trasmiera* and set roots in Cuba. As soon as he arrived, he moved to the village of Las Puentes, in the province of Matanzas (Bonera Miranda 2000). There, he began working for Don Antonio de Galindez y Aldama, a relative, who was director and owner of the firm Galindez y Compañia, a business that was dedicated to the export of molasses. Arechabala apparently saw few prospects in this arrangement, and so he moved to the port city of Cárdenas, which was becoming one of the most important industrial centers in Cuba.

In 1878, Arechabala founded his distillery, which produced rum and other spirits using the leftover molasses from Cuba's flourishing sugar industry. As a member of the Basque diaspora in Cuba, Arechabala appears to have maintained a strong emotional bond to his country of origin. Arechabala had named his original distillery La Vizcaya, in reference to his Basque homeland. This sense of place is also encoded on the bottle. The coat of arms of Vizcaya appeared on the labels of all Arechabala products, including the original Havana Club bottles. The coat of arms depicts the sacred tree of Guernica, the Cross of Vizcaya, and two wolves representing the family of López de Haro, founders of Bilbao. Each wolf is carrying a lamb in its mouth. In 1943, Havana Club modified its emblem by introducing a shield with two panels, on the left the shield of Vizcaya, and on the right that of Bilbao.

During its early years, Arechabala's business faced a number of calamities, including a tropical storm that devastated Cárdenas in 1888, Cuba's ongoing wars for independence throughout the late nineteenth century, and continuous economic crises. Despite these challenges, however, the distillery eventually thrived. In 1921, the company was incorporated under the name José Arechabala S.A. and then pursued a strategy of growth and expansion.

In 1934, the company released its Havana Club label, which was part of a larger growth strategy to expand into the U.S. market. Launched just after the repeal of U.S. Prohibition, the Havana Club label was designed to meet a growing demand for Cuban rum. As part of its strategy, the company's Ron Añejo Arechabala 75 would be designated Cuba's domestic brand, while Havana Club would represent the company in U.S. markets. To facilitate its sale in the United States, its label featured an English rather than Spanish spelling (Havana rather than La Habana).

In celebration of its seventy-fifth anniversary, the company produced a corporate history, which touted a diverse portfolio of products that ranged from a popular line of rums to high-proof medical and rubbing alcohol. In addition to touting its current capabilities, the company reflected on its history. In the publication's foreword, there was a palpable sense of optimism about the company's future. The foreword begins with an explanation of the family's motto, "As we were yesterday, we are today, and wish to be tomorrow":

> As we were yesterday, because that is the most exemplary page of our historical cycle; as we are today, because we are sure that we are doing our part with honor—growing, struggling, and proving ourselves worthy of our past; and as we wish to be tomorrow.... We are confident that the future will bring forth the same effort and vitality of action on the part of those who came after us, raising still higher our standard, emblazoned with the slogan and watchword of our founder: 'Never falter; never retreat; Always to the front! Always forward!' (Sainz 1954)

In hindsight, the company's optimistic view of the future seems misguided. In just nine years, Arechabala's assets would be confiscated by the state and the family forced into exile. Yet the publication gives insight into the business decisions that would ultimately make the company vulnerable to state expropriation. Unlike Bacardí, which diversified its assets abroad, the Arechabala family invested heavily in Cuban infrastructure. After a hurricane devastated the port of Cárdenas in 1933, José Arechabala S.A. financed efforts to deepen the harbor and construct a modern and permanent port facility, which transformed the city of Cárdenas into an industrial port complex. Arechabala also developed a network of railroad tracks and paved avenues, which allowed for easier handling and transportation of its products.

In short, the Arechabala company opted for a strategy of investing in physical assets and distribution infrastructure, and for a time, these strategies appeared to be successful. Gradually Havana Club was able to make a name for itself in the United States and Europe, but within the city of Cárdenas, the family had left an indelible mark. By the time the company celebrated its seventy-fifth anniversary, the Arechabala family had become key players in developing a formidable rum industry in Cuba. This success would be short lived, and the company would face a significant transformation after the Cuban Revolution.

New Life as a State-Owned Product

On April 3, 1960, the new revolutionary government placed an advertisement in *Bohemia*, a culture and lifestyle magazine published in Havana (Figure 1). The advertisement was meant to publicly announce the relaunch of Arechabala industries under new state ownership. At the center of the advertisement is a statue that sits in the Parque de Libertad in the center of Mantanzas. Created by the Italian sculptor Bruemi, the allegorical statue depicts a woman breaking the chains of oppression, which represented Cuba's struggle for independence from Spain.

The state's appropriation of this image was meant to signify a new kind of deliverance, freedom from capitalist exploitation. The headline for the ad reads, "A Nation with Its Own Industries Is a Free People," and the subsequent body copy equates the health of the nation to a thriving industry helmed by revolutionaries: "The intervention of the Revolutionary government will take this firm to higher levels of relevance. Arechabala S.A. will be a pride of Cuba and will march at the head of the country's progressive industries."

It is apparent that the revolutionary leaders saw José Arechabala S.A. as an important asset for the new government. In 1961, the Junta Central de Planificación would extend these policies to the other rum brands, a process that involved varying degrees of coercion. In his testimony to the U.S. Congress (Senate Judiciary Committee 2004), Ramón Arechabala, the great-grandson of the founder and a sales manager for the company at the time, described the coercive measures involved in the company's expropriation. According to his testimony, Arechabala was jailed and later relinquished the business while being

Figure 1. "Una Nación Con Industrias Propias es Un Pueblo Libre," announcement from the Cuban government. From *Bohemia* (April 3, 1960). Courtesy of the Cuban Heritage Collection. University of Miami.

threatened at gunpoint. He eventually fled Cuba and resettled in South Florida. In exile, Ramón Arechabala attempted to secure the capital for restarting the family business. During this time, he worked as an auto repairman and in sales. In the late 1980s, he set up a freight forwarding company. He retired in 1997 after suffering a major stroke (Senate Judiciary Committee 2004).

Under state leadership, the brand initially stalled, largely due to external pressures. The United States imposed economic sanctions against Cuba in 1962, which devastated Cuban rum exports. However, the Soviet Union eventually filled this void, and between the years 1975 and 1984, they accounted for over 90 percent of Cuba's rum exports, mostly consisting of barter deals (Gjelten 2009). While the support of Soviet countries provided some market stability during this time, the end of communism in Europe and the collapse of the Soviet Union prompted an economic crisis that dramatically reduced the ability of the Cuban State to deliver even the most basic commodities to its citizens. This collapse prompted a series of reforms intended to regain economic stability, what has come to be known as the "Special Period in a Time of Peace." According to Pertierra (2011), these economic reforms resulted in a new kind of Cuban socialism, an unforeseen mixture of socialist and market-driven economic practices that were very different from the paths of other post-socialist "transition economies" in Europe or Asia.

Cuba's food and beverage sector became one of the first targets for joint venture investment. In September of 1993, Pernod Ricard reached a deal with the Cuban state, to launch a join-effort called Havana Club International. Under the terms of the agreement, labor was divided according to expertise. The newly created Corporación Cuba Ron would produce and bottle Havana Club rum and then sell it to the Havana Club International. Pernod Ricard, as the French partner, would provide the marketing expertise and distribution network (Morales and Scarpaci 2012).

Because Havana Club competes in the premium rum category, its marketing strategy is centered on establishing product superiority against other rum brands, several of which also have ties to the Caribbean, including Appleton Estate (Jamaica), Diplomático (Venezuela), and Mount Gay (Barbados). However, Cuba occupies a unique space within popular imagination relative to other rum-producing Caribbean countries. First, the brand benefits from scarcity. Havana Club is one of the few Cuban brands available in the global marketplace. Its unique status as a genuine Cuban product is encoded on the packaging. All bottles of Havana Club rum feature a bright red banner with the phrase "El Ron de Cuba," and the brand's logo features La Giraldilla, a figure that has come to signify the City of Havana (Scarpaci, Segre, and Coyula 2002).

Second, as a state-produced product, the brand is uniquely poised to benefit from the government's unique link to Cuban artists, musicians, and filmmakers. The state's proprietary relationship Cuban artists was something the agency believed could be exploited for their advantage. According to the executives at M&C Saatchi, their goal was to "make Havana Club the icon of Cuban culture.... We wanted to embody Cuban culture and become the reference" (Cannes 2016). Over time, the brand has been able to make unique claims to

Cuban authenticity, but this strategy is not necessarily new. The practices of exploiting Cuban culture for commercial purposes dates back to the late nineteenth century.

Commodifying Cuba

The idea of leveraging Cuban culture to sell rum would have been unimaginable during the early days of the revolution. The new government made clear that Cuban culture was meant to enlighten, not sell. By removing the arts from marketplace logic, the new revolutionary government had hoped to advance a new definition of mass culture—a powerful assemblage of individuals that was free from the coercive influences of the marketplace. "When we speak of mass culture," state officials put it in 1972, "it is not in the sense in which the term is used by advertising, i.e. a culture to satisfy the tasteless wants, cheap-jack, vulgar, undistinguished, simulated by an entrepreneur avid to create consumer needs" (Otero and Martínez Hinojosa 1972).

This articulation of Cuban culture may be seen as a response to a long history of economic and cultural exploitation of Cuba. Shortly after the Spanish-American War, U.S. marketers began to express a strong interest in the island. Seeing the opportunities for American businesses, U.S. trade commissioner J. W. Sanger wrote enthusiastically about Cuba. In a 1919 report called *Advertising Methods in Cuba*, Sanger articulated the potential for businesses to capitalize on the Cuban market because of its proximity to the United States:

> Cuba, one of the most densely populated and one of the richest of all Latin American countries, lies only seven hours from Key West, Florida, which is connected by a daily ferry service, carrying both passengers and freight.... Importing nearly everything it consumes, and exporting nearly everything it produces, this island offers a tempting field for manufacturers and foodstuffs, textiles, machinery, musical instruments, chemicals, drugs and other important products. (6)

Sanger's invitation for U.S. businesses to enter the Cuban market was already well underway almost as soon as Spanish occupation ended. As Louis Pérez (1999) notes, under U.S. occupation, a wide array of commodities flooded the Cuban market, including soap, toiletries, patent medicines, clothing, and household goods. But rather than attempt to understand Cuban cultural identity, or to market products to meet the needs of everyday Cubans, many U.S. marketers simply marketed U.S. products as they were intended for a U.S. market.

The trick to selling American products, according to Sanger, was to somehow overcome the deficiencies of Cuban culture. To Sanger, the imagined Cuban consumer was defined by their Otherness. Unlike the Anglo-Saxon consumer, who was presumed to be rational, the Cuban consumer was characterized as emotional, and decidedly less analytical. It was simply in his nature. "The Cuban is a Spanish-speaking Latin," Sanger wrote, "whose ancestry, customs and climate, have given him an almost Oriental tendency" (22).

While Sanger saw Cuba's multiracial identity as a deficiency, some U.S. marketers came to realize that Cuba's "Oriental" qualities could be an asset. Businesses and their advertising agencies began to actively promote Cuban culture. From the mid-1920s onward, images of Cuba frequently appeared in newspapers and magazines in the form of advertisements for airlines, hotels, and rum companies. For North American consumers who were seeking novel experiences, Cuba was presented as an exotic destination that offered a complete sensory experience: warm weather, the taste of sugar and rum, the scent of tobacco, and the sounds of Cuban music (Mogul 2019).

When the Castro regime took control of the island, there was an abrupt end to marketing practices on the island, and for decades almost no attention was paid to marketing. Morales and Scarpaci (2012) point out that most advertising was prohibited. Because even a small sign would be subject to a fine, word of mouth became the main way to promote products. A halt to advertising practices on the island, however, appears to have been a decades-long interruption. When Cuba's economic situation became dire after the collapse of the Soviet Union, the state began to reintroduce, to a limited degree, marketing practices. Suddenly, state officials began to reconsider the transactional value of Cuban culture. As Fernandes (2006) points out, state officials began seeking investment in Cuba through the foreign licensing of records, joint film productions with foreign production companies, and the sale of Cuban art to international buyers. These practices allowed the state not only to generate revenue needed to help stabilize the economy but also to contribute to the development of the island's tourism industry.

Selling Rum in the Global Marketplace

Authenticity is essential in the premium spirits category, which include some of the oldest global brands in existence. However, claiming authenticity has become more challenging in a globalized context, in which the production of alcoholic beverages is no longer contained to a single location. In addition to the urgency to link their brands to physical space, distilleries and wineries must also tout their long-standing histories by featuring antiquated buildings, pastoral landscapes, and family coats of arms or by placing emphasis on hand-craft methods, rituals, and ceremonies. For example, both Appleton Estate (established in 1749 in Jamaica) and Rhum Clement (established in 1887 in Martinique) depict their original buildings (Smith 2005).

The industry's continued fixation on the past reveals a tension between progress and tradition. To remain competitive, rum producers have necessarily modernized their production and distribution processes. However, the actual process by which rum is produced must not disrupt the illusion of being an artisanal product. In his research on the wine and spirits industry, Michael Beverland (2005) found that producers downplay their modern practices, which are built for scale and efficiency, and instead promote the fantasy of craft production, handmade methods, intuitive expertise, and historical continuity. In doing so, they attempt to portray themselves as small craft producers that use time-honored ways and natural ingredients as a means of competitive differentiation.

These tactics are inextricably linked to larger anxieties about modernity. What was once produced locally is now mass produced in factories made for large-scale production. These large, efficient factories are owned by corporations that produce homogenized goods that are intended for mass markets. Furthermore, marketplace logic has extended into culture itself. We are said to have transformed into a consumer society, in which we are beholden to the marketplace for all the material objects that surround us. Marketplace logic has infiltrated all facets of social life, indelibly transforming our notions of love, community, self-worth, and even religion.

As corporations have become more successful selling mass-produced goods, consumers have responded by seeking out genuine feelings and experiences they believe to exist outside the purview of the marketplace. Ironically, it is the advertising agency that has stepped in to satisfy this demand. In her study of consumer cultures, Sarah Banet-Weiser (2012) argues that marketers commonly attempt to invest their products with authenticity in order to distinguish themselves within a crowded marketplace. However, authenticity is more contrived than real. Brands, working in conjunction with advertisers, musicians, filmmakers, photographers, and designers, bolster claims of authenticity by positioning themselves as somehow being outside the purview of the marketplace.

Much of this work is accomplished semiotically. Advertising executives, and their creative partners, are skilled at attaching brand names to images that possess specific social and cultural meaning. These practices involve highlighting some truths, while obscuring others. For example, in her discussion of the modern production of tequila in Mexico, Marie Sarita Gaytán (2014) argues that large, transnational liquor conglomerates deliberately recast themselves as small enterprises committed to preserving Mexican culture. In their advertising materials, tequila marketers often use the image of a *jimador*, a pastoral laborer, to serve as a stand-in for the faceless, modern, corporation.

But authenticity is not fixed. Within the competitive landscape, claims to authenticity are constantly being contested. Given the intense competition within the marketplace, various brands attempt to establish cultural meaning for their brands while attempting to divest their competitors of theirs. Because authenticity is closely attached to the concept of originality, competition for authenticity can be a zero-sum game.

Given its perceived distance from capitalism, Cuba satisfies a Western desire for authenticity, and Havana Club has deftly leveraged this insight. Cuba is seen as noncommercial, compared with rum brands that are produced in other Caribbean countries such as Jamaica, Martinique, and Barbados, countries that are often associated closely with Western tourism. Images such as 1950s-era automobiles or the patina of its historic buildings help to substantiate consumers' perceptions of the island as one that is less visibly marked by overconsumption.

But the more that Havana Club finds success by claiming Cuban authenticity, the more competing rum companies will attempt to strip the brand of its strategic advantage. Brands such as Bacardí and Matusalem also have origins in Cuba, but have reinvented themselves in exile. Through their advertising, these companies have attempted to delegitimize the Cuban State, thereby undermining Havana Club's value as an authentic Cuban product. Consider an advertising campaign that was produced on behalf of Matusalem rum by Kaspen, a Prague-based agency. The campaign was highly pointed in its critique of the Castro regime, and through a series of print executions depicts Fidel Castro as a buffoon who ruined the country by plundering its resources and driving out the country's best rum producers. "The Caribbean Has Never Seen a Pirate like Fidel," reads the headline for one of the print advertisements. "He Stole an Island and Threw away the Treasure." Originally established in Santiago de Cuba in 1872, Matusalem is now based in the Dominican Republic. Yet the company has embraced its role as a Cuban brand in exile and has carved out a place in the marketplace with a messaging strategy that promotes its Cuban heritage while being decidedly anti-Castro.

The strategy of critiquing the Cuban State, however, has been more effectively employed by Bacardí Ltd., the largest rum producer in the world. Since the early 1990s, Bacardí has invested significant legal resources toward challenging the Cuban State's rights to the Havana Club trademark in the United States, where it is currently not recognized. By promoting their own version of Havana Club rum, Bacardí has been effective at appropriating and diluting the brand of a direct competitor, while also using advertising as a platform in which to openly critique the Cuban government.

Positioning of This Book

This book lies at the intersection of two lines of inquiry. First, it follows in the tradition of other scholarship, which has looked at how national and regional histories are embodied in the production, consumption, and promotion of their alcohol. For example, Frederick Smith's *Caribbean Rum: A Social and Economic History* (2005) traces rum's evolution from a cottage industry in the small islands of the Lesser Antilles to a multibillion-dollar industry controlled by multinational corporations. Sidney Mintz's *Sweetness and Power* looks at how commercial sugar production reflected contested relationship that existed between the European elite and their colonial subjects.

John Gust and Jennifer Mathews's *Sugarcane and Rum: The Bittersweet History of Labor & Life on the Yucatan Peninsula* (2020) examines the exploitative nature of sugar and rum production as both products became more widely available in the Caribbean. Gaytán's *Tequila: Distilling the Spirit of Mexico* (2014) demonstrates how cultural producers, including filmmakers, musicians, and marketers, have helped to reposition tequila, from a form of mezcal produced in Jalisco to a drink that has come to embody Mexican national identity. Finally, Tom Gjelten's widely read *Bacardí and the Long Fight for Cuba* (2009) explores the inextricable link between Cuba's history and that of the Bacardí family.

Given my focus on cultural production, I also draw heavily on Pierre Bourdieu's (1993) theory of practice. According to Bourdieu, there is a symbiotic relationship between culture and the marketplace, whereby consumers look to commodities to distinguish themselves from one another. In turn, cultural producers, working on behalf of corporations, reify social distinctions by embedding commodities with cultural meaning. In his critique of taste, Bourdieu (1986) describes the process of distinction, arguing that consumers employ various strategies, consciously and unconsciously, to differentiate themselves from others. Therefore, one's tastes in food, cosmetics, clothing, or home decoration are opportunities to, in Bourdieu's words, "experience or assert one's position in social space, as a rank to be upheld, or a distance to be kept" (1986, 57).

Branded products play an important role in helping to substantiate consumers' self-concepts. As Grant McCracken (1989) argues, consumers are constantly canvassing the object world for goods with useful meanings. The world of brands and commodities, in turn, gives consumers access to workable ideas of gender, class, age, personality, and lifestyle. The marketplace offers a vast repository of possible meanings, in which consumers construct their self-identities. This system of meaning becomes evident in the common practice of product positioning, in which corporations exploit this system of differences to their advantage. Corporations invest significant resources to distinguish their product from others in the marketplace. To ensure that their brand occupies a privileged position in the minds of the consumers, they may differentiate based on any number of factors, including price point, country of origin, and class status.

In his work on cultural production, Bourdieu (1993) attends to the specific role of cultural intermediaries, who work in professions such as advertising, fashion, and art. These practitioners shape consumer tastes by linking commodities and services to symbols that carry cultural meaning, a process that becomes evident in packaging, design, and messaging. But critics of Bourdieu have argued that Bourdieu's theory ignores the institutional, political-economic context of the cultural industry, as well as the division of labor that has developed within these fields (Maguire 2014).

To address this deficit, scholars have built on Bourdieu's concepts by conceiving of cultural mediation more broadly. This process is complex and involves more than just the creation of symbols in advertisements. Instead, we must think of advertising practitioners as engaging in a broader array of activities that interlink, overlap, and conflict with one another. This this kind of mediation is not restricted to the interaction between agencies and their clients, but also includes other sectors, including finance, media, government, and the creative arts (Cronin 2007).

However, dynamics within fields of cultural production are never entirely independent of dynamics within the larger field of power. Bourdieu characterizes fields as both "spaces of possibles" and "fields of struggle" (Bourdieu 1993), meaning that actors who hold dominant positions within the field will ultimately seek to maintain the current social order, but others will seek to alter it. However, fields are also dynamic, marked by a constant influx of new agents who struggle to challenge the status quo. Whereas challenges to the status quo are met with resistance from those who are vested in the current system, newcomers may benefit from shocks and changes from neighboring fields.

Havana Club may be seen as one of these newcomers. The political and economic disruptions in the geopolitical landscape have motivated the Cuban State to reintegrate into global markets, giving Havana Club the potential to disrupt current marketing practices by infusing new sensibilities into the process. In this book, I am interested in the ideological nature of such practices. In the process of investing goods and services with specific meanings, cultural producers promote capitalist ideologies by naturalizing and disseminating the legitimacy of private ownership and exchange. However, as an enterprise that is co-owned by a socialist state, Havana Club raises unique considerations. By advancing the corporate interests of a state-run enterprise, the agency creating advertising on behalf of Havana Club is negotiating two sets of political ideologies, brokering between socialist values and commercial imperatives. A unique set of players are involved in this process, including clients, agency executives, state bureaucrats, and cultural tastemakers.

At first glance, Havana Club's unabashed use of Cuban culture to sell rum may seem to be evidence that the Cuban state cannot maintain control of its own cultural production in the face of globalizing forces. However, Nicola Miller (2008) pushes back on the argument that Cuba is simply submitting to the pressures of neoliberalism. Instead, she argues that the revolution must be seen as an ongoing project and that Cuba has been experimenting with different forms of socialism. Cuban intellectual Rafael Hernández (2003) makes a similar point, arguing it is more insightful to understand the revolution not as a single movement but as several revolutions, in which state actors have attempted to navigate the country through continuous crises of economic, political, and social change.

In this book, I do not lay claims about authentic Cuban culture. Instead, I am interested in which aspects of Cuban culture are deemed most compelling, and therefore most profitable, by corporate marketers. As Hernández (2003) rightly points out, too often much of the research on Cuban politics and culture is produced by those living outside the island. Instead, the book most directly engages the work of scholars, including Louis A. Pérez and James Clifford Kent, who examine the role of Western journalists, illustrators, photographers, and advertisers, who have, over time, cultivated an image of Cuba that is meant to serve Western needs and desires. This study contributes to this scholarship by examining the ways in which various actors in a global economy collude to represent a distorted image Cuba to audiences who live outside the island.

Studying Cuban Rum

In this book, I examine how Cuban authenticity is constructed by cultural intermediaries based in Britain, France, and the United States, as well as the ideological negotiation that is involved in this process. Because case studies are designed to bring out details from various points of view, I drew from multiple sources of data. First, I drew heavily on corporate documents, both historic and current, that outline the brand's communications strategies which are designed to meet economic goals that have shifted over time. The internal forms of communications included annual reports, corporate responsibility reports, and award entries—forms of communication that are designed to facilitate the sharing of information to various stakeholders. External forms of communication included press releases and public statements made to news organizations by various actors involved in the production of Havana Club.

Second, I analyzed the advertising campaigns, public relations efforts, music projects, and art installations that have been produced under the auspices of the Havana Club brand. Here, I focused on two kinds of cultural production. First, I examined products of what Bourdieu terms large-scale cultural production, what is sometimes referred to as mass or popular culture. This form of culture is sustained by a large-scale, complex culture industry, and its dominant principle of hierarchy involves economic capital. These include various forms of marketing communication, including advertising, public relations, social media, trade books, and events. By contrast, the field of restricted production concerns what we normally think of as high art (museums, music, film, visual arts, etc.). These forms of cultural production are not overtly commercial, but they play an indirect role in selling the product.

Finally, I conducted field research. I first traveled to Havana, Cuba, in 2019 and attended the Thirteenth Havana Biennial, an international showcase for Cuban artists, including several artists who have been involved with the Havana Club Visual Arts Project. I was also interested in the featured role

INTRODUCTION

that Havana Club plays in promoting Cuban tourism, and so I visited the Havana Club Museum of Rum, which lies in the center of Havana's historic district. I returned to Havana in 2023, after the pandemic, whose devastating impact was evident. By that time, the tourism sector in Havana had been diminished. I traveled also to Trinidad, a colonial city in central Cuba that has focused its economy on tourism.

I also traveled to Gordejuéxa, in the northern part of Spain, where José Arechabala had launched his journey at the age of fifteen. I then went to Cárdenas, Cuba, the port city where Arechabala eventually settled and created his rum-making empire. Finally, I traveled to two locations that were important is destinations for the Cuban diaspora after the Revolution. The first is San Juan, Puerto Rico, where the Bacardí family established their largest working factory. The second is Miami, Florida, where members of both the Arechabala and Bacardí families relocated. Today, Miami is home to over 1 million residents of Cuban origin, many of whom are actively involved in shape Cuban politics from.

OUTLINE OF CHAPTERS

The product of this research is organized into six chapters. In chapter 1, I focus on the specific role of advertising agencies, which broker between consumers on the one hand and corporate executives, cultural tastemakers, and state institutions on the other. Because advertising is a persuasive form of communication designed to sell rum, it is a form of cultural production that is most explicitly subject to economic pressures. Focusing on three different Havana Club campaigns produced over the course of a decade, I argue that advertising practitioners have exploited preexisting perceptions of Cuba that exist within Western imagination as a uniquely authentic space that exists outside of modern capitalism. I further argue that due to changing dynamics in the marketplace, Cuban authenticity is continuously being rearticulated in new ways. Finally, I argue that what began as an expression of socialist values has, over time, become more conventional and commercial in nature.

In chapter 2, I focus on *Havana Cultura*, an extension of the Havana Club brand that serves as a platform for promoting contemporary Cuban musicians, filmmakers, and visual artists. I begin by analyzing Havana Club's partnership with BBC Radio deejay and producer Gilles Peterson and his record label, Brownswood Recordings. Specifically, I explore the ways in which Havana Club executives, working in direct partnership with the state, have tapped the potential of "undiscovered" musicians for economic and strategic purposes. In the second part of the chapter, I focus on the Havana Cultura Visual Arts Project, an initiative that provides funding to emerging Cuban artists. Leading this effort is British curator Flora Fairbairn, who has tapped into a growing interest in Cuban art by collectors who are seeking products that exist on the periphery.

To exploit this market, Fairbairn educates Cuban artists on how to position themselves as commodities that are available for consumption in the global marketplace.

In chapter 3, I focus on the contested nature of Cuban authenticity in the global marketplace. Focusing on the Bacardí brand, I examine the ways in which Cuban cultural producers, working from the diaspora, advance their own notions of Cuban authenticity that are disconnected from fixed spatial concepts and based more on marketplace logic. In this chapter, I focus on Cuban expatriates, who demonstrate what Benedict Anderson (1998) refers to as "long-distance nationalism," a general sense of solidarity that binds together immigrants and their descendants into a single transborder community. However, I argue that Bacardí's assertions of Cuban identity are shaped directly by profit motive. Corporate executives, marketing practitioners, and artists, working in the diaspora, are motivated to define Cuban authenticity as it exists in another time and another place. I further argue that these marketing practices have political implications. In the process of staking out its position within the marketplace, Bacardí is advancing a particular ideological point of view, based on private ownership.

In chapter 4, I examine the role that corporate museums play in articulating Cuban authenticity. Based on field research conducted in Cuba and Puerto Rico, I focus on the Havana Club Museum of Rum, located in the city's historic district, and Casa Bacardí located at its distillery in Cataño, just outside the capital city of San Juan. Both museums purport to educate visitors on rum's role in Cuban history, but each presents a different version of history that reflects its political ideologies. I further argue that these ideologies become evident in specific curatorial decisions. After all, deciding what to include in a national history of rum necessarily involves a process of deciding what to exclude.

In chapter 5, I address the racial politics that surround the Havana Club brand. The history of rum is one of exploitation, involving the violent use of slave labor. I begin with an analysis of how European artists and writers represented Cuba's mixed-race society to European audiences. I follow with a discussion of how Cuban rum marketers have encoded Black and white bodies with different symbolic meanings for marketing purposes. I then turn my attention to Havana Club's contemporary efforts. Here, I argue that the brand has featured Afro-Cubans in its marketing materials to serve a variety of needs, first to advance the ideals of the revolution by advancing a notion of Cuban national identity based on racial unity. But the brand has also benefited from racial difference. The depiction of Black and brown bodies helps to position the rum as a subcultural product.

In chapter 6, the final chapter, I examine the various forms of labor that Havana Club performs on behalf of the state. As a joint venture that has tremendous presence abroad, the brand is uniquely poised to serve simultaneously as a

INTRODUCTION

form of diplomacy. Even though Cuba lies at the geopolitical periphery, its government has been effective at employing soft power, using Cuban music, art, and commodities to generate solidarity with outside nations. In this way, Havana Club's efforts may have the direct goal of selling rum to outside markets, but the campaign serves much larger goals that go beyond a conventional marketing effort. Havana Club's promotion of Cuban art, music, and film has helped the island fulfill other, equally important national interests, including the attraction of tourists, which in turn generates hard currency. Thus, the function of advertising executives, art curators, and record producers is not simply symbolic. They serve a direct role in advancing the Cuban State's strategic and political interests.

CHAPTER 1

Advertising and Authenticity

Cuba is perceived as exotic, and exoticism is about clichés. When you think Cuba, you think beaches and communism. Beaches are appealing, but not differentiating for rum. Communism is differentiating, but not appealing for a global premium spirit brand. . . . We wanted to depict the Cuba of today, in a non-touristic and non-political way. —M&C Saatchi, 2013

In 2010, executives at global advertising agency M&C Saatchi commissioned New York–based fashion photographer Guy Aroch to lead the visual look and feel of an advertising campaign that would help relaunch the Havana Club brand. By that time, Aroch had garnered a professional reputation for developing high-profile, global campaigns for brands such as Coca-Cola, Victoria's Secret, H&M BOSS, and L'Oreal. His work has appeared in publications including *Maxim*, *GQ*, *Harper's Bazaar*, and *Vogue*.

According to executives at M&C Saatchi, the goal of the campaign was to generate interest in Havana Club by linking the brand to authentic moments that reflect Cubans' appreciation for simple pleasures. To accomplish this, Aroch was given free license to wander the streets of Havana looking for moments of surprise that involved "real Cubans." In the agency's words, they gave Aroch "carte blanche to capture a truly spontaneous Havana" (Cannes 2013). Aroch's photos for the campaign feature a racially diverse cohort of Cubans in serendipitous moments. There is a group of older men playing chess in a public park, a pair of ballerinas stretching in front of a bus stop, and a jazz band driving a 1950s-era convertible, with a cello visible in the back seat.

To produce the video portion of the campaign, the agency hired American director Harmony Korine, a darling of the independent film scene. Korine's commercials have a similar verité quality that creates the illusion of captured moments. One commercial features three friends seated around a kitchen table and making music with found objects, including tin cups, glasses, and spoons. Another video also depicts a newly married Afro-Cuban couple riding a bike down a quiet street in Havana. Along with the ambient sound of the city, we hear the whirring of the bike as it passes by the camera.

The Black and brown bodies, the patina of the Havana landscape, and the expressions of joy and contentment all communicate the socialist ideal that love and happiness are independent of material wealth. The only presence of branding is the Havana Club logo, which itself can be seen as a symbol of love. It depicts la Giraldilla, a statue that has sat atop the Castle of the Royal Force in Havana's old quarter for almost four hundred years. La Giraldilla is the embodiment of Isabel De Bobadilla, who is said to have spent her days looking beyond Havana's harbor, waiting for her husband to return from sea.

The campaign is notable for the absence of any overt commercial messaging. There are no product shots, no price points, no calls to action. Nothing that would mark this as a conventional advertising campaign. But however implicit its appeals, the campaign is ultimately a form of marketing communications. Therefore, these images may be seen less as real, unaltered snapshots of Cuban life, and more as a collection of signifiers, whose meanings are orchestrated to communicate a particular albeit somewhat contradictory set of messages.

As a state-produced product, Havana Club, more than other rum brands in the marketplace, has come to represent Cuba itself. But as discussed in the introduction, Cuba has ambivalent meaning in the geopolitical landscape. As Rafael Hernández (2003) points out, the idea of Cuba has often been reduced to a political system, which has been reduced to the Communist Party, which has been reduced the figure of Fidel Castro. For some, Cuba is associated with human rights abuses and suppression of free speech. Others across the Spanish-speaking world express support for the Cuban Revolution and its achievements. For them, Cuba is a model for resisting U.S. hegemony (Bustamante and Sweig 2008).

The challenge for advertisers, therefore, is to cultivate a version of Cuban authenticity that is most conducive to selling rum to international markets, which involves the process of divesting Cuba of its more controversial elements while focusing on the images, sounds, and other signifiers that establish Cuban authenticity in more appealing ways. In doing so, advertising agencies do not attempt to represent Cuba as it is but rather to invoke positive associations that already exist in the minds of Western consumers.

In this chapter, I examine the ways in which advertising practitioners have invoked various iterations of Cuban authenticity in response to their shifting strategic and economic objectives. I focus on advertising agencies because of their central role in mediating between clients, who are said to lack the necessary creative skills to promote their products, and consumers, who agencies claim are difficult to reach and persuade without the aid of agency practitioners (Cronin 2007). However, the role of advertising practitioners as cultural intermediaries goes beyond mediating between producers and consumers. In the process of creating advertisements, agencies also broker with financial, creative, media, and governmental organizations.

I further argue that producing Havana Club advertising involves a kind of ideological negotiation. As one of the "fixers" of capitalism (Thrift 1987), the advertising industry has become an essential institution for enacting and legitimizing capitalist ideologies. Advertisements openly celebrate consumer choice and portray consumer satisfaction in its idealized form. "Advertising is capitalism's way of saying I love you to itself" is how Michael Schudson puts it (1984, 232). But Havana Club advertising also represents a different kind of political system altogether and, therefore, one might expect that the Cuban state's joint ownership of the Havana Club brand would ensure the same recognition of socialist values.

Focusing on three different brand campaigns produced over the course of a decade, I argue that Havana Club's messaging has over time become increasingly subject to economic pressures. Havana Club's partnership with M&C Saatchi initially yielded a campaign that did not look like conventional advertising, not only because of its celebration of socialist values but because of the notable absence of marketing. As the urgency to sell the product has become more pronounced, the agency has responded by rearticulating Cuban authenticity in ways that directly relate to the product and are more appealing to the lucrative youth market. In doing so, the agency has relied more heavily on creative partners that have a proven record in selling lifestyle brands. But this has come at a cost. The gravitational pull toward commercialization has begun to undermine the brand's strategy of establishing and maintaining its authenticity.

Rum and Symbolic Consumption

In *Sweetness and Power*, Sidney Mintz (1985) reminds us that our capacity to symbolize, to endow anything with meaning, is universal and intrinsic to our nature. However, which artifacts we endow with cultural significance are unpredictably subject to social and historical forces. For much of colonial history, what and how one ate and drank had profound social implications. What specific foods mean to people and what people signal by consuming them have historically been associated with social differences of all sorts, including those of age, gender, class, and occupation.

In her discussion of tequila production in Mexico, for example, Marie Sarita Gaytán (2014) notes that the Spanish elite consumed alcohol that reflected their privileged position in society. They chose to adopt the drinking habits of the old country, preferring wine, brandy, and sherry. Scarcity added to their appeal. Imported drinks often failed to survive the long sea voyage from Europe without being tainted or lost at sea. Furthermore, distance, taxes, and shipping costs made imported alcohol beyond the reach of most early colonists.

Whereas the elite had some access to scarce goods, most settlers in the Caribbean subsisted almost exclusively on foods produced within its borders.

There was certainly a racialized component to these distinctions. Gaytán also points out that in the New World, the consumption of alcohol reflected a clear system of distinction between two ethnic sectors of governance: the República de los Españoles (the Spanish nation) and the República de los Indios (Indian nation). The indigenous of Mexico drank pulque, which was made from agave. It was widely drunk and commonly used for religious ceremonies. To Spaniards, who considered themselves *gente de razón* (people of reason), the indigenous community's consumption of pulque was evidence of their inferiority, whom they considered *gente sin razón* (people without reason) (Gaytán 2014).

There were similar distinctions in colonial Cuba. Originally, rum was considered a common product, consumed by slaves and poor whites. Conversely, the white Spanish elites continued to drink wine, brandy, and sherry. However, there were race and class implications in how alcohol consumption was controlled. Rum was associated with paganism, public drunkenness, and other illicit activities, and so the colonial government declared it a public nuisance and restricted its access (Smith 2005). By the mid-nineteenth century, however, rum had begun its path toward legitimization. Distillers had hoped to develop international market by transforming Cuban rum into a respectable product. This was accomplished through innovations in production as well as a greater use of marketing. Originally, the inconsistency in its production meant that the quality of the product was unreliable. Most consumers drank the equivalent of "gut rot," but over time, various entrepreneurs, scattered across the Caribbean, began to experiment with new methods of distillation.

Facundo Bacardí, the founder of Bacardí rum, is often credited with improving Cuban rum by removing impurities in the distillation process, which likely involved a combination of charcoal and sand (Gjelten 2009). As the production of rum became more refined and consistent, the product category began to take on a new system of distinction, based on quality and age. Ron Añejo, aged rum, was seen as superior to aquardiente de caña, a simple bottom-shelf cane juice distillate. In the French Caribbean, rhum agricole, which was made from pure sugarcane juice on sugar plantations, was considered more of a craft product. This kind of rum was distinguished from rhum industriel, made from molasses in big urban distilleries. Rhum industriel became by far the most distributed rum on the island.

As branding became a more widely used practice, rum began to take on new meanings. In time, generic, unmarked goods held less appeal for consumers, and so distilleries borrowed a tactic from winemakers and began to include logos on their bottles as well as the barrels used to transport their goods. Some distilleries utilized the images of family crests and international awards, including Ron Escarchado and José Arechabala S.A. These images drew on legitimacy through institutions outside the island, drawing attention to the European heritage of these businesses.

Other Cuban distillers branded their logos on real world referents. Matusalem Rum, founded by Eduardo and Benjamin Camp, used the image of the *golondrina*, or barn swallow, which is said to have occupied the barrel-aging warehouses. The Camp brothers felt that the swallow was an appropriate symbol of the company, since it was considered a free-flying spirit, possessing beauty and elegance (Matusalem 2022). Similarly, Bacardí's infamous bat logo is said to have been inspired by a colony of fruit bats that were attracted to the sweet fumes of the fermenting molasses. The bat was a symbol of good fortune to both the Catalans and the native Taínos.

Bring in the Brokers

In the late nineteenth century, Cuban rum producers relied heavily on newspaper advertising. However, the technological limitations of the time constrained what advertisers could communicate. Newspaper advertising was initially limited to written appeals, with the exception of some simple, black-and-white illustrations. By the early twentieth century, however, advertising was transformed by innovations in communications technology, including chromolithography, color rotogravure printing, and the halftone press. These technologies gave rise to new kinds of marketing, including magazine advertisements and trade cards, which enjoyed wide popularity during the nineteenth century. Consequently, art direction became increasingly more sophisticated, enabling advertisers to promote the product in more vivid ways.

These technical innovations coincided with the arrival of a new class of professionals, who brought with them advertising practices developed in the United States. According to Louis Pérez (1999), George Benson, an American identifying himself as an "advertisement contractor," established one of the first advertising agencies in Havana in 1898. Almost ten years later, the Liga Cubana de Publicidad, a professional trade association, formed with Walter Stanton as president and Rafael Fernández and J. A. González as vice presidents.

As Cuban rum brands began to make inroads into U.S. and European markets, advertising started to take on the additional task of distinguishing Cuban rum in the international marketplace. Some of these distinctions were related to the product itself. Cuban rum became synonymous with light, crisp rum, making it conducive to cocktails such as the daiquiri and rum collins (Curtis 2006). Jamaican rums have a bolder flavor profile, whereas rums from Barbados such as Mount Gay occupied the space between Cuban and Jamaican rums. Similarly, rums from the Virgin Islands also occupied this middle space and were best when served in mixed drinks. But these distinctions were also symbolic. Havana Club would join a number of different Caribbean rum producers who began to tap into the positive associations linked with their countries of origin.

ADVERTISING AND AUTHENTICITY

HAVANA CLUB ENTERS THE U.S. MARKET

In 1950, José Arechabala S.A. placed an advertisement in its corporate publication, *Gordejuela*, which was circulated throughout Cárdenas and given to the company's workers, investors, and other professionals involved in the sugar and rum industries (Figure 2). "Traves de Los Años" (Through the Years), reads the

Figure 2. "A Traves de Los Años," print advertisement. From *Gordejuela* (April, 1950). Accessed through Liburuklik Digital Library.

headline, suggesting that the advertisement was meant to celebrate the company's long-standing heritage. The focal point of the advertisement is an illustration of an hourglass with a trail of the sands of time tying together two dates: 1878, when the company was founded, and 1949, when the advertisement was placed. The supporting body copy draws parallels between the company's longevity and the aging process that is essential to producing a superior-quality rum: "el tiempo es uno de los factores más importantes que contribuye a la superior calidad de un ron" (time is one of the most important factors that contributes to the superior quality of a rum).

When José Arechabala S.A. began exporting Havana Club rum to U.S. markets, the responsibility for advertising the product did not directly fall to Cuban professionals. Instead, the company worked closely with brokers, based primarily in New York. For example, the company established a partnership with New York–based W. A. Taylor and Co., which served as Havana Club's distributor in the United States (*New York Times* 1940). That company, in turn, hired Charles W. Hoyte, a New York–based advertising agency, to handle the advertising for Havana Club.

Executives at Havana Club had hoped to make inroads into the U.S. market by positioning their rum as a premium product intended for consumers with cosmopolitan taste sensibilities. In 1939, Havana Club ran a series of advertisements that were placed in the *New York Times* and the *New Yorker*. Each advertisement focuses on a different pair of American consumers who were returning from a trip to Cuba on a different cruise line: the Panama Pacific, the Swedish American, the Cuba Mail Line, and so forth. For example, one of the advertisements (Figure 3) depicts a conversation between two men aboard the Statendam passenger line, touting the authenticity of Havana Club rum. "I took a trip to Cuba to show me the difference in Rum Drinks," one man says to the other. "Until I went to the Havana Club Bar, I never knew how good a rum drink could taste—now I know, and boy, what a difference between theirs and the ones I'd been used to."

Each advertisement featured the recipe for a different Cuban cocktail, but its media placement provides insight into the audience that Havana Club was targeting at the time. When Harold Ross cofounded the *New Yorker* in 1925, it was unabashedly directed toward a highly selective reader, one who was educated and urbane (Lepore 2010). Placed in the publication at this time, the Havana Club advertisement would have been surrounded by a constellation of advertisements for luxury commodities, including fashion and travel. There were also advertisements for premium spirits such as Melrose Whiskey, Courvoisier, and Rhum Negrita.

By the early 1940s, Havana Club had begun working with RC Williams as its U.S. distributor, and together they pursued a different positioning strategy. Instead of positioning Havana Club as a mixer, the brand was now positioned as a premium sipping rum. Now included in the media buy was *Esquire*, which

Figure 3. "It Took a Trip to Cuba to Show Me the Difference in Rum Drinks," print advertisement. From the *New Yorker* (October 28, 1939). Retrieved from the *New Yorker* digital archives.

at the time was a relatively new men's fashion magazine with literary ambitions, having solicited contributions by Ernest Hemingway, F. Scott Fitzgerald, and Julian Huxley. The publication was designed for an educated, affluent reader, what the *New York Times* would later call the "Esquire Man" (Williams 2017), an urbane, well-groomed, cocktail-sipping male with cosmopolitan sensibilities.

This strategy was evident in an advertisement for Havana Club that ran in the September 1943 issue of *Esquire* magazine. The advertisement focuses on exclusivity, with an image of a key next to a bottle of Havana Club rum. "Here's Your Key to the Private Stock Rum from Cuba's Finest Distilleries," reads the headline, as if inviting the reader to exclusive access to the Arechabala family's private cellar. The copywriting goes on to position Havana Club as a prestige spirit, describing it as one of "Cuba's Choicest Rums." Furthermore, the designation "Straight Cuban rum" is not incidental. The term appropriates the language of other premium spirits, such as "Straight Bourbon whisky." This message of exclusivity would have been appealing to the *Esquire* reader during this time. The advertisement ran as World War II was coming to an end, and scarcity would have been a real issue.

However, Havana Club was competing in a crowded space. In that same September 1943 issue of *Esquire*, readers would have been exposed to advertisements for brandy (Chevalier and Leroux Blackberry Flavored Brandy), bourbon (Old Grand-Dad, Old Forrester, and Kentucky Tavern), and gin (Booth's House of Lords, Graves, Gordon's, and Gilbey's). The most widely advertised spirit was whiskey (Four Roses, Vat 69, Schenley Royal Reserve, I.W. Harper, Paul Jones, Park & Tilford, King Black Label, and Johnny Walker).

The magazine also included advertisements from competing rum brands that offered a more explicit connection to the Caribbean. For example, Ron Marno signified its Cuban heritage by featuring two oak barrels placed on an empty beach. Similarly, an advertisement for Myers's Rum, which ran with the headline "The Order of the Day," touts its Jamaican heritage. The advertisement features two contrasting images that are meant to connect the U.S. and the Caribbean. The main image depicts an interaction in New York between a patron and a bartender, who is pulling a bottle of rum from the top shelf. The inset image serves as a contrast by depicting a tropical island setting and the image of a Afro-Caribbean server pouring a bottle of Myers's Rum. "Whenever Americans meet in relaxation," the ad reads. The order of the day is 'The Rum Must be Myers's.'"

The Party's Over: Havana Club Branding under Socialism

By 1960, efforts to court wealthy American drinkers had come to an end. When Fidel Castro assumed control of the island, Cuba's economy was almost completely dependent on outside markets, and the new government felt an urgency to diversify its economy. In his now-infamous speech delivered at El Punto de Este, Uruguay, in 1961, Che Guevara explicitly drew the connection between economic policy and national sovereignty: "The nation that buys, commands; the nation that sells, serves. Commerce must be balanced to assure freedom. A nation that wants to die sells to one nation only, and a nation that would be saved sells to more than one. The excessive influence of one country over another's commerce becomes political influence" (as cited in Deutschmann and García 2022).

The new regime was committed to addressing Cuba's vulnerability as a monocrop economy. However, the U.S. government responded aggressively, and in February 1962, President John F. Kennedy proclaimed an embargo on trade between the United States and Cuba. With established export markets now shut off, the new revolutionary government would not have been able to survive had it not aligned itself with the Soviet Union, the only major power at the time that was not beholden to the United States (Hernández-Reguant 2012).

After the revolution, Havana Club was reinvented as a state-owned product, and when state officials took control of Havana Club, they divested the brand of the Arechabala family's presence by removing the Vizcaya coat of arms, a symbol that had previously appeared on the labels of all Arechabala products. In its place, the redesigned bottle now featured Havana's recognizable statue, La Giraldilla, which signaled Havana Club's transformation from a private commodity into a public good.

When the Soviet Union collapsed, however, the Cuban government again was forced to reinvent itself by engaging in a series of economic reforms. The state amended the constitution to allow new forms of private and corporate property, regulate foreign investment, and decriminalize the circulation of the U.S. dollar. International tourism was identified as a promising strategy, and state companies remodeled old hotels, worked with international partners to build new ones, and revamped small airports near beach areas to accommodate seasonal flights from Western Europe and Canada. These reforms also included turning state companies into for-profit enterprises, while actively seeking transnational partnerships with Western corporations. The country's rum sector seemed an ideal opportunity, and so the government sought out a partner that could help with the promotion and distribution of Havana Club rum.

As one of the largest spirits marketers in the world, Pernod Ricard seemed an ideal partner. Like Havana Club, Pernod Ricard is an example of a family-owned enterprise that has evolved into a large, global conglomerate by establishing partnerships. In 1805, Henry Louis Pernod founded the Pernod-Fils Company, which primarily distilled absinthe, a spirit that had become a popular in France's artistic circles. Paul Ricard had started his own distillery in 1932, producing Pastis, another anise-based drink. The two companies merged in 1975, and largely through a series of acquisitions, Pernod Ricard has gone on to become one of the largest global spirits distributors in the world.

The inclusion of Havana Club rum in Pernod Ricard's product portfolio is part of the company's ongoing strategy of acquiring brands with national heritage and continuing to leverage their family histories and country-of-origin. For example, Pernod Ricard also markets the Jameson brand, an Irish whiskey that was established in Dublin in the eighteenth century. Despite the transnational nature of its new owner, the brand is still marketed as an Irish whiskey, with a label that bears an Irish coat of arms and the words, "established 1780." Pernod Ricard has used similar strategies to market authentic British gin (Beefeater), Mexican tequila (Avión), and Spanish rioja (Campo Viejo).

Havana Club was meant to be Pernod Ricard's "Cuban rum," but here the company could lay claim to a true point of difference. For over two decades, Havana Club was the only brand in the global marketplace that was distributed outside Cuba. Therefore, Havana Club executives could legitimately claim to be the rum of Cuba. Havana Club International considered this an asset, but it needed agency partners that could exploit this difference.

By 2005, Pernod Ricard recognized that it needed the help of a global advertising agency to help raise the profile of the Havana Club brand. And so it invited a number of advertising agencies to pitch the account, including Euro RSCG, M&C Saatchi, Ogilvy & Mather, and thenetworkone (*Campaign UK* 2005). The new business pitch is an industry ritual, in which a client sends out a request for proposals, inviting competing agencies to deliver a detailed account of how they would solve the client's problem, including strategic and creative development.

Ultimately, it was M&C Saatchi that won the account. The agency positions itself as a creative start-up but with the experience and organizational structure to have a global impact. As it states in its pitch materials, M&C Saatchi has "local, regional or global capability—more powerful than solo boutiques, more creative and agile than conglomerates." With over thirty-one offices worldwide (M&C Saatchi 2022), the agency had the organizational structure to market Havana Club in international markets. This global structure was necessary, since Pernod Ricard had planned to launch the campaign in thirty countries (Effies 2012).

Headquartered in London, M&C Saatchi has regional offices in all the major continents. At the same time, the agency was not part of a large advertising conglomerate, so it could claim to offer the personalized and local service that the client needed. It was determined that the agency's Paris office, M&C Saatchi.GAD, would lead the effort due to their close proximity to the client. Pernod Ricard's global headquarters was based in Paris and having a satellite office nearby would ensure the agency's continuous presence.

Contemporary Advertising

In practice, a typical full-service agency is generally organized around five key disciplines: account management, strategy, media planning, creative, and production. Determining the business objectives of the advertising is largely the purview of the account executive, whose job it is to make sure that the advertising meets the client's needs but at a profitable return for the agency. The account executive generally manages the team that will eventually take on the task of ensuring that the advertising fulfills its marketing function.

The role of the strategist is to help the agency achieve its goals by understanding the lifeworlds of potential consumers. To make these assessments, account planners utilize a variety of primary and secondary research, which includes syndicated research, focus groups, surveys, social media data mining, ethnographies, and interviews. This research will be distilled into a creative brief, which provides the blueprint for what the campaign will ultimately become. The efforts of account managers and strategists are supported by the media department, who determine where the advertising will be placed so that it can reach the right people, at the right time, and in the right place.

It is the creative team, however, that produces the most visible labor of the agency. Composed generally of an art director and a copywriter, the creative team delivers on the strategy by attaching commodities to a particular set of images and words that have specific cultural meaning. According to Linda Scott (1994), the creative process is rhetorical in nature. Copywriters and art directors craft their messages in anticipation of the consumer's probable response using shared knowledge of various vocabularies and conventions as well as common experiences. Consumers use this same body of cultural knowledge to read the message, infer the sender's intention, evaluate the argument, and formulate a response. Shared cultural knowledge thus provides the basis for clear communication. But the creative team is not acting alone in this process. To help it execute its creative vision, an agency will often work with the production team, which in turn will enlist photographers, filmmakers, musicians, and so forth, to help execute the creative vision.

When M&C Saatchi began working on the Havana Club account, the strategy team had identified a target audience, which it termed "Urban Cultural Explorers," primarily men between ages twenty-five and forty-three (*Guardian* 2010). These consumers were both premium spirits drinkers and opinion leaders (Effies 2012). According to the agency, these consumers socialize often and are motivated to seek out "undiscovered" music, films, and brands.

A secondary objective was to develop Havana Club into a "hot brand" among bartenders and restaurant owners who are important gatekeepers to the product (Cannes 2013). Consumer advertising, business-to-business communications, and public relations are practices that are considered essential when competing within a marketplace that can be unforgiving. "Generally, for a spirits brand to be successful they need to market to not only consumers but also taste makers," Noah Rothbaum, a journalist who covers the spirits industry, told me. "So, in the liquor world that means targeting bartenders, journalists and influencers. These people have a lot of sway over the public's perception of a brand and that's key to its popularity" (personal interview 2023).

Today's marketplace is marked by plurality, in which there are a vast number of brands that are competing for visibility. Of these, Bacardí dominates the world market, selling in over 170 countries globally (Bacardí 2022a). But the strategy team at M&C Saatchi had identified a weakness. Category leaders tend to be seen more as ubiquitous and commercial and, therefore, less genuine. Consequently, Bacardí's dominant position within the category had undermined its ability to claim Cuban authenticity. Havana Club's advertising was designed to exploit Bacardí's vulnerability as a brand that had little connection to place. According to internal documents, Havana Club was positioned as an apolitical, Cuban brand against Bacardí, which they believed consumers considered to be the embodiment of globalization (Effie 2012). In other words, Havana Club's priority was to position "Havana Club as the genuine Cuban brand against the vaguely-Latin Bacardí" (Effie 2012). In doing so, M&C Saatchi had hoped to position Havana Club as an artisanal drink for discerning consumers while counterpositioning Bacardí as a generic product meant for mass consumption. As the agency stated, "Bacardí was the mainstream rum for mainstream partygoers and Havana Club wanted to become the preferred alternative for the more premium and discerning spirits drinkers" (Cannes 2013).

M&C Saatchi had inherited a brand that had varying degrees of success marketing Havana Club as an authentic Cuban product. Before the agency acquired the account, Havana Club advertising had utilized a number of slogans, including "The Authentic Cuban Rum" and "The Soul of Cuba." In 2004, the brand ran a series of print ads with the tagline "Havana Side of Life," which were essentially lifestyle advertisements depicting young, attractive drinkers in a beach or club setting. The challenge for M&C Saatchi was to communicate Cuban authenticity in a way that would be compelling and believable.

Nothing Compares to Havana

It is one thing to claim authenticity but something entirely different for consumers to find it believable. M&C Saatchi's first global campaign was titled "El Culto a La Vida" (The Cult of Life) and included television, online, and print advertising, as well as nontraditional marketing such as music sponsorships and events. In its annual report to investors, Pernod Ricard (2006) touted the campaign: "After several years of communicating around its Cuban origins, *El Ron de Cuba*, the brand decided to develop a new, more emotion-based campaign around Cubans' irresistible vital energy and unique attitude towards life." The campaign attempted to associate Havana Club with a contemporary Cuba by featuring young, attractive (presumably Cuban) models in sexualized poses. As a branding device, each model's head was surrounded by a red aura, a visual based on the Havana Club logo. The campaign appears, however, to have generated little success in meeting its objective of positioning Havana Club as an authentically Cuban product. As the agency later acknowledged, the campaign did not resonate with consumers because it presented Cuba in a way that was not ownable. In the agency's words, the campaign was "selling too much joie de vivre, and not enough Cubanness" (Cannes 2013).

It soon became clear, however, that Havana Club was struggling to establish its distinctly Cuban identity, and so the company began work on a major rebranding effort. The centerpiece of the effort was a global advertising campaign that explicitly linked Cuban culture to the rum. The campaign, which included television, print, outdoor, and public relations (Effies 2012). Ran with the headline "Nothing Compares to Havana" and showcased "real Cubans" who were filmed at unexpected moments. Implicitly, the campaign was designed as a critique of modern capitalism. According to agency executives, the idea for the campaign was inspired during an agency trip to Havana. While there, members of the advertising team suddenly found themselves caught in a rainstorm. This moment was captured in a photograph that was included as part of its industry case study: One hot afternoon during a three-day immersion trip to Havana, a huge tropical storm fell upon us in the street. We ran for shelter in nearby entrances. At the same time, groups of young Cuban students were starting to emerge from adjacent schools, seemingly not disturbed by the rain pouring hard. Suddenly, some of them took off their uniforms, and started to run and jump (Cannes 2013). There is a similar photograph of children playing in a rainstorm in *Looking at Cuba*, Rafael Hernández's (2003) reflections on civic and political life on the island, from an insider's perspective. The photograph is one of several images meant to illustrate the complex lives and resilience of the Cuban people. Hernández also includes photographs of a street protest and a state-run ration store. Similar to the Havana Club advertising campaign, there is an image of a wedding couple wading through water during a hurricane. The agency's reading of this type of moment, however, is telling, because it articulates Cuban-lived experience in terms of Western anxiety. From the team's perspective, this moment was evidence that Cubans had retained an innate joy, something that had been lost in Western culture. According to the agency, consumers had become disillusioned with Western capitalism. They were too caught up in the rat race. As they describe it, "people had come to realize that they are so busy dealing with their lives, they forget about living it."

In his research on advertising during the global recession, Matthew McAllister (2010) had found that during this same time, marketers attempted to capitalize on consumers' dissatisfaction with capitalism. In the wake of the crisis, the agency held up Cuba as a superior economic model, and there is evidence that Havana Club and its partners made a conscious effort to present Cuba in a way that would appeal to Western audiences. As executives at M&C Saatchi stated, "Cubanness is a tricky thing to 'sell'" (Cannes 2013), given the island nation's association with communism and its contested place in the geopolitical landscape. The agency is, in many ways, expressing the perspective of some cultural critics who have argued that modern society has become too complicated, competitive, and exploitative.

Havana Club deliberately set out to showcase Cuban joy as the remedy to Western preoccupation with consumer culture. According to the agency, the goal was to "infect the world with the pulse of Havana, spread its spontaneity and humanité" (Cannes 2013). Agency documents reveal that the brand had hoped to tap into Western anxieties about the failures of capitalism during the height of the economic crisis. According to the agency

> Cuban difference is not just a product of ideology or geography, but about a different set of priorities. These priorities echoed new aspirations in the Western world. Back in 2010, the subprime crisis had just hit the world. The Western model was severely questioned, and it was going to last. This crisis acted as a catalyst for various emerging trends: the urge to opt out of the rat race, the quest for more meaning, and authenticity. (Cannes 2013)

Rather than depict a contemporary Cuba, however, Havana Club decided to present a version of Cuba that had already become vivid in the minds of Western consumers, what James Gilmore and Joseph Pine (2007) call "referential authenticity." Over the course of the twentieth and early twenty-first centuries, the idea of Cuba in the Western imagination has been constructed predominantly around North American representations of the country (Kent 2019). These conceptions draw from Cuba's colonial past, the glamour of the Republican era, the revolutionary period that followed. These images have become fused with modern conceptions of the Havana's ruin and decay, what has been referred to as the post-"Special Period aesthetic."

Beholden to this perspective, the Western gaze becomes fixated on the vintage American cars, the colonial architecture, and the crumbling buildings. The visual style was crucial to the way that the advertising functioned. For example, Saatchi hired New York–based photographer Guy Aroch to provide the images for the print portion of the campaign. For its video footage, the agency turned to U.S.-based film director Harmony Korine. According to the agency, the advertising campaign was filmed on location and, in the agency's words, "featuring genuine Cuban people, expressing their different sense of priorities."

There is a print advertisement that focuses on two ballerinas who are stretching in front of a public bus stop. The erosion of Havana's buildings is clearly visible in the background, which is consistent with the post–Special Period aesthetic. The consumer is led to believe that these are real ballerinas, as opposed to models hired for commercial purposes. Presented as a spontaneous moment, the advertisement creates the illusion that the distinctions between high culture and mass culture have been diminished, thereby promoting the socialist ideal of a classless society.

As Kent (2019) points out, Aroch utilized a filtering process meant to simulate film formats associated with analog cameras, giving them a vintage feel reminiscent of the Ektachrome, a type of "chrome" slide film. This film format launched in the 1940s and was popular among National Geographic photographers. A second effect is the use of the lens flare, which is reminiscent of inexpensive and disposable cameras, like the Polaroid. Both techniques have a pseudo-verité and nostalgic quality associated with the popular picture magazines of decades past (Kent 2019).

The video portion of the campaign offers a different, but complementary, visual point of view. The director, Harmony Korine, brought a noncommercial sensibility to the campaign. Instead of using professional actors, Korine's videos utilize quirky, everyday Cubans. One commercial, titled "Piropo," focuses on the art of flirting. The protagonist is an older Cuban gentleman who is charming and confident. We follow him as he readies himself in his small, modest apartment. Impeccably dressed, he strolls along Havana's Malecón before arriving at a small, unairconditioned bar. The spot concludes with him successfully asking a young woman to dance.

The videos are distinctive in the commercial marketplace simply because they do not feel like commercials but rather like captured moments of lived, Cuban experience. Furthermore, the focus on Cubans who have little material wealth may be seen as a reflection of socialist values, which rejects the bourgeoisie and the fetishization of material objects. In other words, the advertisements were distinctive in the marketplace because they simply do not overtly sell the product. At this point in time, it becomes evident that the agency was investing in building the brand, not necessarily in overtly promoting the product. This would change as economic pressures began to increase.

You Just Know When It's from the Heart

The "Nothing Compares to Havana" campaign may have been effective at branding the company, but it appears as if there was pressure to focus more explicitly on the product. In 2015, Havana Club launched a follow-up campaign that featured the tagline "You Just Know When It's from the Heart." In the new campaign, the agency rearticulated Cuban authenticity in ways that tied directly to the island's physical landscape. Instead of focusing on everyday life in socialist Cuba, the new campaign promoted the island's unique climate that resulted in superior extract ingredients. To tell this story, the new campaign focused on "the workers" who support the rum industry rather than on the "Cuban people." These individuals were positioned as stewards of the land, craftsmen who employed age-old methods for distilling rum, and service workers who labored simply for the love of work.

Intended to be an update to "Nothing Compares to Havana," the new campaign barely registered a mention in Pernod-Ricard's annual report for that year. A press release from Havana Club, however, provides a glimpse into the strategic motives behind the campaign:

> Through the passion of a musician playing, the laughter of a couple dancing, the care of a Cantinero making a Mojito or the emotion of our Maestro Ronero talking about what rum means to him, the creative embodies the authenticity and creative energy of the Cuban culture, expressed in each and every bottle of Havana Club 3 Year Old Rum. (Havana Club International 2015)

As indicated in the press release, the goal of the campaign was to position the product as the embodiment of Cuban cultural values. This kind of commodity fetishism had been avoided in the previous campaign but was embraced in "From the Heart," in part by focusing on the extract ingredients that come directly from the land, what Gilmore and Pine (2007) refer to as "natural authenticity." Havana Club touts itself as the only brand that is 100 percent made in Cuba and claims that its rum benefits from Cuba's rich soil and warm weather, which produce quality sugarcane.

Havana Club's claim is not without merit. Arguably, Cuba's rich volcanic soil, tropical climate, regular rainfall, and abundant sunshine make it an ideal island for growing sugarcane. But the natural ingredients are only part of the story. Equally important to the narrative is the process by which the rum is made. This strategy is not necessarily unique. Brands within the spirits category often portray themselves as small craft producers that use time-honored ways and natural ingredients as a means of competitive differentiation. These messages are meant to communicate the notion that distilleries operate purely for the love of the craft rather than for commercial considerations (Beverland 2005).

Although the video portion of the "From the Heart" campaign focuses on Cuban laborers, the project was helmed by filmmakers based in the United Kingdom. The video portion of the campaign was directed by Nick Rutter and produced by London-based Sonny Productions. Over the course of multiple videos, consumers are exposed to the life cycle of a Havana Club cocktail through rum's division of labor. The first video in the series celebrates the agricultural workers who harvest the sugarcane. Simply titled *Claudio*, the first video documents a day in the life of a single sugarcane worker.

Figure 4. Scene from *Claudio*, directed by Nick Rutter.

The commercial begins as Claudio, the protagonist of the video, starts his day in a run-down tenement in Cuba's sugar country. Claudio is shown riding with other workers in the back of a truck that is headed toward the sugarcane fields, where he cuts the cane by hand with a machete. There are close-up shots of Claudio's weathered hands and sun-kissed skin. Despite the hard labor, the laborers appear happy cultivating the land. Later that evening (Figure 4), the sugarcane workers enjoy the fruits of their labor: eating, dancing, and drinking the rum Claudio helped to cultivate.

In some ways, Claudio embodies Che Guevara's notion of the "New Man," one who commits to hard work not for pay but for the good of the community. According to revolutionary discourse, moral incentives are meant to overcome the lack of material incentive. Cuban sugarcane workers may not be well-compensated for their labor, but they are obliged to work for the love of their "socialist country." The video concludes with Claudio enjoying his time with friends and family. The consumption of rum, of course, is a key factor in bringing them together.

The next stop in the rum division of labor is the master blender. Titled "Maestro Ronero," the commercial focuses on Asbel Morales, Havana Club's master rum maker. In the video, we spend a day with Morales from the time he leaves his home in Havana, to his time in the sugar-fields, to the warehouse, where he tests the quality of rum. Morales's dialogue is written to describe the qualities that are unique to Cuban soil:

> I think I would describe the rum as Cuba. We have such a beautiful land for sugarcane to grow. This place is full of mysteries that, with time, you will get to discover. Rum is . . . Color. It's time. It's Aroma. It's not just a written recipe. It's so much more. It's a pleasure passed down through generations. I know it's a passion for all Cubans. Because I live it. Because I feel it. Because I share it, with everyone. It's a legacy that is passed from Cuban to Cuban. The rum *is* Havana. (Havana Club International 2012)

By avowing its commitment to traditional methods, the brand is asserting the point of view that only Cuban rum made by Cubans, using traditional Cuban practices, can be considered truly authentic. In the campaign, Havana Club's "Maestros del Ron Cubano" are framed as stewards of the land and guardians of long-kept secret processes.

The final stop in the process is the bartender, who brings all the ingredients together to make the perfect Cuban cocktail. A spot titled "Mojito" focuses on Chino, a former-boxer-turned-bartender. Speaking directly into the camera, Chino engages in a personal dialogue about what goes into creating an authentic mojito. While he focuses on the essential ingredients for a true mojito (the lime, the mint, and so forth), Chino makes sure to point out that it is the spirit of Havana that makes an authentic Cuban mojito. Interspersed within Chino's dialogue is a montage of a young, well-dressed bartender, readying himself for work. The spot concludes with the moment of consumption: cocktails being served to young, attractive Cubans.

The accompanying print campaign, however, appears to have been designed with a different strategic objective altogether. Instead of focusing on the worker, the print component fixes its gaze squarely on the consumer. The campaign was shot by British photographer Adam Hinton, who seemed to be an intuitive fit for this campaign. Hinton has developed a strong portfolio photographing "real" people in the Global South. His work has centered on foundry workers in Dhaka, Palestinian refugees at a camp in southern Beirut, and the Roma living in Bulgaria.

Hinton's commercial work for the "From the Heart" campaign, however, looks much more like conventional lifestyle advertising. The print campaign is essentially a series of portraits that feature young, attractive Cubans in festive settings. One print advertisement depicts a young percussionist, while another depicts an attractive couple, dancing in a nightclub. There is a print ad with a stately bartender pouring a drink. The campaign makes use of models, which is a notable shift from the "Nothing Compares to Havana" campaign, which featured real Cubans. Furthermore, the previous campaign had a captured moment aesthetic, but the new advertisements were clearly art directed. The most notable shift, however, is the greater prominence of the product. In the new campaign, a bottle of Havana Club 3 Años is clearly visible.

Cuba Made Me

By 2018, executives at Havana Club determined that the brand was not making significant inroads with its target audience of young, urban drinkers. And so M&C Saatchi launched a third global campaign, which articulated Cuban authenticity in yet another way. Launched with the headline "Cuba Made Me," the campaign focused on Havana's youth culture. As with the previous two campaigns, the agency wanted to avoid tired tropes of the city. At the same time, the agency wanted to appeal to a younger demographic by linking the Havana Club brand to urban, street style. According to the agency's press materials:

> As an authentically Cuban rum brand, Havana Club is ubiquitous in and around the streets of Havana. To help with audience appeal and a desire to convey a more authentic and gritty aspirational aesthetic, the campaign distances itself from the tourism clichés of beaches, vintage cars and salsa and instead focuses on the young Cubans uniquely shaped by Havana, its culture, and its streets. (Little Black Book 2018)

Jeremy Hemmings, chief client officer at M&C Saatchi, believed that Havana Club was uniquely poised to make this claim. "Many brands aspire to associate themselves with gritty, urban street culture," stated Hemmings. "But few have the credibility to pull it off. Havana Club is ubiquitous throughout Havana—in the bars, clubs, and streets, so you could say that this campaign is as authentic as you get."

Hemming's description of Havana's "gritty, urban street culture" connects to ongoing claims that in contemporary society, authenticity is no longer found in other times or far off places but rather in urban centers. With their multiracial inhabitants, large cities are believed to have become repositories of new forms of creative expression. In the campaign, there is also a notable shift in focus on young Afro-Cubans, which was certainly a strategic choice. Within popular imagination, exotic urban spaces are marked by the prevalence of racial and ethnic Others, who develop nonsanctioned cultural art forms, such as fashion, music, and art.

The ethos of campaign is reflected in a one-minute video that launched the campaign. The video is essentially a montage of young Afro-Cubans taking to the streets of Havana (Phillips 2021). In the very first scene, we see a young teen leaving his apartment, quickly stuffing a can of spray paint and a bottle of Havana Club rum into a backpack. It becomes apparent that he is on his way to rendezvous with friends, who are painting over the roof of an old building, creating a form of street art that can only be seen from the sky. Both the art direction and copywriting suggest that this kind of creative expression is not entirely state sanctioned. There are images of the teens running under the cover of dark. The use of bodies that are clearly marked as the ethnic Other is essential to the campaign. The early portion of the video serves as a sort of anthem for Cuban identity with title cards that read,

> Cuba Made Me Brave
> Cuba Made Me Create
> Cuba Made Me Original
> Cuba Made Me Rebel

Halfway through the video, however, the action pivots to a nightclub, and it is here where the true marketing work of the commercial begins. There are images of young, attractive Afro-Cubans dancing and drinking in a club setting. The tone of the advertisement shifts from rebellion to fun, with copy that reads,

> Cuba Made Me Wild
> Cuba Made Me Alive
> Cuba Made Me Rebel. Shine. Chill. Fresh. Unique. Proud.

Creatively, the advertisement is leveraging Cuban pride, but by the end of the commercial, the focus is squarely on the product. The action centers on the bartenders pouring Havana Club rum into cocktails. The video concludes with the logo, the tagline, and product shots of Havana Club 3 Años and their Añejo 7 Años.

Since the campaign was meant to court young, urban consumers, older Cubans are nowhere to be seen. This was a notable departure from the previous two campaigns, which included more age diversity. The campaign's youth orientation was also evident in the media strategy, which primarily utilized social media platforms, such as Facebook and Instagram, which featured the campaign hashtag #CubaMadeMe. Multiple short videos were produced for these platforms, and they featured young Cubans exploring Cuban streetstyle, street art, street food, and club scenes.

The online portion of the campaign was complemented by a print effort that focused on bartenders. This is not the first time Havana Club had photographed bartenders as part of its advertising, but there is a clear shift in how bartenders were represented in the new campaign. The bartenders in the "Cuba Made Me" campaign were decidedly younger, aspirational, and more stylish. The campaign was also decidedly more explicitly commercial, each execution featuring a product shot of a Cuban cocktail. This portion of the campaign was shot by Los Angeles–based photographer David M. Helman, who has built an extensive portfolio of work for youth-oriented brands like Nike, New Balance, and Adidas.

The anthem video was directed by British director Courtney Phillips and produced by London Alley. According to his representatives, "Courtney Phillips has become one of the UK's most emerging young directors. With a deep understanding of youth culture and urban style." It was perhaps his deep understanding of urban culture that motivated longtime competitor Bacardí to hire Phillips to direct its own youth-oriented commercial. Titled "Do What Moves You," the Bacardí advertisement is very similar to "Cuba Made Me." Both commercials are essentially music videos, and both commercials depict young, ethnic consumers in urban settings. And herein lies the problem. A focus on urban youth makes the "Cuba Made Me" campaign less distinctive. The city of Havana, as it is depicted in this campaign, could be any large city in the Global South, populated for the most part by non-whites. It is only the reggaeton music, which serves as the soundtrack to the anthem the video, that marks this being part of the Spanish-speaking world.

Advertising and Shifting Ideologies

In his critique of capitalism, Michael Schudson (1986) compares advertising to "socialist realism," a type of state-sanctioned art that presented optimistic depictions of life under Soviet leadership. According to Abram Tertz (1960), a defining characteristic of socialist realism is its truthfulness, in the representational sense. Artists were encouraged to present "authentic" scenes of the everyday life of the proletariat. However, Tertz further argues the art must also involve the education and ideological transformation of the citizen. Thus, socialist realism art is meant to be purposeful by supporting the aims of the state and the party.

By contrast, Schudson characterizes advertising as "capitalist realism," a commercial art form that celebrates a different political economic system altogether. According to Schudson, advertising does not claim to picture reality as it is but rather as it should be. The consumer, rather than the worker, is the focal point of advertising, and individuals are often presented as the embodiments of some larger, desired market category. Furthermore, consumption is presented in its ideal form and the product becomes the solution to individual needs and desires. Orchestrating all this, of course, is the corporation that is presented as the embodiment of progress.

At first, M&C Saatchi attempted to bridge the gap between socialist realism and capitalist realism. Their "Nothing Compares to Havana" advertising campaign may have followed the conventions of modern advertising by celebrating the product, but it simultaneously put a benign face to the revolution. Created as a direct response to global capitalism, "Nothing Compares to Havana" promoted an alternative economic model as the pathway toward human fulfillment.

The result of these efforts was something that looked much different from typical Western advertising, which focuses disproportionately on the wealthy or middle class. Instead, the focus of the campaign is on the proletariat, which has been a consistent hallmark of Havana Club advertising. Whether it is a pair of ballerinas in the "Nothing Compares to Havana" campaign or the sugarcane workers depicted in the "From the Heart" campaign, none of these are wealthy people. The campaign is also purported to be truthful in the representational sense in that it claims to depict authentic lived experience. Stylistically, this is accomplished through the photojournalistic approach to photography, which defines the aesthetics of the campaign. It is also evident in the campaign's focus on "real Cubans" rather than professional models and actors typically used in commercial advertising.

The agency's subsequent campaigns, however, have become increasingly stylized and oriented toward the product and the targeted consumer, which is characteristic of fields of cultural production. According to Bourdieu (1993), fields of cultural production are structured around the opposition between the heteronomous pole representing forces external to the field (primarily economic) and the "autonomous" pole representing the specific capital unique to that field (artistic or scientific skills). Because advertising is a form of marketing communications, there is great pressure to make sure the advertising delivers on its goal of generating sales. As there is increasing pressure in the marketplace to sell the product, the agency has adapted by rearticulating Cuban authenticity in new ways. By the time of "Cuba Made Me" in 2019, there was a much more concerted effort to tout the unique qualities of the rum and to become more appealing to the coveted youth market.

Agencies, along with the photographers and filmmakers they hire, are adept at selling products, and to accomplish this, they are continuously drawing on the recurring tropes and images in their repertoires. But there is a contradictory logic at play. Advertising executives attempt to make their brands stand out in a saturated marketplace, yet they naturally gravitate toward creative partners with a proven track record in selling similar kinds of products. But the more agencies hire the same cultural producers to meet their needs, the more their advertising campaigns begin to look alike. The whole thing is circular in nature. But these practices become even more pronounced when advertising agencies are faced with market pressures. Despite the industry's rhetoric of innovation and creativity, advertising agencies are in fact conservative institutions, which deliver a product that is characterized not by difference, but by sameness.

CHAPTER 2

Selling Cuban Culture

Culture has a use value, and therefore an exchange value as well. But the political economy of culture cannot be reduced to the market . . . The need to think and to know, to imagine and to create value is what can distinguish a worker from a consumer, a citizen from a client, a real person from merely an instrumental one.
—Rafael Hernández, Looking at Cuba

In May of 2012, a crowd of several dozen journalists, marketing executives, and members of Havana's arts community gathered at the Havana Club Museum of Rum to celebrate the opening of the art exhibit "Un Olor Que Entra Por Mi Ventana" (A Smell That Comes through My Window). According to the exhibition's curators, the title was meant to evoke a note of populism, referring to the aromas emanating from neighbors' kitchens that can often drift into surrounding homes. It was intended to be a metaphor for the new aesthetic and thematic trends among young Cuban artists; what is being "cooked" in terms of art in Cuba. The show included Alejandro González's photo portraits of Cuban youth, Orestes Hernández's sculptures that looked to be made of shaving foam, and a video installation by Reinier Nande that re-created a drive through different Havana neighborhoods (*Slanted* 2013). The exhibition was organized under the auspices of Havana Cultura, an extension of the Havana Club brand, which is designed to promote Cuban music, literature, film, design, architecture, and visual and performing arts. But while the Havana Cultura platform is meant to develop and promote Cuban cultural products, executives at Havana Club have made clear that such efforts should ultimately be in the service of the brand. In a press statement describing the platform, François Renié, communications director at Havana Club International, made the link between Cuban culture and the product: "At Havana Club, we are proud of our Cuban roots and culture, and believe that it is essential to support our artists by promoting their work internationally. Contemporary Cuban culture is extremely vibrant, whether it's Cuban music, visual or performing arts, cinema, or literature—it all adds magic to our brand and flavour to our rum" (Pernod Ricard 2016).

The Havana Cultura Visual Arts Project represents the kind of Anglo-Cuban collaborations favored by M&C Saatchi. The project was coproduced by British curator Flora Fairbairn and Sachie Hernández, director of the Centre for the Development of the Visual Arts. A total of six artists were selected by a jury of professionals that included Jorge Fernández, director of the Havana Biennial; Roberto Cossío, specialist at the National Council for Visual Arts; and Lázaro Saavedra and René Francisco Rodríguez, who are both prominent visual artists and professors at the Higher Institute of Arts.

The project leverages several of Havana Club's assets, including a promotional apparatus for showcasing Cuban artists, a set of British tastemakers to guide creative projects, and a dedicated space for exhibition purposes. In turn, artists benefit in multiple ways. Not only do they receive the financial resources to develop their creative work, but they also have opportunities to make their work visible to international audiences and buyers. The timing of the first exhibit was meant to coincide with the 2012 Havana Biennial, one of the largest international visual arts events, which brings together artists, buyers, curators, journalists, and tourists.

The artists themselves are astutely aware of the importance of this kind of exposure. Mabel Poblet Pujol, one of the featured artists, described the exhibition's significance. "I think this exhibition can open many doors for us because of the number of visitors," she stated during the opening exhibit. "We're at the 11th Havana Biennial, and part of the official exhibition program" (Havana Club International 2012). Visual artist Abel Barreto echoed this sentiment, stating, "The Havana Cultura project is very pertinent. Not only for the production of the piece, but because of the promotion strategy, and being included in other kinds of exhibitions. Not only in Cuba, not only during the Biennial, but also in other international spaces" (Havana Club International 2012).

In this chapter, I examine the ways in which Havana Club has utilized Cuban culture both as a kind of experiential marketing and as a form of cultural diplomacy. The state's use of Cuban culture for strategic purposes is an extension of an ongoing project. Since the revolution, Cuban culture has been employed as a form of soft power that advanced the ideals of the revolution to publics in Europe, Latin America, and Africa (Schwall 2012). As a joint venture, however, Havana Cultura represents a new kind of diplomacy that involves both state officials and marketing executives. Therefore, diplomatic relations are not entirely driven by state officials, but involve Western marketing executives, who are conceptualizing Cuban culture within the logic of capitalism.

In his discussion of cultural production, Pierre Bourdieu (1993) distinguishes between fields of restricted production, which include what we normally think of high art (museums, visual arts, etc.), and fields of large-scale production, which include fields such as popular music, movies, journalism, and advertising. Fields of restricted production are relatively autonomous, meaning that they are free from external pressures, including those of the state and the marketplace. By contrast, fields of large-scale cultural production are sustained by an extensive and complex culture industry, in which the dominant principle is economic capital or the bottom line.

Whereas the Havana Cultura platform featured a wide array of artistic products, I focus on two kinds of cultural production that involve a different set of actors. I begin with an examination of the commercial music component of Havana Cultura, which has been developed under the guidance of British deejay Gilles Peterson. I then follow with an analysis of the Havana Club Visual Arts Project, which was developed by British curator, Flora Fairbairn and was intended to draw attention to Cuba's visual arts scene. Finally, I examine the ways that Havana Club's use of Cuban culture has, over time, become more influenced by economic pressures, which in turn have determined the kinds of creative collaborations in which the brand invests.

Revolutionizing Cuban Culture

During the Republican era, Cuban artists produced a remarkable body of work that was beginning to gain currency in the international marketplace. Cuban visual arts reflected the nation's multiracial background, drawing from both Spanish and African traditions (Martínez 1994). Furthermore, much of this art reflected the ongoing struggles of a relatively young nation that was in the process of defining itself. Cuban artists addressed themes such as Cuba's changing political and social reality, the continued intervention of the United States, and the country's economic reliance on sugar production.

Cuba's influence extended into popular cultural art forms as well. During the 1940s and 1950s, Havana had emerged as one of the most important centers of commercial radio and television production in Latin America. According to Yeidy Rivero (2009), the importance of Havana as a production center was due to a combination of the city's economic wealth and the emergence of a middle-class audience, who had the money to spend on arts and entertainment. Havana's entertainment industry also benefited from its close ties to the United States, which exported its production, programming, and advertising practices. As a result, a workforce of Cuban professionals emerged in Havana, who had mastered the technical, business, and creative aspects of broadcasting production.

It is clear, however, that not all Cuban artists benefited equally during this period. Deborah Hernández (1998) argues that Cuba was highly racist during the Republican era and that biases against Afro- and mestizo Cubans manifested themselves in a number of sectors, including education, housing, and recreation. In his analysis of Cuba's music scene, Robin Moore (2006) notes that despite his wide popularity in Cuba, Afro-Cuban musician Benny Moré was excluded from performing in exclusive venues such as the Havana Yacht Club and Casino Español.

Given the racialized politics of prerevolutionary Cuba, not all cultural art forms were considered equal. White, middle-class Cuban audiences adopted the taste sensibilities of the European elite, meaning that cultural art forms such as ballet, were considered to be superior art forms and reserved for predominantly white performers (Schwall 2012). Conversely, many middle-class audiences dismissed the country's African traditions as primitive, which meant that Black performers were often shut out of opportunities with Cuba's elite academies and troupes.

After 1959, however, the new revolutionary government began to advance a very different notion of Cuban culture. According to state officials, the revolutionary government inherited a cultural system that was "corrupted" by commercialization. Under the new government, Cuban culture would serve its true function, which was to enlighten, not sell. To ensure this, cultural production was overseen by the state. Since 1959, cultural policy has been conceived of as a branch of education, and for almost a decade, it was under the supervision of Cuba's Ministry of Education (Grenier 2017).

When describing the importance of art to the revolution, state leaders argued that culture should be easily made accessible, while also promoting the values of the revolution. Of course, Cuban culture, of course, should be entertaining. Otherwise, it would fail in its capacity to reach the masses. But it should also be educational. This mission was later explained by Cuba's Consejo Nacional de Cultura:

> The cultural policy of Cuba is based on complete freedom for the creative artists. Each one makes his own choice among trends, manners, and styles according to his needs of expression, thus ensuring variety and spontaneity in the manifestations of artistic creativity. At the same time, the State relies on each artist's sense of responsibility for a close reconciliation of his freedom of expression and his Revolutionary duty, setting a barrier against the subtle ideological infiltration whose final goal is the destruction of the institutions that guarantee and promote his freedom. (Otero and Hinojosa 1971)

Whereas the Soviet countries required that art depict socialist themes and conform to realism in style, Cuban artists were relatively free to express themselves in their own ways (Levinson 2015). That said, under the new revolutionary government, artists were expected to assume some responsibility for educating the masses and promoting a new kind of consciousness. Art forms that were once used for marketing purposes (graphic design, film, illustration, and others) were now used to encourage Cubans to save water, to save electricity, to study, or to embody a new kind of citizen under the revolution. Cuban artists promoted health messages, urged recycling, taught history lessons, and urged citizens to privilege collective over individual interests (Levinson 2015).

Cuban arts under the new revolutionary government also began to reflect a new racial politics. Fidel Castro and Che Guevara made strong statements against racism, and in 1959 the newly installed government passed new legislation, which mandated the desegregation of all neighborhoods, parks, hotels, clubs, and beaches. As part of this effort, state officials also began to invest more heavily in promoting Afro-Cuban art forms. The revolutionary government recognized that African-derived art forms uniquely embody Cuba's unique character and could serve as a powerful populist symbol of the nation.

Cuban art also served the interests of the state by serving as a form of cultural diplomacy, promoting the socialist model to international publics. According to Elizabeth Schwall (2012), artists became full-bodied investments in political projects, helping to advance the ideals of the revolution. By performing abroad, Cuban artists were instrumental in the state's exercise of soft power by creating a dialogue between Cuba and Africa, while also highlighting the island's connections to Europe and Latin America. Furthermore, Cuba's use of artists as evidence of racial inclusivity served as a clear point of difference with the United States, where the civil rights movement drew worldwide attention to the country's legacy of racism.

Cuban Cultural Production and Marketplace Logic

During Cuba's Special Period, financial support for the arts in Cuba was severely impacted. The Cuban government could no longer provide even the most basic support for its citizens. In turn, prospective audiences no longer had the resources to support the arts. The overall lack of functional, public transportation made attending live performances extremely difficult for most Cubans. Simply buying records and cassettes was out of reach for many Cubans, which devastated an already struggling market for Cuban recordings (Hernández 1998). Furthermore, Cuban artists could no longer count on state funds for professional development, purchasing equipment, or renting rehearsal space.

The Cuban arts were also negatively impacted by the Cuba's shifting political environment. The economic crisis made the state vulnerable to critique, which in turn led to a series of conflicts between artists and state officials. For example, Cuban artists previously had a degree of independence that allowed for free artistic expression and even critique. However, when faced with growing public dissent, state officials began to exert more pressure on artists who were critical of the regime. Consequently, there was an exodus of Cuban artists, who left the island in search of opportunities abroad. For those artists who remained on the island, many sought alternative exhibition spaces beyond the state-run galleries, including private homes and public spaces (Levinson 2015).

This period is also notable for the reintroduction of marketplace logic into the realm of Cuban cultural production. As Sujatha Fernandes (2006) points out, during Cuba's Special Period, state officials were forced to make concessions to the international market by allowing some degree of foreign market investment, partnerships, and privatization. The Cuban government recognized that it could earn much-needed resources by marketing Cuban art forms to international audiences by seeking out partnerships with businesses that could help them develop creative projects and market them abroad.

With their work now more readily available for sale in the global marketplace, the state once again began to reconsider the transactional nature of art. State officials began to recognize that Cuban cultural products could generate much-needed revenue. But to sell, Cuban culture had to satisfy the preferences of audiences who were culturally and linguistically removed from the island. Perhaps more important, Cuban cultural producers had to create work that would appeal to the industry gatekeepers who ultimately determine which creative projects are worthy of investment.

It is the perceived foreignness of Cuban culture appears to be a significant part of its appeal. According to Dermis León (2001), Cuban art has become an attractive investment for curators, gallery owners, and collectors, who seek out alternative art that is produced in Asia, Africa, the Middle East, and Latin America. Consequently, Cuban visual artists find themselves competing with artists based out of other "Third World" countries, which host their own biennials. Collectively, these artists are competing for the attention of critics, curators, and artists who are in the market for art from the Global South.

In the field of music production, Cuban musicians also benefit from the niche of Otherness. The longstanding popularity of Cuban music is partially a result of Cuba's continued investment in Afro-Cuban musical traditions, which promoted all types of Cuban music, from rural guajira to Afro-Cuban rumbas to Son Cubano to modern jazz. Artists, including Celia Cruz and La Lupe, are examples of Afro-Cuban artists who later found acclaim in the United States. These efforts were meant to address long-standing policies of discrimination, and to promote the revolution's key theme of racial equality. But the unintended consequence was a proliferation of music that translated well for the global audiences, who had developed a taste for "undiscovered" music that had the ideal mix of First World and Third World traditions.

Hernández (1998) similarly argues that the marketing of contemporary Cuban music is grounded in racial difference. Often designated as "World Music," "world beats," or "Latin Alternative," various genres of Cuban music are collapsed into categories that signify its difference from Western mainstream music. Within an international music industry that is dominated by U.S. popular music, some Cuban musicians have learned to exploit the system of differences to their advantage, but as Ignacio Corona (2017) notes, this system of difference is based on both capitalist and racial ideologies. Cuban music must sell, but to sell, Cuban must be dissimilar to mainstream popular music in its introduction of "foreign" sounds and rhythms, language, and other ethnic markers.

An increasing reliance on Cuban culture as a revenue generating mechanism, however, represents a significant shift in thinking. The revolutionary government's original mandates were to make Cuban culture available to the masses and to direct resources away from the capital and toward communities on the periphery. After Cuba's Special Period, however, state officials realized that Cuban culture could be profitable, and so they began redirecting resources toward Havana and other tourist destinations. This, in turn, has put Cuban arts and culture out of reach for many Cubans, who do not have the economic resources to see live music or to purchase cassettes or CD's of popular artists.

Havana Cultura and a New Kind of Cultural Brokering

Within the global marketplace, mere artistic talent is no guarantor of success. Instead, artists participate in a system of production that will ensure that some cultural producers will receive the funding and exposure that will allow them to compete ably in the global marketplace and that others will not. Furthermore, the success of any given artist would not be possible without the help of cultural intermediaries who possess the knowledge to navigate the commercial landscape and have access to the relevant, professional social networks. Those players will differ, depending on the field.

These cultural intermediaries possess a "professional habitus," or the mastering of a specific professional game in a specific professional field. It means thinking about the creative industries as a game in which one must be able to master the rules of that game. Within the realm of visual arts, for example, it is a knowledge of how to navigate the networks of artists, gallery owners, auction houses, collectors, museums, and journalists. Conversely, commercial music is a field of large-scale cultural production, which involves a greater number of players. The promotion and distribution infrastructure for commercial music is carried out by a connected network of musicians, agents, independent and commercial record labels, concert and music festival presenters, radio deejays, producers, performance venues, magazines, and streaming platforms.

It is here where an advertising agency such as M&C Saatchi brings value. In her analysis of advertising practices, Anne Cronin (2007) argues that the role of advertising agencies as cultural intermediaries extends far beyond brokering the relationship between producers and consumers. Rather, advertising agencies often serve as brokers between media, financial institutions, producers of goods and services, and professional creatives working across industries. As a global advertising network, M&C Saatchi has also developed strong working relationships with music executives, photographers, film directors, graphic designers, and others who contribute to the process of advertising.

I found there to be in an incongruency in how Havana Club described their search process in their press materials, and the actual practice of selecting Cuban artists to participate in the Havana Cultura platform. In the press surrounding the launch of the event, the process of finding undiscovered Cuban talent was described as an exhaustive search in which it was possible for any Cuban artist to be discovered. Consider the following excerpt from an essay that ran in *Slanted* (2013) in which journalist Randall Koral describes the process as an extensive search for the best talent across fields: "The Havana Cultura team took that cue to explore every corner of modern Havana, roaming from Alamar to Zamora, from uptown art galleries to underground dance clubs, from Yissy, the drummer to Yusa, the soul singer." The actual process of selection, however, was less democratic. To even compete for the opportunity to be part of the project, the Cuban artists up for consideration would likely have already achieved some level of recognition within Havana. Therefore, Havana Cultura's scouts did not scour the entire island for undiscovered artists, but rather tapped into existing networks that had already identified talent.

Furthermore, not every Cuban art form was considered equal. It was essential that scouts working on behalf of Havana Club identified talent that would resonate with Western music producers, who would serve as brokers between Havana Club and their core audience, which was identified as men between the ages of twenty-five and thirty-four who lived in urban centers. These consumers were described by the agency as "experience seekers," for whom music and socializing are an important part of their lives. They were believed to have discriminating tastes and wanted exposure to contemporary artists who had not yet been discovered by mainstream audiences (*The Guardian* 2010).

To bridge the gap between European consumers and Cuban artists, the brand enlisted the help of British tastemakers with established industry connections and who had experiences developing art from the Global South. To draw attention to Cuba's contemporary arts scene, two ambassadors were hired to legitimize the initiative and raise its awareness: BBC deejay Gilles Peterson, who produced numerous Havana Cultura albums and concerts, and Flora Fairbairn, an art curator who set up in 2010 the Havana Cultura Visual Arts Project. Peterson and Fairbairn, in turn, relied heavily on Cuban insiders who had already developed working relationships with artists who had commercial potential.

The Anti–Buena Vista Social Club

When the Havana Club platform first launched, the brand invested in an aggressive public relations campaign, which yielded mentions in the United Kingdom's largest newspapers, including *The Guardian* and *The Telegraph*. The challenge was to make the project legible to primarily British audiences by invoking something they already knew. The Buena Vista Social Club became an important referent against which the Havana Cultura project was defined. Consider the following piece that ran in *Slanted* (2013), an international publication focused on the arts:

> If you suspect there's a lot more to the Cuban capital than Buicks, *barbudos* and the Buena Vista Social Club—*ya está*, now you're on the right track. If you understand that Havana today is a powerhouse of inspiration for cubatón, rockoson, and Afro-Cuban jazz; for the Havana Biennial art fair, and the Cubadanza festival, for films like *Suite Habana*, *Habanastation*, and *7 Days in Havana*, for poster artists and *chateo* (satire) artists, for the *Trilogia sucia de la Habana* by Pedro Juan Gutiérrez—if you know all that, then chances are you're already acquainted with Havana Cultura, the pre-eminent arts showcase for 21st century Havana.

Invoking and then evading the Buena Vista Social Club was a consistent talking point in the promotion of the Havana Cultura platform. The Buena Vista Social Club was a project developed by American guitarist and record producer Ry Cooder, who brought together an ensemble of performers of traditional Cuban *son*, many of whom had played during the 1940s and 1950s. The original *Buena Vista Social Club* album was recorded for World Circuit Records, a British World Music record label, and was produced over the course seven days in Havana's infamous EGREM Studios. A documentary directed by Wim Wenders (1999) soon followed, garnering more attention for the project.

Overall, the Buena Vista project was a creative and financial success for Cuba. In 1998, the album won the Grammy Award for Best Traditional Tropical Latin Album and generated multiple spin-off albums. The project also sold millions of records internationally. As the owner of the copyrights on each of the album's tracks, Editora Musical de Cuba, a government-owned publishing company, has benefited financially from direct sales of the disc abroad (Fernandes 2006). But the album was also a boon for Cuba's tourism industry. The success of Buena Vista was due, in part, to how Cuba was depicted as a country that had remained almost unchanged from the 1950s, which was appealing for foreign tourists (Bustamante and Sweig 2008).

The project, however, was not without its critics. The Buena Vista Social Club has been denounced for how it portrayed Havana as a city lost in time. Others expressed concern over the apolitical nature of the project and the fact that there was no mention of the negative impact of the U.S. embargo on Cubans. As Moore (2006) noted, critics of the film argued that it promoted a First World/Third World narrative by juxtaposing dilapidated buildings in Havana with the modern, well-maintained buildings in Manhattan's business district. Others argued that the project's focus on prerevolutionary artists rather than on contemporary Cuban artists was a form of imperialist nostalgia (Moore 2006).

Executives at Havana Club wanted to avoid the pitfalls associated with the original project. Instead of looking at Cuba's cultural past, the architects of Havana Cultura wanted to focus on contemporary art and music. "At Havana Club, we're proud of our Cuban origins," stated Communications Director François Renié, who runs the initiative at Havana Club. "Havana is one of the world's most buoyant cultural scenes—particularly when it comes to music—and we were eager to give a bigger voice to a generation of young artists whose work is decidedly modern, yet firmly anchored in the richness of Cuba's musical tradition" (Pernod Ricard 2016). To "give voice" to this young generation of Cuban artists meant that the company needed cultural brokers who had experience making Cuban art and music appealing to non-Cuban consumers.

Gilles Peterson and the New Cuban Sound

Given its proven success within the international marketplace, it is no surprise that commercial music has become the centerpiece of the Havana Cultura platform. To help launch the effort, Havana Club and M&C Saatchi partnered with BBC Radio deejay and producer Gilles Peterson. In this role, Peterson served two functions. First, he traveled to Cuba to oversee the development of Cuban musicians with the purpose of creating an album that could be marketed globally. Second, Peterson served as an advocate for the platform in the global media outlets to which he had access. According to François Renié, international communications director for Havana Club, "We decided that we needed to find a credible ambassador to help us spread the message. When we met Gilles, we knew he was the perfect man for the job" (Cantor-Navas 2015).

Here, it is important to consider what exactly made Peterson the perfect man for the job. Gilles Jérôme Moehrle was born in France but grew up in London, where he later took on the name Peterson. In his youth, he became an avid fan of music, but in interviews, he has made clear that he had a particular interest in different genres of ethnic music, describing himself as drawn to Black London musicians who were featured in UK magazines like *Black Echoes* and *Blues and Soul* (*Resident Advisor* 2022).

As a youth, Peterson worked as a deejay in South London's Electronic Ballroom, where he was inspired by the work of deejay Paul Murphy, another British deejay who made a name for himself by fusing jazz, soul, and Latin music. "It was the ghetto Black club, and there were very few white boys," Peterson recalled during an interview with *Resident Advisor* (2022). "In the main room it was Paul Anderson with George Power, jazz, funk, imports, and early electro. Upstairs was this little ghetto room. Paul Murphy was in there playing mad fast speed jazz records. Really nutty, rare fusion Afro-Cuban stuff."

Peterson's self-positioning as one of the "few white boys" in Black spaces has served him well, allowing him to claim a proprietary understanding of musical traditions that appear to be out of reach to white, mainstream listeners. Over the course of his career, Peterson has become proficient in developing music produced within the Global South so that it is appealing to British ears. In 1998, he began working as a deejay for BBC Radio 1, and in 2016, he launched WorldWide FM, a platform for eclectic international music, which at its peak was broadcast in fifteen countries. In addition to his work as a deejay, Peterson has established a number of record labels, including Acid Jazz, Talkin' Loud, and finally Brownswood Recordings, which released the Havana Cultura albums.

Through his Brownswood Recordings label, Peterson has been able to capitalize on a number of international collaborations. The label's catalog boasts a number of artists who fuse traditional sounds with contemporary Western rhythms, including the Owiny Sigoma band, a London-based group working with Kenyan artists; Anushka, a British American sitar player; and Shabaka and the Ancestors, a collaboration between a British saxophonist and an ensemble of South African musicians.

Gilles Peterson Presents . . . Sonzeria: Brazil Bam Bam Bam, which was released in 2014. is a good example of the process that Peterson has been able to perfect as a producer. He creates connections between British producers and musicians from the Global South. He blends traditional music with contemporary sounds. And he rebrands the effort under his own name. The album was produced in collaboration with Brazilian singer and songwriter Alexander Kassin, a member of the band Orquestra Imperial. During the project, Peterson traveled to Rio de Janeiro to record an album that mixes the old and new and features appearances from Brazilian musicians. The project also reflects Peterson's strong market sensibilities.

The album was partially driven by economic interest. Brazil was hosting the World Cup at the time, and the album was meant to capitalize on the interest in Brazilian culture and music. However, Peterson positions these projects as creative endeavors. "Out of all the world musics," he said in an interview with *Sounds and Colors*, "I think Brazilian music is the one music that British people are the most inclined to go for. I've done African, Latin records, and the ones that have always sold the best, by far, are the Brazilian records. I think it's because the British people en masse have a love affair with football, they love all the intrigue and excitement of Brazil" (Slater 2014). Peterson is careful, however, not to come across as mercenary. When promoting his albums, he often describes them as labors of love.

For example, in interviews during the launch of *Gilles Peterson Presents . . . Sonzeria: Brazil Bam Bam Bam*, Peterson stated that this Brazilian music was one of his first loves when he broke through as a deejay on pirate radio in the 1980s and that it has been a big influence on him ever since (Slater 2014). In a similar way, Peterson has described his attraction to the Havana Cultura project as a produce of his love of Cuban music. Consider the following statement that was included in Pernod Ricard's press materials surrounding the launch of *Gilles Peterson Presents: Havana Cultura Anthology*, a double CD that highlights music from the first eight years of the project: "The Havana Cultura project gave me the chance to go deep in a country that had intrigued me ever since I was digging for Latin records as a young DJ. From the first release up to now, it's been about taking that spirit of the Buena Vista Social Club to show a new generation of artists and opening it up to as big an audience as possible" (Pernod Ricard 2016).

Peterson has delivered on his promise to generate public interest in the Havana Cultura platform. Largely due to his professional reputation, Peterson has the stature to garner the attention of the United Kingdom's largest media outlets. He is a regular contributor to both the BBC and *The Guardian*, which makes him a particularly effective spokesperson for the brand. This was evident in an essay he authored for *The Guardian*, which ran under the title "From our Correspondent: Gilles Peterson's Havana" (Peterson 2009). Overall, the piece reads as a sort of travelogue, in which Peterson introduces British readers to Cuba's tourism hotspots. Describing the capital city as "Old school baroque Havana meets Disney," Peterson recommends specific hotels and restaurants. He also makes sure to entice readers to visit the Havana Club Museum of Rum, where they will have an opportunity to "understand the roots of the drink and down a cheeky mojito."

As an authority on music, Peterson also highlights the best and worst of Havana's music scene. In the article, Peterson encourages the reader to patronize specific venues such as the Casa de la Música de Centro Habana ("the best live venue in Cuba"), and to avoid others, such as El Zorro y El Cuervo ("one of the worst designed clubs I've seen, but people seem to love it"). Meanwhile, Peterson dutifully promotes the Havana Cultura project and his own record label, which will produce the first album.

At the time, Peterson was involved in the production of what would go on to become the project's first album, *Gilles Peterson Presents Havana Cultura: New Cuba Sound* (2009). The double album was recorded at Havana's legendary EGREM studios and featured a collection of more than fifteen established and up-and-coming musicians, including Danay Suárez, Telmary Díaz, Los Aldeanos, Gente de Zona, Harold López-Nussa, Descemer Bueno, Kelvis Ochoa, Yusa, Doble Filo, Ogguere, Kumar, Wichy de Vedado, Tony Rodríguez, Mayra Caridad Valdés, Cubanito, and Free Hole Negro.

That same year, Gilles Peterson recorded *Danay Suarez: Havana Cultura Sessions* (2010), a highly praised four-track album. Suárez, a Havana-born artist who has been featured on several of the Havana Cultura albums, was backed by pianist and album coproducer Roberto Fonseca. Long known as "la Reina del

Hip Hop Cubano," Suárez has, under Peterson's supervision, begun to fuse hip-hop with several other styles, including jazz, reggae, soul, and traditional Cuban music. Since her involvement in the project, Suárez has gained international popularity the United States, the United Kingdom, and France.

Suárez was also featured on the first Havana Cultura album and has contributed to other albums produced under the Havana Cultura label, including "Noche Sueños," a track on the album *Mala in Cuba*. It is clear that Suárez has benefited from her involvement in the project. In 2014 she released a CD under her name, and that year, Billboard named Suárez one of their ten "up-and-coming" reggaeton artists. In 2017, she was nominated for four Latin Grammys in various categories, including Best New Artist and Album of the Year.

Suárez's visibility has risen since her involvement in Havana Cultura, but Peterson cannot fully be credited with discovering Suárez. Instead, her early career was due to relationships with producers living in Havana. In 2007, Suárez arrived unannounced at the home of X Alfonso, an influential Cuban fusion artist and music producer, and delivered a compilation of demo recordings representing her work. Clearly impressed by what he had heard, X Alfonso invited Suárez to record with him. It was X Alfonso who brought Suárez to the attention of Peterson, demonstrating the importance of Cuban producers in the project, something that has been downplayed in Havana Cultura's press materials.

Also instrumental to the process was Robert Fonseca, a renowned Cuban pianist, vocalist, multi-instrumentalist, composer, producer, and bandleader. Fonseca was born in Havana and has been a prolific artist. He has released nine solo albums and has been nominated for a Grammy Award. Prior to working with Peterson, Fonseca had toured with the Buena Vista Social Club and has worked with Cuban artists such as Rubén González, Ibrahim Ferrer, Cachaito, Guajiro Mirabel, and Manuel Galbán.

In an interview with the *Irish Times* (2009), Peterson acknowledged Fonseca's role in the project, yet he positions Fonseca more as production support than as a true creative partner. For example, Peterson credits Fonseca with possessing the necessary linguistic skills, social connections, and understanding of Cuban music that ensured the project could be produced within a short timeframe. Peterson went on to describe how Fonseca booked time at EGREM studios and brought in the technicians required to complete the project. Peterson also noted Fonseca's proficiency in English, which was instrumental in ensuring that Peterson could direct the Cuban musicians.

At the same time, Peterson has elevated the role of British producers, which was evident in his collaboration with Mark Lawrence, a deejay and record producer who goes by the professional name Mala. Like Peterson, Lawrence grew up in South London and made a name for himself in the UK dance music scene. In 2010, Peterson invited Lawrence to travel to Cuba and produce an album that would blend traditional Cuban sounds with his own style of British dubstep. The product of that collaboration became *Mala in Cuba*, which follows in the project's tradition of blending traditional Cuban music with contemporary European musical styles, what Lawrence has described as "South London meeting Havana" (Purdom 2012).

Peterson has asserted an ongoing claim that he develops a deep understanding of a people and their culture through their music, but Lawrence has admitted to knowing very little about Cuba or its music before entering the project. He also admits that the creative process was not particularly collaborative. As Lawrence has described it in interviews, the production of *Mala in Cuba* was not necessarily a true cultural exchange. Instead, he was given a preselected set of tracks and then tasked with converting them into a sound that reflected contemporary British dance music. "What they had in mind was that they would record traditional Cuban rhythms for me," he stated in the piece. "Then I would take those rhythms home and try to start twisting them up in my style, and that's when I went home with a hard drive of the music they had recorded for me" (Davison 2012).

Lawrence expressed his appreciation for the musicians involved in the project, but he is careful not to claim that he has produced a Cuban album, but rather a British album with some Cuban influences. "Well, I have to be me, I have to do it my way," he stated in *Inverted Audio* (Davidson 2012). "At first, I was like, I want to do a Cuban record, because I want to use all this music the Cubans have given me. But at the same time, I'm not Cuban. I'm half Jamaican, half English."

Whatever misgivings Lawrence may have had about developing the music from the Global South a seems to have diminished. Since developing *Mala in Cuba*, Lawrence has followed in Peterson's footsteps of taking traditional Third World music and blending it with contemporary British sounds. In 2016, Lawrence released *Mirrors* through Peterson's Brownswood Recordings label, which features Peruvian music and artists. By that time, Lawrence had adopted Peterson's practice of claiming an ongoing love for a type of regional music and then claiming it as universal. "I was introduced to music from the jungle, music from the mountains, Andean sounds, native sounds, Afro-Peruvian music," he said in an interview with *Sounds and Colors* (Slater 2016). "It all goes back to the roots and the rhythms, and I related instantly. That primal rhythm is in all of us."

These kinds of collaborations between British and Cuban musicians, producers, and deejays have proven lucrative for both Peterson and Havana Club. By 2022, over a dozen records had been produced under the Havana Cultura brand. The musicians involved in the project also went on to tour globally, which has served as a kind of experiential marketing. For example, Peterson also supervised the launch of Havana Cultura Live, a series of concerts by artists associated with the project. The group has toured in France, Belgium, the United Kingdom, Denmark, Austria, the Netherlands, Germany, Chile, and Spain—all key consumer markets for the brand.

The Havana Cultura Visual Arts Project

When the Havana Cultura platform first launched in 2007, Cuba's visual arts scene was intended to be an important component. Associating a brand with high art is not necessarily unique within the premium spirits category. Absolut Vodka, Tequila Herradura, and Ron Zapaca are just a few brands that have collaborated with painters, illustrators, street artists, and photographers. These kinds of collaborations can invest products with authenticity by emphasizing the company's role in safeguarding cultural heritage and by embodying the cultural expression of a period and a region (Cetino, Karlsson, Lu, and Yao 2018).

To establish itself as the face of Cuban arts, the Havana Cultura Visual Arts program grants scholarships to emerging artists. According to Havana Club (*Slanted* 2013), the Visual Arts Project was initially designed to accomplish a number of objectives. First, executives at Havana Club sought to encourage the production of contemporary art by young, emerging Cuban artists by granting artistic scholarships. Second, they wanted to build a corporate collection of Cuban contemporary art and show it around the world. Finally, they wanted to establish an exhaustive database of young Cuban artists.

While it was not explicitly stated, an unstated goal was to utilize Cuban visual arts to promote tourism by leveraging the Havana Club Museum as an exhibition space. "From the beginning Havana Club wanted to transform it into a space for the promotion of contemporary Cuban art," said Sachie Hernández, director of the Centre for the Development of the Visual Arts (Havana Club International 2012). "Especially contemporary artists that are part of the Havana Cultura Visual Arts project, and the visual arts residencies included in this program. Our idea was to reopen this space during the Havana Biennial, which was obviously an important moment to show the result of the first two editions of the residencies."

To lead the Visual Arts Project, Havana Club International turned to Flora Fairbairn, a British curator with a background in architecture. Over the course of her career, Fairbairn has helped artists to get their work into a wide range of public and private collections around the world, but she has also developed a professional reputation for curating exhibitions in architecturally unique spaces, such as La Casa Encendida in Madrid, and the vaults underneath the courtyard of Somerset House, London. This kind of expertise was beneficial for the Visual Arts Program, since a secondary objective was to create a corporate art collection that could be exhibited at the Havana Club Museum of Rum.

Born into an influential British family, Fairbairn possessed the requisite economic, social, and cultural capital to thrive in the exclusive world of art. She is a graduate of the Royal Drawing School, and in 2001, she posed as the model for a portrait painted by British artist Lucian Freud, whom she has stated was instrumental in sharpening her understanding of the creative process. She was also friends with Robert Loder, a prominent businessman, philanthropist, and art collector who had built a prominent collection of African art and whom she has described as a mentor who provided her with global contacts.

Another important contact was Philippa Adams, who worked for Charles Saatchi as a curator. Charles Saatchi, who along with his brother Maurice would go on to establish the global advertising agency M&C Saatchi, Havana Club's agency of record, is himself a patron of the arts. In 1985, Charles Saatchi established the Saatchi Gallery in London, which initially drew heavily upon his private collection. The museum routinely showcases new work from emerging artists and has become a recognized authority in contemporary art globally.

Unlike Peterson, who directly shapes the music, Fairbairn's goal was to give unestablished, Cuban artists the resources to develop and promote their own work. However, the actual requirements for participating in the program were broadly defined. According to Havana Club, artists must be young, must reside in Cuba, and must have limited previous international exposure and unlimited artistic potential (*Slanted* 2013). According to Fairbairn, she also wanted to provide them with the professional skills to market themselves. "This project is especially important for young artists without the means to publicize their work," Fairbairn stated during the interview, "to buy an ad in an art magazine, or to attend an international art fair."

Photographer Alejandro González, who was part of the initial residency program, is a good example of the kind of artist who was supported by the Havana Club Visual Arts program. His installation, titled *Cuba Año Cero*, included a series of photographs of Cuban teenagers who were born after the year 1990. According to González, this generation was born during Cuba's Special Period, a pivotal point in Cuban culture. "This was right after the disappearance of the Soviet bloc," González stated in a video produced by Havana Club (2012). "It's a generation that grew up in very particular circumstances, where official discourse contradicts reality. This generation lived during the Special Period, and they don't have any knowledge or memories, of the sweeter period of the Revolution of the 1980s."

González is referring to the revolution's "Golden Age," a period of relative economic and political stability. The artist presents a nostalgic vision of Cuba before the incursion of marketplace dynamics. González's series may be seen as a critique of Cuba's economic policy in the years after the Special Period, but it is hard to deny that González himself has benefited from some of the economic concessions that were made during this time. Over the course of his career, González had proven adept at creating content that is coveted in international markets According to León (2001), in a landscape in which there are a number of products from the Global South, Cuban artists must offer something more than just Third World art. To appeal to international buyers, Cuban artists must produce work that is "critical" of the state, and calls into question, the concept of a socialist utopia.

González's art certainly fits this description, however, it is not accurate to say Havana Cultura launched his career. By the time he had participated in the residency program, González had already achieved some level of international recognition, despite the requirement by Havana Club that participating artists have limited exposure outside Cuba. In 2000, González debuted with his first solo exhibitions "Quién" (Who) and "Donde" (Where), a black-and-white series showing unidentified people or places in Havana. He also took part in group exhibitions in Cuba as well in Los Angeles and Tel Aviv. In 2002, González was invited to an artist-in-residence program at the Kunsthohschul für Medien Köln (Academy of Media Arts) in Cologne. González continues to participate in national and international exhibitions and art fairs and is represented by Galeria Servando in Havana and Galeria Art Forum in Bologna, Italy.

That said, the monetary support and international promotion that he received for his work were not inconsequential. According to González, Havana Club gave him the resources to complete his project. Perhaps equally important was his access to international buyers. The first exhibition of Havana Club–sponsored artists was specifically timed to coincide with the 2012 Havana Biennial, which took place in the city's museums, cultural centers, galleries, and public spaces. Since its first edition in 1984, the Havana Biennial has become a major artistic event specializing in visual arts from Latin America, Africa, and Asia. Celebrated every two years, the Havana Biennial has become a major showcase for "Third World" art.

While some of the artists associated with the project have done well on the international market, the Havana Cultura Visual Arts Project has never become a defining feature of the Havana Cultura platform. Furthermore, Fairbairn never became the public advocate for the brand in the way that Peterson has. Nor has the Havana Cultura Visual Arts Project delivered on its promise of converting the Havana Club Museum of Rum into an important exhibition space. During my visit to Cuba during the 2019 Havana Biennial, the Havana Club Museum of Rum was not on the official program. And when I visited the museum in 2023, it was not an exhibition for contemporary art in the way that it was originally envisioned. Instead, there was a sporadic display of artistic works that had been commissioned to feature the Havana Club product. Thus, it appears as if the Havana Club Visual Arts Project has struggled with its ability to blend art and marketing, in the same way that other brands have been able to achieve. Whatever artworks are there are not formally curated for aesthetic purposes, nor are they effective at attracting visitors to the museum.

Perhaps it is because of its poor return on its investment that the Havana Cultura Visual Arts Project has, over time, taken on a more diminished role.

Fairbairn's collaboration with the project was also short-lived, and she does not recall the project in favorable terms. During an interview with *The Telegraph* (Gleadell 2021), Fairbairn stated that it was difficult to work with limited infrastructure, including internet services that were inadequate for sending high-resolution images for promotional purposes. Fairbairn stated that she felt as if she were constantly being monitored and that government officials exerted too much control over the creative process.

In 2020, Fairbairn and Sachie Hernández collaborated on another exhibit that was also meant to showcase Cuban artists. Titled "The Weight of an Island, the Love of a People," the exhibition was not affiliated with the Havana Club Visual Arts Project. Together, Fairbairn and Hernández developed an exhibit that was much more critical of both the United States and the Cuban State. Cuban artists were working through a variety of subjects, including the effects of the pandemic, the country's reliance on tourism, and the continued impact of the U.S. embargo under the Trump presidency. The exhibit was also meant to draw attention to Cuban artists, creatives, and activists, who were calling for greater freedom of expression in Cuba. "The situation there is electrifying," Fairbairn stated during an interview with *The Telegraph* (Gleadell 2021), "with Cuban artists demonstrating outside the Ministry of Culture, and Miami-based Cuban rappers taking on the government."

Cuban Culture Goes Global

Executives at Havana Club have positioned the Havana Cultura platform as a way to promote Cuban art, dance, and music to various audiences abroad. In this way, Havana Club can be seen both as a marketing effort and as a form of cultural diplomacy, and there is some evidence that the platform is working in this way. British coverage of the platform has largely been favorable. "The cold war ice continues to melt in Cuba," began a review of the project in *The Guardian* (Spencer 2009) in its coverage of the first two albums. *Clash* magazine (Green 2016) went even further, by describing the project as a necessary form of cultural exchange. "As Cuba takes to the global stage," *Clash* magazine reported, "a whole host of foreign musicians will be exposed to its lush musical history. Compositions like these show that Cuba has much to give musicians around the world, and musicians around the world have much to give to Cuba."

The belief that a corporate brand can serve in this capacity is predicated on the assumption that Havana Club is an extension of the state and therefore serves the interest of the Cuban people. However, it is better to think about Havana Cultura as a repository of multiple, complementary brands, each with competing interests. This was most evident in the music component of the platform, which receives most of the company's resources. First, there is the overt corporate branding. Havana Cultura is a sub-brand of the larger Havana Club brand. Both names are ubiquitous in all marketing communications: on the albums, in the press releases, and throughout the promotional videos that showcase anything involving the artists.

Then there are the musicians themselves, who serve as brands in their own right. However, not all Cuban musicians involved in the project are promoted equally. Most of the records produced under the Havana Cultura banner are anthologies, and the individual artists are generally presented as part of a larger ensemble. In limited cases, singular artists who have been identified as lucrative have been featured. Both Daymé Arocena and Danay Suárez have produced individual albums under the Havana Cultura banner.

Then there is Gilles Peterson, who is, of course, the most important brand of all, along with his record label Brownswood Recordings. The entire enterprise is meant to showcase emerging Cuban talent, but it is Peterson who takes center stage on these albums. This is evident in the artwork for the first album, *Gilles Peterson Presents: Havana Cultura, the New Cuban Sound*. The album cover features an image of Peterson standing with a mic on a busy Havana Street, staring directly at the viewer. In the background are passersby, presumably Cubans, who are rendered as a blur. Peterson is the only figure that is clearly in focus. A follow-up album, *Havana Cultura: The Search Continues*, depicts Peterson standing front of a mural of Cuba's revolutionary heroes, Che Guevara, Camilo Cienfuegos, and Julio Antonio Mella.

By making Peterson the face of Cuban music, the Havana Cultura project replicates some of the problems associated with the Buena Vista Social Club, the project on which it was implicitly modeled. At the time, critics chafed at making Ry Cooder the central figure in Wim Wenders's documentary, making him the face of Cuban culture despite his relative lack of knowledge of Cuba, its language, and its history (Bustamante and Sweig 2008). But Peterson essentially serves the same role, traveling to an unknown land, discovering new talent, and sharing it with the world, all despite having limited knowledge of the island's language, its history, its politics, and its culture.

As a global product, however, Peterson is a necessary branding device. He serves as a reassuring and recognizable face for a primarily Western audience that is unfamiliar with Cuban culture. Coverage in the United Kingdom has unreflectively invoked colonial images. "Our man in Havana" is how *The Guardian* refers to Peterson, a reference to the 1959 Graham Greene spy novel of the same name. The *Irish Times* (2009) called Peterson a "man on a Cuban mission" and then goes on to describe him as a sort of sonic explorer, traveling to exotic places and bringing unfamiliar sounds that can be consumed by British audiences. "The globetrotting DJ has travelled to the four corners of the planet" is how he is described in the article, "bringing his passion for jazz, soul, World Music and what-have-you to numerous far-flung places."

According to Peterson, it is his deep understanding of music that allows him to confidently make these kinds of assertions. By focusing on the universal qualities of music, he can transcend all kinds of boundaries: geographic, linguistic, and cultural, but most importantly political. "I've been coming here for almost 10 years now," he stated in 2018, "and finally felt a movement that was neither restricted by politics (hip hop), tradition (jazz) or Eastern European techno (yawn)" (Peterson 2018).

Peterson is alluding to the apolitical nature of the project. As Sujatha Fernandes explored in her book *Cuba Represent!* (2006), popular musicians on the island generally fall into two categories. First, there are commercial rappers, like the members of the hugely popular group Orishas, who tend to portray Cuba as an exotic getaway, while shying away from explicitly political themes. The second category includes more political groups who advance critiques of materialism, globalization and the country's unequal relationship with the United States.

Peterson's project has, to varying degrees, attempted to upend familiar tropes that have relegated Cuba to the past. Yet the project stops short of engaging in the kind of thoughtful reflection and critique that is necessary for serious art. After all, politics gets in the way of sales, and Peterson is, if anything, an astute businessman. The kind of music Peterson has produced on behalf of the project adheres to what Barber (1996) calls "the market imperative," in which marketers avoid parochialism, isolation, and political fractiousness, or anything that might disrupt the flow of commodities across borders.

Consider how the artists themselves negotiate political issues that inevitably come up. For example, during interviews Suárez has shied away from addressing Cuban politics, because in her words, "politics are very unpredictable and manipulative." When pressed, however, Suárez has attempted to strike a balance between the capitalist sensibilities of her Western fans and the socialist sensibilities of state officials. For example, when asked about the potential thawing of the relationship between Cuba and the United States, Suárez was optimistic that artists like her might find more opportunities. But then she expresses some concern if these opportunities reflected a fundamental shift in values. "It would be wrong if this means that Cuba will become a capitalist society where people start living just to make rent and to buy a bunch of material goods that in the end they won't be able to enjoy," she stated during an interview with *Remezcla*. "Where you don't even have enough time to look at the clouds or the mountains, or you can't talk to your neighbor, or that we'll have extreme poverty" (Hassan 2015).

Peterson's work deemphasizes political and cultural differences in favor of a universal musical experience (Lipsitz 1994), which as Steven Feld (2000) argues, is the ethos of global music. By removing music from its specific sociohistoric context, producers can more easily create a product that can flow seamlessly across national boundaries. It is the detachment of sound from its context that also allows British producers like Peterson and Lawrence to claim ownership over Cuban music without being fluent in Spanish or having a deep understanding of Cuban culture and history.

Furthermore, Peterson's strategy of blending traditional rhythms with contemporary sounds has become a proven strategy within the genre of World Music. As Feld (2000) argues, the very appeal of World Music is that it allows listeners to imagine an idealized past, while simultaneously envisioning the possibilities for a better future. Ultimately, however, World Music also reflects the logic of globalization, which is driven by a need of expansion. This was evident in the platform's more current creative collaborations with artists from other countries.

By 2020, the Havana Cultura platform turned away from the island and began cultivating relationships in other countries. In 2022, Havana Club launched Havana Club Grounds in Brussels, a series of creative workshops, talks, and classes. The goal was to tap into Brussels's creative community by hosting three creative workshops, which focused on deejaying, fashion, and photography. From a marketing standpoint, the objective was to gain visibility for the product in the Belgian market. The event concluded with a party, in which Havana Club rum was showcased.

These kinds of collaborations were positioned as goodwill efforts, but Havana Club has made sure to capitalize on them by establishing direct links to the product. In 2022, Havana Club collaborated with Joseph Junior Adenuga, who goes by the name Skepta. Born in Ogun, Nigeria, Adenuga moved to Tottenham, England, eventually becoming an MC, rapper, and record producer. This collaboration also yielded its own limited-edition rum, named Havana Club x Skepta. According to Havana Club, the connection between Yoruba and Afro-Cuban cultures is reflected in the concept of Aché, which they describe as "a creative, universal energy that brings us all together" (Hypebeast 2020). To make sure to capitalize on this connection, a uniquely designed bottle of Havana Club was released, featuring several Nigerian symbols: Ewe Oshun leaves that are used in Yoruba rituals, cowrie shells, and Guiro textiles.

A year later, Havana Club collaborated with Francis Junior Edusei, a Ghanaian-Dutch rapper who goes by the name of Frenna. The rapper was the centerpiece of a campaign titled "A Toast to The Culture," which included a music track and a music video. The collaboration also integrated a variety of auxiliary artists. The campaign itself was photographed by Calvin Pausania, who had made a name for himself by working on campaigns for Nike, Converse, and Valentino (Numéro 2022). Havana Club also commissioned an oil portrait to be painted of Frenna by British artist Hannah Vernier. Finally, a limited-edition bottle of Havana Club rum was created by Amsterdam designer Julian Roebling, which included the Ghanaian flag, and seven adinkra symbols to signify greatness, bravery, creativity, wisdom of the past, strength, and hatred (Kiely 2022).

That same year, Havana Club engaged in a similar collaboration with Alba Farelo I Solé, professionally known as Bad Gyal, a Catalan singer who blends trap, reggaeton, and dancehall music. According to Havana Club, the collaboration made sense because Bad Gyal embodied the urban authenticity that the brand was known for (Brooker 2022). To make a connection between the artist's "urban energy" and the product, Havana Club brand released "Havana Club 7 x Bad Gyal," a limited-edition rum that is positioned as a "tribute to parties, music and people" (Havana Club International 2022).

The move away from showcasing undiscovered Cuban musicians to featuring international artists with established reputations marks a notable shift in strategy. But the specific kinds of collaborations in which Havana Club engages is not arbitrary. Executives at Havana Club have sought out partnerships that are intended reinforce the brand's authentic credentials by connecting the brand with artists who themselves possess urban and Third World authenticity. But Havana Club has been increasingly effective at mining these connections. It is not just the music that serves the brand, but also the marketing materials that surround the music.

These collaborations reflect a new strategy for communicating Cuban authenticity, one that looks outward rather than inward. Havana Club's strategy has shifted from promoting Cuban artists to European audiences, and the new strategy is to employ a two-way exchange in which Cuba becomes a receiver of culture rather than an exporter. Another significant shift is the move away from "undiscovered artists" to those who have already achieved international exposure. Havana Club's more recent collaborations are with artists who are undoubtedly products of the commercial music system. This shift in strategy seems to undermine the very idea that Cuban culture is meant to enlighten its citizens and to develop sympathies with various publics. Instead, this use of Cuban cultural products seem designed to cultivate consumers in markets that are of economic importance to the brand.

CHAPTER 3

Long-Distance Nationalism and the Logic of Capitalism

My life was changed forever on New Year's Day 1960 when the Castro government took over the rum business that my family founded in 1878. The Revolutionary regime called it intervention. They promised us we would eventually be paid, but we never got a red cent. The simple truth is our property was stolen.
—Ramón Arechabala, 2004

In 2018, *Amparo*, an immersive theater experience, debuted in New York, then later in Miami. Written by Vanessa García and directed by Victoria Collado, both Cuban Americans, *Amparo* centers on the Arechabala family in the days before its business was expropriated by the Cuban State. In Miami, audiences gathered at a historic villa, which was transformed to look like a prosperous home in Cuba, just at the onset of the revolution. Over the course of ninety minutes, the audience follows various members of the Arechabala family as they confront the loss of their country and their business.

Named after Amparo Arechabala, the family's matriarch, the play is a view of the revolution from the perspective of the entrepreneurial class that fled Cuba. The exercise of state coercion is made dramatically throughout the play, and to bring audiences into the moment, actors portraying armed guerrillas direct members of the audience into a jail cell. The denouement of the play is a scene depicting Ramón Arechabala relinquishing his family's business at gunpoint.

However, the play ends on an optimistic note. The audience learns that despite having lost everything, the family resettled in the United States, having smuggled its original recipe for Havana Club rum out of Cuba. In Miami, the Arechabalas do what Cuban expatriates do: They build connections with other Cuban families who have lost everything. With some help from the Bacardí family, the Arechabalas resumed their mission of making quality rum.

According to Paul Ramírez, executive creative director of Team Enterprises, commissioning *Amparo* provided "the opportunity to tell the Cuban exile experience, through this one family's experience. The universal through the specific" (Cuban Research Institute 2020). *Amparo*, which also means refuge, can be seen as a counternarrative to Havana Club's advertising, which presents the revolution as a success. "The Arechabala story is a story of having everything, it being taken, then being erased, and I think that's the crucial story," García stated. "The idea of an entire history being erased, being veiled and being covered. And the desire of our generation to say, no, no, no. Let's scrap this and unveil this thing, because there is so much history that people don't know about" (Immigrant Archive Project 2019).

Amparo might be seen as a political commentary were it not for the fact that it was sponsored by Bacardí Limited, longtime competitor to Havana Club. After the revolution, Havana Club offered little competition, but when the Cuban State entered into its partnership with Pernod Ricard in 1994, the brand suddenly posed a viable threat. In order to impede the entry of Havana Club into U.S. markets, Bacardí purchased the Arechabala family's rights to the Havana Club name, in the hopes that it might undermine the Cuban State's claim to the trademark.

In its press materials for *Amparo*, the Bacardí company positions itself as a kind of benefactor to the Arechabala family. The play frames both families, once longtime rivals, working in solidarity against an oppressive state. In this way, the play is more overtly political than most conventional advertising. According to Bacardí executive Rick Wilson, the purpose of the play was to openly criticize the Cuban government for its suppression of the right to private ownership. Wilson stated, "[*Amparo* can help] educate the public about the wrongdoings of the Cuban government and their business partners, Pernod Ricard, against the Arechabala family, the original owners of Havana Club rum" (Wong 2018).

To establish its own rights as legitimate owners of the Havana Club brand, Bacardí needed to call into question the idea of Cuban authenticity itself. During a panel discussion at Florida International University, Ramírez gave a glimpse into what the brand was trying to accomplish. "As marketers we get briefs from our client. Okay, here's the challenge. We want to reach these people by saying this thing," Ramírez told the audience. "The problem was that there was a Cuban Havana Club that already existed, that was authentic. And that is a challenge, because we're saying 'no, this is the real one. Even though it says Puerto Rico on the bottle'" (Cuban Research Institute 2020). According to the agency, the marketing problem was simple. On its website, the agency expressed the problem this way: "How do we connect the real story of Havana Club to an audience that believes only Cuba produces real Cuban rum, and convince them that although distilled in Puerto Rico, Havana Club is #forevercuban?" (Team Enterprises 2022).

In this chapter, I examine the ways in which Cuban cultural producers, working from the diaspora, advance specific conceptions of Cuban authenticity, which are congruent with their political and economic interests. I focus specifically on Cuban expatriates, who demonstrate what Benedict Anderson (1998) refers to as "long-distance nationalism," a general sense of solidarity that binds together immigrants and their descendants into a single transborder citizenry. However, I argue that this articulation of Cuban authenticity is filtered through the logic of capitalism. Corporate executives, marketing practitioners, and artists, working in the diaspora, are motivated to define Cuban authenticity in ways that disconnect the island from fixed spatial concepts. I further argue that these marketing practices have political implications. In the process of staking out its position within the marketplace, Bacardí is advancing a particular ideological point of view, based on private ownership.

In chapter 2, I discussed the various ways in which executives at Havana Club and their marketing partners have asserted various iterations of Cuban authenticity by linking the brand to images, words, and sounds that possess social and cultural meaning. I have also argued that signs are not fixed but rather change depending on the strategic objectives of the organization. I build on this argument by exploring the competitive nature of sign building. In a mature sign economy, competing brands routinely unhinge signifiers from signifieds so that new meanings can be fashioned. In a practice that Robert Goldman and Stephen Papson (1996) describe as "sign wars," corporations will often appropriate, reappropriate, or tarnish the meanings of competing brands.

As the dominant player in the rum category, Bacardí has attempted to divest Havana Club of its unique point of difference by appropriating the brand and delegitimizing the Cuban State. I begin by examining Bacardí's marketing efforts prior to the Cuban Revolution in which it promoted its Cuban heritage, while negotiating its relationships with Spain and the United States. I then examine how Bacardí's messaging strategy has shifted in exile to reflect a more global ethos. Finally, I examine Bacardí's efforts to appropriate the Havana Club trademark and to reinvent it as a brand in exile. In doing so, Bacardí has reconceptualized Cuban authenticity, not grounded in a specific place, but in a time that existed before the revolution.

A Tale of Two Families

The story of Cuban rum has been framed as the story of two families. Both the Bacardí and the Arechabala families emigrated from Spain during the nineteenth century. One from Catalonia, the other from the country's Basque region. Both families settled in port cities, and along with other Spanish entrepreneurs, helped to create a formidable market for Cuban rum. Both families prospered under U.S. occupation, and to meet the needs of American and European markets, they built new relationships with American and Spanish businesses. In the process, they became some of the first transnational businesses. According to Javier

Lázaro (2016), on the eve of the 1959 revolution, Cuba's rum industry hinged on these two large family-run companies.

Both businesses were nationalized by Fidel Castro's government in 1960, but it is here where their paths diverge. Many of the Arechabala family's assets were invested in Cuban infrastructure, which ultimately left the business vulnerable to expropriation. The family fled Cuba, but its financial assets became property of the state, leaving the family economically depleted. Attempts to restart the Arechabala family business in exile never came to fruition, and the family faded into obscurity.

Both families were part of the first wave of postrevolution immigrants—members of Cuba's upper and upper-middle class who were adversely affected by the nationalization of private industries in 1960. According to Silvia Pedraza (1996), over 90 percent of those who left immediately after the revolution were white. But the Bacardí family has prospered in exile. The Cuban State attempted to expropriate the Bacardí family's business but was unsuccessful because the company had already established its presence abroad, enabling it to reorganize and resettle in Puerto Rico, then later in the Bahamas. In exile, the Bacardí family has flourished owning the largest privately held spirits companies in the world (Bacardí 2022b).

Today, Bacardí Limited has evolved into a large, transnational organization. The company is headquartered in Hamilton, Bermuda, but also has a significant corporate presence in Coral Gables, Florida. Most of Bacardí's rum is produced in Puerto Rico, but with sugarcane that comes from Mexico and as far away as India. During Cuba's Republican era, Bacardí's advertising unequivocally positioned the brand as a product of Cuba, but after the revolution, Bacardí's advertising has reflected a conflicted, sometimes ambivalent, relationship with the island.

Crafting the Bacardí Narrative

The Bacardí family history has been well documented by writers working across a number of genres. Jorge del Rosal's *The Rise of Bacardi: From Cuban Rum to Global Empire* (2020) offers an insider's view of the business aspects of the company, whereas journalist Tom Gjelten's *Bacardi and the Long Fight for Cuba* (2009) provides a history of the Bacardí family and its involvement in Cuban politics prior to its exile. Allan Schulman's *Building Bacardi: Architecture, Art and Identity* (2016) focuses on the family's collaboration with architects and artists in the design of its various properties across the globe.

But the Bacardí corporation itself has been the primary curator of its own history, having produced countless marketing materials designed to tell the family story for a variety of stakeholders, including restaurants, bartenders, consumers, and the media. Like all histories, the process of cultivating the Bacardí family history involves a series of strategic choices about what to tell and what to leave out. It is a blend of fact and myth, which elevates one man as being singularly responsible for inventing Cuban rum.

"The story begins with the birth of Facundo Bacardí Massó in the Spanish coastal town of Sitges, Catalonia in October 1814" is how it is written in *Bacardi: A Tale of Merchants, Family and Company* (Dawson and Argamasilla 2006). The authors of the book situate the company's founder as the moral center of the Bacardí company and family. In his sentimental portrait of the company's founder, Jorge del Rosal, himself a member of the Bacardí family, invests Facundo with significant moral authority, describing him as "a young man who migrated from Spain to Cuba in 1829 with nothing but his values, his dreams, and the will to succeed."

In actuality, Bacardí's fortunes were less a function of his moral fortitude and more due to the economic and social capital to which he had access. Bacardí's wife, Lucía Victoria Amalia Moreau, was the granddaughter of Pedro Benjamin Moreau, a French coffee plantation owner whose family had fled to Cuba after the Haitian Revolution. Facundo opened his distillery partially with capital inherited by his wife (Bonera 2000). In addition, he relied on the expertise of José León Boutellier, a local distiller and confectioner of French descent (Gjelten 2009).

Bacardí also benefited from membership in the Catalonian diaspora. Santiago de Cuba had developed a successful rum-making community from liquormakers who also came from Sitges. According to Lázaro (2016), newly arrived Catalonian immigrants benefited from access to social and cultural capital, which enabled them to flourish in their new country. By the mid-nineteenth century, Catalonian immigrants living in Santiago de Cuba had created a number of social and economic institutions where entrepreneurs could get legal advice, have access to spaces in which to conduct business, and to cultivate professional networks. Santiago de Cuba's distance from Havana meant that these Catalonian institutions were more invaluable than Spanish institutions, which had little authority in the region.

Bacardí's Shifting Connections to Place

In *Bacardi and the Long Fight for Cuba* (2009), Tom Gjelten expertly connects the history of the Bacardí family to the history of Cuba itself. Certainly, the Bacardí family was a key influence in Cuban politics and society during the late nineteenth century and into the Republican era. However, I found that the Bacardí company has, throughout its history, emphasized and deemphasized its ties to Cuba depending on its strategic goals.

Bacardí initially began as a local brand. Laborers working at the seaport of Santiago de Cuba found Bacardi's rum superior to the low-grade version of rum that they had previously been drinking. Under Spanish rule, soldiers stationed in Cuba were a ready market for Bacardí rum, and over time, the company made important business connections with Spanish authorities, which led to export opportunities in Spain.

In late nineteenth-century, advertising was not essential to how rum was bought and sold in Cuba. Rum was generally sold at the doors of the distiller, where customers brought their own bottles and jugs (Bonera 2000). The first documented bottle for Bacardí dates to 1909 but includes all the basic elements that it has retained over the years. The original bottle included the words "Santiago de Cuba," the region where it was manufactured. Also present is the brand's recognizable logo of a black bat contained within a red circle.

The origins of the bat logo have been the subject of some debate. One theory is that the logo might be based on the coat of arms of Valencia, Spain, which features a bat with wings spread over a crown. The more prevalent theory is that the origin of the logo refers to the fruit bats that fluttered around the original distillery in the evenings. According to Bacardí, the bats were attracted to the sweet fumes of the fermenting molasses, and so the locals started calling Bacardí rum the "Bat Drink."

A more banal explanation is that Bacardí's rum was first sold in cans repurposed from a brand of oil that had a bat as the logo. Locals had become accustomed to asking for the Ron del Murciélago, and so Lucia Victoria Amalia Moreau suggested they adapt that image. But the logo also carried significant cultural meaning. In either case, the Catalans and the Taínos thought it was a sign of good fortune. According to Bacardí, Amalia liked the idea of the bat, believing that it meant good fortune, good health, and family unity.

By 1868, Bacardí rum was sold on a large scale in Havana, but the company had also begun to take advantage of U.S. occupation. Among Bacardí's first forms of advertising were a series of postcards that date back to the late 1890s, when large numbers of U.S. servicemen were stationed in Cuba. These postcards showcased the city of Santiago de Cuba, its buildings and monuments, including the distillery. According to del Rosal (2020), these early forms of marketing were meant to prompt export sales. Bacardí had hoped that the American soldiers stationed in the region would use the postcards to send messages back to the United States, thereby increasing its brand awareness abroad.

As the company began expanding internationally, Bacardí became increasingly adept at marketing and promotion, making prolific use of newspaper advertising. Like José Arechabala, Facundo Bacardí was born in a region of Spain that has its own unique identity and language, yet there is little evidence that Bacardí ever positioned the rum as a product with Catalonian heritage. Instead, Bacardí had hoped to position its rum as globally respected rum by invoking imagery associated with the Spanish crown.

To cultivate its export markets, Bacardí took to the international awards circuit, which was a relatively novel approach. Until the late nineteenth century, Habano Tobacco was the only Cuban brand that competed in international fairs. Cuban rum first competed in international competitions during the Centennial Exposition of 1876 in Philadelphia, which was organized by the U.S. government to mark the hundredth anniversary of the American Revolution (Bonera 2000). That year, Bacardí y Compañia won their first award for their cognac and aged rum, at the time named La Tropical.

Throughout the rest of the nineteenth century, Havana Club would go on to fare well in similar kinds of expositions, including the Exposición Universal Barcelona in 1888, the Exposición Universal Paris in 1889, and the Exposición Mundial Colombiana de Chicago in 1893. These award competitions serve as what Bourdieu calls "circuits of legitimation" (English 2002), in which an industry invests itself with merit and, therefore, power. Awards of these types can serve as a kind of objectified capital, which can then be converted into economic capital.

Bacardí was not the only Cuban distillery on the international awards circuit (Bonera 2000), but it has proven to be the most effective at leveraging these awards over time. Perhaps the most lucrative of these awards have been the gold medals earned at the Exposición Universal de Barcelona in 1888, which allowed the brand to emphasize its ties with the Spanish monarchy. In its marketing materials, Bacardí likes to claim that by winning the award, Queen María Cristina granted the company the right to claim to be "Purveyors to the Royal Spanish Household." This recognition also allowed the company to place the Spanish Royal Coat of Arms on their label (Bacardí 2024).

During this time, the company began to utilize the tagline "BACARDÍ: the King of Rums & the Rum of Kings," further creating the perception that the Bacardí family was part of the royal household. For example, Bacardí likes to tell the story of how Spain's King Alfonso XIII fell ill with a fever in 1892. Because it was commonly believed that alcoholic spirits had strong medicinal value, the royal court physicians began looking for the highest-quality spirit to give to the king. The next morning, the king's fever had passed, and he quickly recovered. According to lore, the royal secretary of Spain wrote to thank the Bacardí Company "for making a product that has saved the life of His Majesty."

It is difficult to verify the truth of this story. According to Bonera (2000), the precise dates of the affair have changed over time in Bacardí's press materials. More important, the relationship between the Bacardí family and the Spanish monarchy appears to have been much more transactional and conflicted than what was suggested in the company's advertising. Bacardí was initially founded during a time when Spanish tariffs had slowed the growth of the Cuban rum industry (Bonera 2000). Additionally, Cubans were actively engaged in an ongoing struggle for independence from Spanish rule. Bacardí's manager, Enrique Schueg, had been exiled to Jamaica, and Facundo's son, Emilio, was jailed in Spain for revolutionary activities.

Despite these personal conflicts, the company actively advertised in Spanish newspapers. The first known advertisement for Bacardí was placed in *La Ilustración Artística* on January 4, 1886. Intended for a cosmopolitan Spanish reader, the Barcelona-based publication made effective use of illustration, engraving, and later photography. By the early 1900s, Bacardí began consistently advertised in Cuban lifestyle magazines such as *Bohemia* and *Carteles*, while also having a strong presence in cocktail books marketed to U.S. tourists.

As Bacardí began to make inroads into the U.S. market, the company enlisted the help of outside brokers, including New York–based distributors and advertising agencies. In an effort to appeal to North American audiences, Bacardí began to emphasize its Cuban, rather than Spanish, identity. U.S. advertising was largely handled by Schenley Import Corporation, which handled distribution. According to the *New York Times* (1937), Bacardí's advertising in the United States was handled by New York–based agency Lawrence C. B. Gumbinner. A review of Bacardí's U.S. advertising during this time indicates that the brand began to link the product with imagery that had been consistently circulated by the tourism industry, which drew upon a vast inventory of visual tropes that blended Cuba's Spanish colonial heritage and Afro-Cuban cultural art forms.

In its advertising. Bacardí included images that reinforced American consumers' perception of Cuba as a tropical paradise. Consider the following advertisement (Figure 5) for Bacardí that ran in the *New Yorker* in 1934. "Wouldn't You Like a Bacardi Cocktail as We Mix It in Cuba?" reads the headline. That advertisement was part of a series of print ads that depicted Cuban waiters and bartenders, dressed in rumba attire, who are touting the benefits of Bacardí rum to an unseen American tourist. While the copywriting invokes the Cuban voice, it is important to note that the advertisement was written by marketers living in New York for an imagined audience of North American consumers. The advertisement was placed in a New York–based publication and sponsored by Schenley Importation, Bacardi's distributor in the United States. The advertisement's visual design was developed by George de Zayas, a Mexican-born illustrator who had settled in Manhattan. To ensure the reader clearly understands that the setting is Cuba, de Zayas included a number of visual cues, which signal a sense of place: a set of palm trees, the mambo attire, and an outline of Cuba.

The purpose of the advertisement is to position Bacardí as the only rum that can complete a truly authentic Cuban cocktail. "Señor, please do it this way," the copy reads before providing a simple recipe for a daiquiri. "So, now you can treat your guests to the real, true Bacardi cocktail that every visitor from Cuba has always talked about." The advertisement reflects a common strategy for Cuban brands at the time, which was to leverage a country-of-origin effect, in which brands capitalize on the positive associations made between a nation and a commodity. However, those connections would become severely upended by the 1959 Revolution.

Figure 5. "Wouldn't You Like a Bacardí Cocktail as We Mix It in Cuba?," print advertisement. From the *New Yorker* (December 8, 1934). Accessed through the *New Yorker* digital library.

La Grán Familia Bacardí

When the Bacardí family left Cuba, they began to reconceptualize their relationship to the island. With no formal connections to Cuba, the brand began to build community around its various business assets. In its corporate history, *Bacardí: A Tale of Merchants, Family and Company* (Dawson and Argamasilla 2006), the company describes its evolving relationship to place: "Without their country, the Bacardí family adopted Bacardí company as their nation. Scattered around the world, the Cuban Diaspora soon began forming itself into a powerful network of connections based on family and friends. In unison with Mexicans, Puerto Ricans, Americans, Europeans and Brazilians, the concept of La Grán Familia Bacardí (The Great Bacardí Family) was born."

It becomes clear that Bacardí's new understanding of home was no longer based on country of origin but rather on its consumer markets, its organizational structure, and its business relationships. This conceptualization of space is highly consistent with the logic of global capitalism in which identity is based on consumer markets and nodes of production. But this sense of displacement began to alter its brand perception. The Bacardí brand had become loosely associated with the Caribbean but was no longer inextricably linked to Cuba in the way it had been during the Republican era.

In its U.S. advertising, Bacardí tended to depict American occupation in a favorable light, which was no doubt, meant to appeal to the political sensibilities of U.S. consumers. In doing so, they minimized the actual role that Cubans played in creating their own rum industry. In 1966, for example, Bacardí produced a print campaign that linked the U.S. military occupation to the invention of Cuban cocktails. One advertisement featured the headline "This Is How the Daiquiri Was Invented" and goes on to tell the story of an American mining engineer who quenched his thirst by adding lime and sugar to Bacardí to rum and then named his invention after the Daiquirí mines where he worked. A similar advertisement ran with the headline "How the Rum and Coke Was Invented," credits the invention of the drink to a U.S. soldier working in the office of the Chief Signal Officer. To establish its legitimacy, the ad claims to show an affidavit from Fausto Rodriguez, who witnessed the event as a young boy.

A variation of this story was later produced as a television commercial that aired in 2013 (Figure 6). Filmed in sepia tones, the advertisement is written from the perspective of a U.S. soldier who is a member of Teddy Roosevelt's Rough Riders. A title card informs the audience that the year is 1900, which would have been the final years of Cuba's fight for independence. Rather than depicting the soldier as a member of an occupying force, however, his presence is characterized as part of a good-will mission. "I was there helping the Cuban people from the Spanish," is how the soldier puts in voice-over. The storyline of the com-

Figure 6. Scene from *Cuba Libre*. From BBDO, 2013.

mercial involves an encounter between the soldier and a sultry, creole Cuban woman, who is a member of Cuba's armed resistance against Spain. When the soldier offers the her an unbranded bottle of Coke, she responds fiercely by taking out her flask of clearly branded Bacardí rum, pouring it into her Coke, and declaring, "Cuba Libre."

The creative concept is that the Cuba Libre was born through the perfect marriage of American and Cuban resourcefulness, however, the depiction of Cuba as a sultry, creole woman builds on an ongoing tradition of representing Cuba from the North American perspective. As Louis Pérez (2008) notes, this representation gained currency during the Republican era, in which Cubans were seen through the North American sexual gaze. However, the commercial serves a political purpose by minimizing the importance of Cubans in their own history, while amplifying role that the United States played in achieving victory. As Ada Ferrer (2021) points out, the United States was not necessarily a partner in the struggle, but more of an occupying force that ensured its economic interests. Furthermore, a focus on intrepid Americans who invent Cuban cocktails obscures the actual role that Cubans played in developing their country's rum industry.

COMMODITY SIGNS AND THE POWER OF TRADEMARK

In her discussion of corporate trademarks, Katya Assaf (2009) describes the symbolic and legal aspects of brands. At a practical level, trademarks are designed to enable the consumer to identify, without confusion, the source of various goods and services. But at a deeper level, trademarks act as a kind of commodity sign (Baudrillard 1988), joining together a product or business with a symbol that has cultural meaning. The cultural meaning of a trademark is carefully built up by its owner by means of advertising and other marketing techniques that create links between the trademark and various positive cultural values such as prestige, freedom, and youth.

But meanings shift. The Bacardí logo may have originally been intended to symbolize good fortune, good health, and family unity, but it has over time has lost its primary meaning. This is partially a function of its own advertising. To deliver on shifting strategic objectives, the brand has come to mean different things in different places over the past century. Early on, Bacardí was a brand that was local to Santiago de Cuba, but the company began to export in Europe, they decided to endow the product with prestige by affirming its Spanish, rather than its Cuban, heritage. When Bacardí sought to cultivate a U.S. market, they found that emphasizing its Cuban identity was more advantageous.

As previously discussed, the meanings associated with brands are also open to contestation from competing brands. Therefore, a trademark must be protected legally, against blurring and tarnishment. According to Assaf (2009), blurring occurs when a trademark's distinctiveness is harmed because it becomes confused with a similar mark or trade name. In other words, a third party's mark weakens the connection between the original brand and the product or service they are selling. Conversely, tarnishment occurs when an infringing trademark puts the infringed trademark in a negative light, such as associating the brand with criminal or other illicit activity (Assaf 2009).

Over the years, Bacardí has been effective at using trademark law for both defensive and offensive purposes. During Cuba's Republican era, Bacardí demonstrated an uncanny ability to make its name synonymous with all Cuban rum by positioning itself as "the rum that made Cuba famous." However, the brand became so successful that it risked becoming a generic term. Bartenders in the United States were serving their guests other brands of rum when they ordered a Bacardí drink. In response the company successfully sued the Barbizon Plaza Hotel and Wivel's Restaurant, two of New York's most desirable establishments (*New York Times* 1936). The move was meant as a declaration to restauranteurs that Bacardí would aggressively protect its trademark.

The ability for Bacardí to use the court system to protect its business interests proved to be a critical difference after the revolution. By that time, Bacardí had already become an international company, allowing it to avoid expropriation. The original Bacardí firm was based in Santiago de Cuba, but it had also established four other companies, each with a separate structure and legal identity. Although they were owned by the same shareholders, these entities were not subsidiaries and were therefore beyond the reach of state authorities in Havana.

In 1957, José (Pepin) Bosch, head of the company, had created Bacardí International Ltd. in the Bahamas with the rights to manufacture and sell rum everywhere outside Cuba, with the exception of the United States. The new company had allowed Bacardí to claim ownership of its various trademarks, by making the case that this subsidiary had not been nationalized by the Cuban State and remained the property of the original owners. The only condition for retaining the rights was that the label of almost every bottle of Bacardí sold in the United States carry the words "Puerto Rican Rum."

By the mid-1990s, Bacardí's legal strategy shifted from protecting its own trademark to challenging the Cuban State's right to the Havana Club name. According to Gjelten (2009), Bacardí had long admired the Havana Club trademark, believing it had significant brand value that could be leveraged. Like "Bacardí," "Havana Club" was easy to say in any language. Havana Club also connoted the lively night scene for which Cuba had long been known. However, there was new urgency to acquire the trademark when Cuba entered into a joint agreement in 1995 with Pernod Ricard, to distribute Havana Club globally. If the United States were to eventually drop the Cuban embargo, Havana Club would be in a position to seriously challenge Bacardí's dominance in the marketplace.

With no tangible connection to the island, Bacardí had no product offering that could challenge Havana Club's claim to Cuban authenticity. When faced with such challenges, James Gilmore and Joseph Pine (2007, 60) advise marketers, "If you don't have any old brands in-house that qualify, consider obtaining the rights to others." And that is exactly what Bacardí did. Bacardí rolled out its own Havana Club rum purportedly based on the original Arechabala formula, which Bacardí claimed to have acquired when purchasing the rights to the trademark. By basing its rum on the "original recipe," Bacardí could counterposition Havana Club International's rum as inauthentic.

The ensuing legal battle has played out on a global scale (Dinan 2002) and has involved a variety of actors, including Bacardí, Pernod Ricard, the U.S. Congress, the World Trade Organization, and the European Union. Bacardí claimed that it owned the trademark because it had purchased the rights to the Havana Club name from the Arechabala family in 1995. However, the Cuban government had registered the trademark internationally in 1973, after the Arechabala family, believing the trademark had no value, had stopped paying to maintain it.

International courts found that the Arechabala family legally did not have the right to sell the trademark to the Bacardí family. Meanwhile, the U.S. Congress enacted legislation to support Bacardí's claims to the patent rights to Havana Club, asserting that the trademark was unlawfully seized. According to Congress, Arechabala family's rights to its trademark was synonymous with supporting the embargo itself, which was deemed to necessary to protect the national security of the United States. It is the tension between national and international law, which has allowed Bacardí to launch its own version of Havana Club in the U.S. marketplace.

Building a More Authentic Havana Club Brand

In 1994, Bacardí began to introduce the Havana Club name in the United States (Stempel 2011), but it was not until 2016 when the company began actively promoting the product on a national scale. The strategy was to position Bacardí's version of Havana Club as the true rum of Cuba while counterpositioning the Cuban State's Havana Club rum as illegitimate. But there were clear barriers to messaging. Bacardí's version of Havana Club could not explicitly claim that it was produced in Cuba. To circumvent the problem of where the rum is produced, the brand and its agency asserted that their version of Havana Club rum was based on the original Arechabala formula, which they claim to have acquired when purchasing the rights to the trademark.

There is a kind of semiotic battle that is evident in the redesign of the bottle. When the Cuban State expropriated the Havana Club brand, it erased the Arechabala family's presence by removing the Vizcaya coat of arms, a symbol that appeared on the labels of all Arechabala products from the foundation of the distillery. In its place, state producers included the image of La Giraldilla, which had become a symbol of Cuba's capital city. But when Bacardí launched its own version of Havana Club, the company engaged in some sign-work of its own, illustrating the ways in which cultural producers appropriate and reappropriate symbols for their own strategic purposes.

Created by Tara Lobonovich, a new New York-based graphic designer, the new logo reestablished the Vizcaya coat of arms as the centerpiece. The packaging was influenced by the brand's original elements, yet had its own distinct look and feel. But in 2023, the brand made a bold move by releasing a limited edition of its Original 86 proof Añejo Blanco, which is almost an exact reproduction of the Havana Club logo as it existed in 1934. The marketing materials promoting the product note that this limited-edition rum is double aged in oak barrels and has notes of vanilla, brown sugar, and roasted nuts, making it even closer to Arechabala's original recipe (therealhavanaclub.com 2023).

By reverting to the original logo, with some modifications, Bacardí accomplished several goals. First, the design affirms Havana Club's positioning as a family-made rum rather than a product of a large corporation. Second, the inclusion of the Vizcaya coat of arms, helps to reposition the rum as product with a long legacy, which is a common practice within the premium spirits category. As Michael Beverland (2005) found, wine and spirits marketers make common use of historic images that predate modern, mass-produced production. Such strategies are meant to distract from the actual scientific and marketing prowess and conformed to the expected rules of and as being above commercial considerations of efficiency, consistency, and scale.

Although they were not directly involved in the production of the rum, the Arechabala family was instrumental to Bacardí's public relations efforts strategy, which quoted the family members at length. In a public statement released by Bacardí (2016), José Arechabala, great-grandson of the Havana Club's founder, expressed his support for the enterprise:

> Our family could not be happier that Bacardí is launching Havana Club Añejo Clásico, which is based on the original recipe created by the Arechabala family in 1934. Our families knew each other before we were both exiled from Cuba, and with Bacardí being the premiere rum company in the world, it's only fitting that they continue our legacy by paying proper homage to the capital city of Cuba, a place we once called home.

Thus, the entire enterprise is positioned less as a commercial endeavor and more as a passion project. Bacardí has made sure to describe Havana Club as a collaboration between two families, meeting on equal footing, rather than an asymmetrical relationship between a powerful corporation and a family that has lost everything. This sentiment was expressed by Fabio Di Giammarco, global vice president for Bacardí, who stated, "This is the ultimate convergence of two Cuban families in exile coming together to continue the legacy of this incredible brand and introduce it to a new generation" (Bacardí 2016).

To publicly introduce the brand, Bacardí hosted a gala that took place at the Saxony Theater Faena Hotel, located in Miami Beach (Montgomery 2016). The event was meant to evoke the prerevolutionary era, when both the Arechabala and the Bacardí families were thriving in Cuba. To create a sense of time and place, the party featured a ten-piece band, which played several of the Cuban standards. There were Cuban-inspired showgirls and elegantly dressed waiters carrying illuminated Havana Club bottles. And to make sure that the event received adequate press coverage, the guest list included notable actors, designers, and social media influencers.

Both the redesign of the packaging and public relations effort coincided with a national print advertising campaign that was created by BBDO. Launched with the tagline "Aged well," the campaign invokes an image of Cuba that is purported to have existed before the revolution. The print campaign evokes the aesthetic of vintage movies posters, and each advertisement features a different headline with typography that is designed to mimic the Victorian Gaslight style. In a press statement released during the launch of the campaign, Bacardí said it wanted to focus on the Cuba that existed in the years spanning 1920 to 1950, which places the campaign squarely during Cuba's Republican era: "Havana

Club rum is based on the original recipe created by the Arechabala family in Cuba in 1934, capturing the exuberant spirit of the Golden Age in Havana, a period of time that spanned from the 1920s, when people flocked to the island during prohibition, through the 1950s when everything stylish and glamorous reigned supreme" (Bacardí 2016).

The campaign, therefore, was not grounded in any specific period, but rather in an unspecified past. This was evident in a print execution titled "Glamour." The focal point of the advertisement is a young, elegant woman holding a daiquiri. She is wearing a summer dress and a large straw hat. In the background is an image of a young, attractive, well-dressed couple. The images within the advertisement evoke different eras, but they are not tied to any particular time period. Similarly, there is no specific mention of place, although the images of palm trees and a 1950s-era automobile suggests Cuba.

The advertisement reflects what Goldman and Papson describe as a "hazy, nostalgic, picture of the past" (1996, 128), in which specific meanings may be rooted in history but are dislodged from their original contexts and then rearticulated for marketing purposes. For historic images to serve commercial purposes, Goldman and Papson argue, they must be decontextualized and depoliticized. But in this case, Bacardí was advancing an inherently political point of view. Explicitly, the campaign is a celebration of capitalism. Like other advertisements developed by Western agencies, the "Aged Well" campaign depicts young, beautiful, and wealthy consumers. This appears to have been by design. According to Bacardí, the campaign was designed to evoke a "glamorous, effervescent feeling" associated with a better, more affluent past, what Bacardí referred to as its "gilded origins" (Bacardí 2016). All advertisements within the campaign feature the tagline "The Golden Age Aged Well," referring both to the aging process that results in a more complex rum and to a time before the Cuban Revolution interrupted the island's market orientation.

The campaign is consistent with larger narratives promoted by the Cuban exile community, which assert that Cuba has not evolved under Castro but merely crumbled (López 2010). The true Cuba, according to this narrative, is the one that flourished under capitalism. Yet, the campaign's reference to the Gilded Age seems disconnected from the political reality of that era. Despite the glamour associated with the era, the Gilded Age was also marked by poverty, unemployment, and corruption in Cuba. The campaign is vaguely situated in the time of Fulgencio Batista, who, while being friendly to U.S. business, was responsible for the excesses and inequities of the era that led to the revolution itself. However, the campaign is decidedly anti-Castro, which is evident in the headline for one print advertisement that features the headline, "Revolution Couldn't Topple the Rum." By focusing on the wealth and glamour during the pre-Castro years, Bacardí is asserting that the true Cuba is the one that flourished under U.S. intervention (Chávez and Valencia 2018). Governments may come and go, the advertisement suggests, but the right to consume should be everlasting.

Constructing Cuba as an Exile Community

In 2018, Bacardí launched a follow-up campaign for its version of Havana Club, titled *Forever Cuban*. Rather than focus on a glorious past, the new campaign focused on the contemporary. Specifically, the agency decided to define Cuban authenticity in terms of the Cuban people. It is telling that the campaign did not focus on Cuban nationals, but rather Cubans living in the diaspora. The new campaign was notably more political than its predecessor, and there is a concerted effort to use "exile" rather than "immigrant." This choice seems deliberate, meant to focus attention on the deficiencies of the Cuban government. The Center for a Free Cuba (2019), a Washington, D.C.–based organization that lobbies for political and economic change, articulates the distinction between these two terms. Immigrants can return to their home country depending on their personal circumstances. By contrast, exiles are unable to return home unless there is political change in their home country.

The issue of lost property is the centerpiece of Bacardí's Havana Club campaign, with an overt focus on of how Arechabala's intellectual and material assets were stolen by the state. This message is consistent with ongoing discourses within Cuban exile, which fixate on the revolution's early nationalization of private property. As Ricardo Ortiz (2007) has observed, when it comes to returning to Cuba, old-guard Cuban exiles harbor a powerful resentment over property long lost to the revolution, which Ortiz, describes as the paradox of exile. In their stubborn refusal to surrender their claim to lost property and capital, Cuban exiles are complicit in delaying their own return home.

Over the course of multiple mediums, Bacardí tells the story of how the Arechabala family lost everything and about how Ramón Arechabala personally transcribed the original recipe, smuggled it out of Cuba, and later sold it to Bacardí. It also tells the story about how Bacardí has helped the Arechabala family retain its legacy. According to Bacardí:

> Havana Club's authenticity is based on the original recipe, great-taste, craftsmanship, technique and passion since the brand was crafted by the Arechabala's in 1934. The Arechabala family has entrusted Bacardí with their recipe, and the brand's goal is to carry on this legacy with the same passion and perseverance that the Arechabala and the Bacardí families are known for, having experienced the same hardship and sharing a common goal.

The centerpiece of the campaign is a sixty-second commercial (Figure 7), produced in English and Spanish. Filmed in black and white, the commercial is shot on a set that is made to look like Old Havana. "Don't tell us we're not Cuban," reads

Figure 7. Title card from "Don't Tell Us We're Not Cuban." Produced by BBDO, 2017.

Cuban American actor Raúl Esparza, reciting lines from "Island Body," a poem written by Cuban American poet Richard Blanco. The poem reads as follows:

> Forced to leave home, but home never leaves us.
> Wherever exile takes us, we remain this body made from the red earth of our island—our ribs taken from its *montes*—its breeze our breaths. We stand with its *palmeras*.
> Don't tell us we're not Cuban.
> Remaining true to our *lucha*, we thrive—oily hands fixing broken beauty
> Pockets filled with the gossamer dew and dust of its sunrises, with the song of its *sinsontes* and its son nested in our souls.
> Don't tell us we're not Cuban.
> Wherever the world spins us, home remains in us. Its sun still sets in our eyes. We walk, carrying the *música* of our island, And the amber rum born from it.
> Don't tell me I'm not Cuban.
> Or him. Or her. Or them.
> Or any of us.

The video concludes with a product shot of Bacardí's Havana Club gold and silver rum with the campaign's tagline, "Forced from Home. Aged in Exile. Forever Cuban." With the visible presence of props, cameras, and crew, the producers of the commercial seem eager to convey the message that this is a set rather than an actual street in Havana. Perhaps to suggest that Cuban exiles are manufacturing their own version of the city abroad. Earlier in the spot, there is a caption claiming that the video was shot in Miami and was written, produced, and directed by Cuban exiles. However, this claim is not entirely accurate. Formal credit for the commercial within industry circles is given to BBDO New York, Bacardí's agency of record, and a creative team that included creative director Joao Unzer, copywriter Kathryn Kvas, and art director Brian Kim.

The anthem video was complemented by a print component, which included three different executions, each focusing on a different prominent Cuban American. There is an advertisement featuring actress Anisbel López, who is identified by the copy as a first-generation Cuban American born in Camagüey. Another features musician Michelle Fragoso, identified as a first-generation Cuban American born in Havana, and finally, Brent Cruz, identified as a second-generation Cuban American born in Tampa. Tying the campaign together is a headline that boldly asserts an alternative reading of Cuban identity. "Don't Tell us We're Not Cuban," reads the copy. "Cuba Lives within Me."

To round out the campaign, Bacardí also created a separate website, with the URL therealhavanaclub.com. The dedicated website seems designed to create the illusion that this is a stand-alone rand rather than a Bacardí property. On one hand, the website serves practical marketing functions. It makes use of the trademark for legal purposes, and showcases the different types of Havana Club rum (añejo and blanco). The website also features a variety of cocktail recipes, as well as a geolocation mechanism for informing the consumer where they can purchase the product in their area. Finally, the website showcases the tagline, "Forever Cuban," which ties the campaign together.

At the same time, the website performs political labor by reshaping the historical narrative. For example, there is a section on the website titled "Learn the Truth: What Is the Story of the Real Havana Club Rum?" where readers are invited to learn more about the expropriation of the Havana Club brand:

> In 1934, the Arechabala family created Havana Club rum in Cárdenas, Cuba. Then, on January 1st, 1959, their world changed. The new Cuban government nationalized the company and stole all their assets without compensation. The family was then forced into exile, leaving behind years of hard work and their family legacy.... To this day, the Cuban government continues to make a rum using the Havana Club name without permission, but what they couldn't take from them was the original family recipe. (therealhavanaclub.com 2023)

What is lost in this narrative is how Bacardí has, in its own way, seized control of Arechabala's assets. The Arechabala family is not actively involved in producing the rum that it created in 1934 and, therefore, has no control over its taste and quality. The degree to which the Arechabala family benefits economically from the sale of Havana Club is uncertain, since whatever profits it receives from the sale of Bacardí's Havana Club rum remains undisclosed. Furthermore, the Arechabala family has lost its capacity to tell its own story. Instead, it is Bacardí's public relations and marketing teams that assume this responsibility.

Consider how Bacardí has been able to appropriate the name, image, and likeness of Don José Arechabala y Aldama, the founder of Havana Club. In 1947, a portrait of José Arechabala was featured in and advertisement placed in

Figure 8. Portrait of Don José Arechabala y Aldama. From *Gordejuela* (November 1947). Accessed through Liburuklik Digital Library.

Gordejuela, José Arechabala S.A.'s corporate magazine (Figure 8). The image was part of a special issue meant to celebrate a century since Don José's birth and to generate renewed interest in the company. In its own marketing materials, however, Bacardí has used a similar portrait of Don José in the packaging and marketing materials promoting their own rum. What was once the portrait of a family patriarch has been reconfigured into a commodity sign that has served Bacardí well.

Bacardí's appropriation of the Arechabala family history for economic gain can also be seen in a section of the Real Havana Club website (2023) titled "Our Story," in which Havana Club's history is laid out, beginning with the founding of the distillery in 1878, touching upon state expropriation, and concluding with a "handshake deal" between Ramon Arechabala and the Bacardí family (The Real Havana Club U.S. 2023). Through its use of the collective "we" and "our," Bacardí conflates its own interests with that of the Arechabala family. "Today there is one genuine Havana Club Rum rooted in honor, and another rooted in deceit," reads the copy on the Real Havana Club website. "Though no longer made in Cuba, we still retain our tenacious Cuban spirit."

Performing Exile

The immersive theater experience *Amparo* was a key component of this campaign. Originally written for bartenders and influencers living in New York, the play was soon rewritten for a larger audience of Cuban expatriates living in Miami. When conducting research for the play, García relied heavily on the testimony of the family, including formal interviews with Arechabala family members that were coordinated by Bacardí. These interviews were later submitted to the Immigrant Archive Project, a Miami-based organization founded by Cuban expatriates, and now serve as a historical record.

García first became involved in the project when she was contacted by Paul Ramírez, a Cuban American advertising executive who was working with Team Enterprises. He was representing the Havana Club portion of the Bacardí line, and the team was looking for a writer who knew something about Cuba. García then enlisted the help of Victoria Collado, a Cuban American, to direct the play.

The Amparo Experience had a successful run, until it was cut short by COVID-19. Then in 2022, the story reemerged in digital form. An Instagram account was created with the handle "therealhavana club," which includes short videos with Collado and Garcia, as well as the main characters of the play. The platform seamlessly blends politics and marketing. Along with messaging about *The Amparo Experience*, there are promotional shots of the product and short videos on how to mix the ideal Cuban cocktail, using Bacardí's Havana Club rum. One post indicates that for every follower of @therealhavanaclub, the company will donate up to $25,000 to the Center for a Free Cuba. "Discover the story of the Arechabala family's exile," reads the post. "And help improve the lives of those that remain."

A Cuban American writer, enlisting the help of a Cuban American director, after having been approached by a Cuban American marketing executive to work on behalf a corporation with ties to Miami, demonstrates the remarkable way in which Bacardí has enlisted a body of Cuban cultural producers, working from the diaspora, to produce a campaign that celebrates Cuban expatriates. Overtly, their work reflects long-distance nationalism, by asserting their membership in a transborder citizenry. But it is the continued political nature of the community that is of interest. Long-distance nationalism is marked by a continued interest in the national politics of their country of origin. As Anderson states of this person, their "political participation is directed towards an imagined *heimat* which he does not intend to live, where he pays no taxes, where he cannot be arrested, where he will not be brought before the courts—and where he does not vote. In effect, a politics without responsibility or accountability" (Anderson 1998).

Assertions about Cuban culture and politics from members of the diaspora are not new. Rafael Hernández (2003) points out that perceptions of Cuba are often shaped by those living outside Cuba, not within it. In doing so, they often delegitimize the perspectives of those living on the island. In Hernández's words, Cuban cultural producers are believed to "lack their own perspectives and capacity for reflective thought. Either they are faint hearted, or they are bureaucrats repeating official discourse. Dissidents, on the other hand, are a splendid species, the product of some mutation: they carry the banner of truth, integrity, and credibility."

Certainly, the cultural producers working on behalf of Bacardí are privileging the perspective of Cubans living in the diaspora. In doing so, they are expressing a distinct political point of view, consistently condemning the socialist revolution for its suppression of freedom and capitalist values. But these condemnations are communicated through advertising, which is a particularly pernicious form of public discourse. The amount of media spending available to advertisers ensures that their voices can be heard while drowning out alternative points of view.

Bacardí is advancing the point of view that the expatriate's voice is more authentic than the voice of Cuban's living on the island, but it is important to recognize that such discourses are ultimately filtered through the logic of capitalism. In the process, Cuba has been reconceptualized not as a nation-state linked to physical space but rather as a nodal point within a larger consumer market. Consider the following testimony from Ned Duggan, senior vice president at Bacardí: "Bacardí is a brand with deep roots in the Caribbean—both in Cuba and Puerto Rico. While the Caribbean is our home, we consider Miami our backyard. Miami is a mash-up of Latin and American cultures—it's a city filled with the same energy, diversity and spirit that embodies the Bacardí brand" (Schubert 2018).

What Duggan describes as a "mash-up" is an example of what Néstor García Canclini (2001) calls "frivolous homogenization," in which distinct cultures are simplified so that they can be used interchangeably. Furthermore, Bacardí is advancing a conception of national identity that is based less on fixed spatial concepts and more as an interpretive community of consumers with varying connections to the island. This conceptualization of space is conducive to the logic of global capitalism in which products, information, and consumers flow more easily across borders. Under current conditions of globalization, borders are no longer markers of national boundaries.

At the same time, there is a sort of double-speak at play. Duggan is both invoking and evading national identity for strategic purposes. For example, Duggan also makes sure to designate its competition as a French rather than a Cuban enterprise by invoking the Cuban State's relationship with Pernod Ricard: "We debuted the campaign not only to engage with the exiled Cuban community but also to reaffirm our place as the true Havana Club rum. Pernod Ricard, a French company, continues to partner with the Cuban dictatorship to produce rum under a stolen name, what makes both Pernod Ricard and the government's rum brand an imposter" (Schubert 2018).

By emphasizing Havana Club International's French ties, Bacardí is both questioning the brand's true authenticity while criticizing what he believes to be a problematic alliance between Pernod Ricard and authoritarian regime. Because the "real Cuba" has been corrupted by the state, Cuban authenticity can only be found in the diaspora. But the constant struggle for defining authenticity is constant in a competitive marketplace. In response to the "Forever Cuban" campaign, Pernod Ricard shot back. In a statement in *The Spirit Business*, Pernod Ricard reasserted its claim that true authenticity lies in physical location: "The real Havana Club rum, produced through a joint venture between Cuba Ron S.A. and Pernod Ricard, is crafted in Cuba, from cane to glass, using the knowledge and expertise passed down from generation to generation of Maestros del Ron Cubano. As such, it is a 100% authentic Cuban rum" (Hopkins 2017).

Today, Bacardí Ltd. and Havana Club International continue to engage in a public battle over which is the truly authentic Cuban rum. For Havana Club International, an authentic Cuban rum is one that is wholly produced in Cuba. Therefore, it was disingenuous for Bacardí to "promote its Puerto Rican rum products in the USA under the name Havana Club Rum" (Eads 2018). For Bacardí, authenticity has little to do with place and everything to do with the Cuban people. Not the Cuban nationals who continue to reside on the island, of course, but those "true" Cubans who left the island after 1959.

CHAPTER 4

Museums and Memory

Cuba is like going to a whole other planet. It's so different, but it's so similar to the United States, to Miami. It's like a doppelganger. It's the mirror image. And I have no doubt that once Cuba becomes democratic, that it will be the favorite tourist destination for Americans.
—Interview with Dr. Henry Louis Gates, Jr.

In 2015, American late-night talk show host Conan O'Brien produced a series of vignettes that were filmed in Havana. The vignettes were part of an ongoing segment titled "Conan without Borders," which depicts O'Brien playing the role of the typical American tourist, learning local customs while fumbling through them. Part comedy sketch, part travelogue, O'Brien performs the role of flaneur, visiting a Cuban cigar factory, strolling along the Malecón, and dining in a local *paladar*.

In one of the vignettes, O'Brien visits the Havana Club Museum of Rum, located in La Habana Vieja, the city's historic district. Much of the comedy during the episode comes from the interaction between O'Brien and Gretel, a brand representative for Havana Club. Throughout the episode, Gretel gives O'Brien a private tour of the museum, attempting to educate him on the history of rum making in Cuba. Instead, Conan is singularly focused on moving on to the actual rum tasting. When O'Brien finally does get to the museum's bar, he has too much to drink and becomes emotional. The episode ends with O'Brien lying top of the piano, singing, and then weeping.

Despite the comedic setup, "Conan in Cuba" provides Havana Club with an opportunity to showcase its brand and its products. During the interaction, Gretel makes sure to describe the unique qualities of Cuba's extract ingredients, and at one point, they discuss Havana Club's featured products: Selección de Maestros, Gran Reserva, and Maximo. But there is clearly a public diplomacy aspect to the episode. According to O'Brien, his primary objective was to reintroduce Cuba to American audiences. During an interview with the *Los Angeles Times*, O'Brien described what he had hoped to accomplish by traveling to Cuba:

I think that mission was accomplished because there's a lot of segments where I'm diving into their culture. I'm trying to do their thing and they find me absurd. They're laughing at me, but the entire time understand where it's coming from. It's nice to know that there's this universal language with this culture that's been isolated from ours for 53 years, they understand this absurd man is terrible at salsa singing, he's terrible at dancing the rumba, he made a terrible cigar, he got drunk on the rum tour, he looks stupid in the motorcycle sidecar because his legs are too long. And I wanted Americans to really see Cuba. (Blake 2015)

To O'Brien, the way to "really see" Cuba was through its tourist destinations, and Cuban officials were eager to help him encourage travel to the island. Despite the heated political rhetoric that can sometimes be exchanged between the U.S. and Cuban governments, executives at Havana Club appeared supportive of the idea of enticing Americans to see Cuba for themselves.

Produced when President Barack Obama was working to normalize relations with Cuba, this kind of outreach seemed part of a larger project to reframe how Americans perceived Cuba. However, when Donald Trump took office, there was a reversion to the Cold War rhetoric, and the administration reversed course. Over the course of his term, Trump's administration employed increasingly aggressive economic sanctions against Cuba, including restrictions on transactions with companies controlled by the Cuban military and the elimination of educational travel for individuals.

These actions were enough to cause some concern. In 2018, Asbel Morales, Havana Club's *maestro ronero*, delivered a public appeal from the Havana Club distillery, calling for an end to petty politics and making an overt appeal to Cuban tourism. Asbel's statement was delivered in part as a response to Bacardí's "Forever Cuban" campaign, which clearly unsettled executives at Havana Club. If only American consumers could visit the island, Morales argued, they could experience true Cuban culture and taste the rum in its intended setting:

So is there anything better than inviting our American friends to come taste a glass of Havana Club, this rum full of pride, truth, and love that brings people together instead of dividing them. Because this is the soul of Cuba, and it lives within each and every one of us and it's everywhere around us. We are looking forward to welcoming them here in Cuba, in La Habana, so that they experience it for themselves. (Pernod Ricard 2018)

To keep momentum going during a time of uncertainty, Morales tirelessly promoted the Havana brand by creating special editions of Havana Club rum, including the 2018 Selección de Maestros and the 2020 Havana Club Tributo. He has also helped launch these products by speaking at a variety of press events that were hosted at the Havana Club Museum of Rum.

Over the past decade, the Havana Club Museum of Rum provides a physical setting for Havana Club event marketing, including press events, art openings, and concerts. Located just one hundred fifty meters from Havana's cruise ship terminal, the museum has become one of Cuba's most popular tourist destinations. Housed in a colonial-era building, the museum is an experiential space where tourists can physically interact with the brand, learn the history of Cuban rum, listen to music, and, of course, purchase the product.

In this chapter, I explore the role of museums and memory. Based on field research conducted in Cuba and Puerto Rico, I focus on two corporate museums. The first is the Havana Club Museum of Rum, located in Havana. The second is Casa Bacardí, located at its distillery near San Juan, Puerto Rico. Here, I am interested in how the museums cultivate a specific kind of organizational memory as it relates to family, the company, and the country. As García Canclini (2001) points out, textbooks, museums, civic rituals, and political speeches have long been the mechanisms by which each nation's identity was formed and its narrative rhetoric consecrated. But as a corporate museum, the Havana Club Museum is primarily designed for tourists who come from Canada, Western Europe, and the United States, who are seeking to escape the mundane by having "genuine" Cuban experiences. But as Dean MacCannell (2013) points out, the function of museums is not entirely determined by what is shown; the way in which the objects are shown is also important. Equally important are the erasures of people, places, and events that are involved when corporations advance specific kinds of Cuban histories.

The Museum as Ideological State Apparatus

Conceptual artist Daniel Buren (1970) has described museums as privileged spaces that serve multiple functions. First, museums offer a unifying aesthetic experience that provides the frame for experiencing the collection being displayed. Second, museums instantly elevate to "art" status the very objects they display. Finally, museums serve the marketplace by giving economic value to the artifacts that it exhibits.

Certainly, museums serve both aesthetic and educational purposes. Visitors enter a physical space where they can encounter material objects and reflect on their significance. In some cases, the spaces themselves are designed to inspire insight and wonder, either having been specifically designed for aesthetic purposes or having been repurposed from former spaces of power, including churches, government buildings, or the former homes of a society's wealthiest citizens.

At the same time, museums serve an important educational function. Visitors can learn about the cultural and natural history through its cultural artifacts. However, it has become increasingly clear that a museum's aesthetic and educational functions are not value neutral. There are ideological implications to what a museum director chooses to present as history, art, and culture, which are reflected in small curatorial decisions. As Benedict Anderson (1983) argues, collections are amassed and given a chronological perspective. Artifacts are arranged, period costumes adorned on mannequins, and facades painted to provide the illusion of context. These seemingly benign decisions draw attention to some aspects of lived experience while rendering others invisible.

These practices also create the illusion that museums are "public" institutions, while obscuring the fact that they have also historically served as spaces through which power is enacted. For example, museums have historically served the interests of powerful families. In his research on museums, Paul DiMaggio (1982) focuses on the unique importance of the Boston Brahmins, a wealthy New England class that thrived during the nineteenth century. According to DiMaggio, the Brahmin class was instrumental in establishing the Boston Symphony Orchestra and the Boston Museum of Fine Arts. Yet despite being "for the public," these institutions ultimately served as exclusive spaces, exerting elite taste sensibilities modeled on European high culture.

During the late nineteenth century, the Bacardí family had gotten into the museum business. By then, the Bacardí family had become influential in Cuba, and so it seemed inevitable that they would follow in the tradition of other wealthy families who built a number of cultural institutions that bear their family names. Named after the founder's son, the Emilio Moreau Bacardí Municipal Museum was established in 1899 and officially opened in 1928. The museum replicated European elite sensibilities in several ways. First, the building was housed in a neoclassical building designed by local architect, Carlos Segrera Fernández. Some of the artifacts hailed from colonial Europe, including one of the three death masks made of Napoleon Bonaparte. The museum also featured the paintings of Sitges by Catalan painter Joan Miró as well as an Egyptian mummy brought to Cuba by Emilio and his wife Elvira in 1912 (Dawson and Argamasilla 2006).

At the same time, the Emilio Moreau Bacardí Municipal Museum was also an exercise in nation building. First opened during the early days of Cuba's Republican era, Bacardí's museum was meant to give legitimacy to the fledgling nation. This may be a reflection of Bacardí's own politics. Emilio Bacardí had been active in Cuba's struggle for independence and went on to become the first democratically elected mayor of Santiago. The museum that bears his name was meant to showcase the promise of a newly independent Cuba, which is evident in collection, which included artifacts from both Cuban Wars for Independence, such as the Cuban flag used by the Cuban nationalist hero José Martí on the day he was killed.

A New Kind of Cuban Museum

In his work on Cuba's museum system, González (2018) points out that even before victory had been achieved, revolutionary leaders had begun to consider the role of museums in advancing socialist ideals. González notes that during the offensive, Cecilia Sánchez, revolutionary hero and lifelong secretary to Castro, sent a letter reminding him of the importance of documenting the revolutionary struggle and collecting artifacts. With the objective of shaping future memory, Sánchez started collecting materials from Fidel Castro, Camilio Cienfuegos, and Che Guevara.

When the new government took control, their vision was that museums might serve a role in cultivating a more ideal revolutionary, one who expressed his individuality through a commitment to the collective. Che Guevara's notion of the "New Man" was conceptualized as someone who was communitarian in his orientation. This new consciousness could possibly be achieved through education and other state efforts. After the revolution, museums were seen as essential to the creation of a new way of thinking. To do so, however, museums needed to correct the ideologies of the past.

As stated in *The Cultural Policy of Cuba* (Saruski and Mosquera 1979), a new way of thinking would occur at the grassroots level, as well as through traditional circuits of production: "To achieve this, a powerful amateur cultural movement has been developed. At the same time, the regular circuits of cultural dissemination have been fostered by the opening of museums, theatres, art galleries and libraries, the formation of orchestras, choirs and theatre companies, the production of books, records and films and the extension of radio and television coverage." Here, state officials called for a reconceptualization of cultural institutions to embody a more ideological mission. By the late 1970s, museums were considered one of several ideological state apparatuses that could reshape human understanding and promote socialist values, second only to schools. To help the state achieve its objectives, museums were established to celebrate Cuban achievements in the arts and sciences. Others were dedicated to telling the history of struggle for independence in Cuba.

This is evident in the Museo de la Revolución, which was designed to highlight the atrocities that were committed under the Batista dictatorship as well as to celebrate the heroes of the revolution. Located just a few blocks east of Old Havana's main thoroughfare is the Museo de la Revolución, which is deliberately housed in the presidential palace, the former home of Fulgencio Batista, to draw attention to the excesses of capitalism. The building included a room of mirrors modeled after the Palace of Versailles and has elements designed by Tiffany and Co. of New York. The opulent setting serves as a contrast to the revolutionary struggle, with artifacts that symbolized sacrifice, including Che

Guevara's beret, Camilo Cienfuego's shirt, and Fidel Castro's boots. A centerpiece of the museum is the *Granma*, a cabin cruiser boat that transported Che Guevara, Fidel Castro, and eighty followers from Mexico to Sierra in 1956 (Dickey 2016).

After Cuba's Special Period, however, the state again began to realize that Cuban museums might be able to advance socialist ideals, while also helping to promote Cuba's bourgeoning tourism industry. To convert some museums into tourist destinations, the Cuban government established La Oficina del Historiador de La Habana Vieja (OHCH), which serves two strategic functions: to become an instrument for generating hard currency through tourism and to reembrace Cuba's colonial heritage as part of its national identity (González 2018).

The decision to leverage museums for tourism purposes involved a shift in policy. Once the center of Spanish power and wealth, La Habana Vieja was initially seen by the revolutionary government as a space that symbolized centers of colonial power. In the years after the revolution, more resources were directed outside the city, leaving Old Havana to fall into decay. But in 1982, Havana Vieja was declared by UNESCO as a World Heritage Site, a status that transformed the colonial section of the city into an asset. In 1993, Cuba designated it as a Prioritized Preservation Zone (ZPC), and a year later, the OHCH drafted a master plan for ensuring the redevelopment of the city center. As González (2018) argues, the goal was to create a tourist-friendly experience that would essentially convert La Habana Vieja into a living museum.

Unlike those of other Cuban institutions, the OHCH's revenues do not come from the state but from commercial activities, which include hotels, restaurants, and real estate management. To achieve its goals, OHCH is given some concessions not available to other institutions, including the ability to grant visas and to negotiate exports and imports without state mediation. La Habana Vieja, the capital's historic district, figures prominently in its efforts. The OHCH manages a network of twenty-nine museums, most of them located in Old Havana.

According to González (2018), there are several types of museums that fall under the auspices of the OHCH. Some museums were taken over from other bureaucratic entities, including the Museo Napoleónico, which features the collection of sugar magnate Julio Lobo, who was fascinated by the French emperor (Rathbone 2010); the Museo de Automóvil (Cars); and the Casa Natal de José Martí. Another group of museums celebrate important Latin American figures that embody the ideals of the revolution, including museums dedicated to Simón Bolívar, Guayas Aman, and Juan Gualberto Gómez. Finally, there are museums that are primarily meant for tourist consumption and which have a strong retail component, including The Museum of Rum, el Museo del Tabaco, and the Museo del Chocolate.

The Havana Club Museum of Rum

The Havana Club Museum of Rum opened in 2000 and is housed in an eighteenth-century colonial building. Originally home to Ramón Herrera y Gutiérrez, the Count of La Mortera and a member of one of Cuba's wealthiest families, the building was later converted into a commercial space. When the Castro regime took power, the building was appropriated and became home to a variety of government buildings, including the Academy of Sciences (1965). In 1968, the building was home to the National Council of Culture.

In some ways, the Havana Club Museum of Rum operates like other corporate museums in that it is an exhibit-based facility, which primarily serves public relations and marketing functions. With tours that are conducted in English, Spanish, French, Italian, and German, visitors are invited to enter into an immersive experience in which the Havana Club brand is the focal point. At the end of the tour, visitors have an opportunity to physically consume the product, by either purchasing bottles of rum in the gift shop or drinking the rum at the museum's bar.

Yet the Havana Club Museum of Rum is distinct from other corporate museums in that it does not focus singularly on José Arechabala. According to Victor Danilov (1991), corporate museums generally construct a historical memory of who the founder was and what he or she has accomplished. His or her values and passions are meant to capture the brand's essence and moral authenticity, which are intended to transfer to the product itself. Whether focusing on the life of Milton Hershey at the Hershey Story Museum in Pennsylvania or that of Sam Walton at the Walmart Museum in Arkansas, these types of museums tend to frame their founders as visionaries who transformed their respective fields.

José Arechabala is only briefly mentioned during the Havana Club tour. Instead, the curators of the Havana Club Museum of Rum have constructed an alternative narrative that positions Cuban rum as the product of a collective effort involving a number of nameless actors. In this way, the Havana Club brand is used as a vehicle for discussing the larger history of rum in Cuba. This concept is established almost immediately. Even before visitors enter the museum, they are greeted by a small-scale replica statue of La Giraldilla, which serves as a branding device for both the product and the city.

The chronology of the tour is important to the narrative. The story of Havana Club does not begin in 1847, when José Arechabala was born, or in 1878, when he established his distillery. Nor does the story begin in 1934, when the Havana Club brand was formally launched. Instead, the story of Cuban rum begins 500 years earlier when Columbus arrived in Hispaniola. Over the course of the tour, visitors are taken through the rum-making process, from harvesting at sugarcane plantations to the final bottling process. Visitors are led into different rooms that simulate the harvesting, fermentation, and blending of rum.

The historical narrative is meant to depict rum production as a collective effort, but it also serves an important marketing function by invoking multiple forms of authenticity. First, the museum tour emphasizes the product's natural authenticity. Early in the process, the curators established the unique importance of place. Tourists learn about the ideal conditions that make Cuba conducive to growing sugarcane. Placards tout the importance of terroir, or the complete natural environment in which the rum is produced. By invoking the brand's natural authenticity, the museum is part of ongoing messaging strategy that distinguishes Cuba from other sugar-producing nations. The presentation of the history of Cuban rum in this way also allows the Cuban State to appear as the curator of local and long-standing traditions.

Second, the museum reinforces its historic credentials by focusing on the traditional rum-making processes. To give the visitor a sense of time and place, historic artifacts that were once used in the distillation of rum are placed throughout the museum. There are stalks of sugarcane and historic tools. There is a rudimentary device for pressing sugarcane, and tourists are invited to make their own cane juice. In the fermentation and distilling rooms there are wooden casks and copper distillation columns and pipes, which demonstrate the production process. These accoutrements are important for creating a sense of time and place.

This kind of curation reflects what MacCannell (2013) describes as "re-presentation," in which museums purport to depict a total situation but in reality only offer a limited perspective based on the artifacts on display. For example, a focal point of the tour is a small-scale model of a sugarcane plantation created by Lázaro Eduardo García Driggs. The model is an exact replica of the Ingenio La Esperanza, an actual distillery that was in full operation around 1930. The display has been designed to represent sugar production during the Republican era, while obscuring the economic and racial politics of the time.

This artifact is meant to make a spatiotemporal connection to another time and culture. According to Michael Beverland (2005), this kind of staging is a necessary component of authenticity building. Like other brands that compete in the wine and spirits category, Havana Club must demonstrate its commitment to historic traditions and its passion for the craft of rum making. In the process of re-creating a particular version of the past, however, the museum deliberately obscures its own modern practices, since the actual production of Havana Club rum takes place over twenty miles away in the distillery at San José de las Lajas. Far away from the tourist gaze (Urry 1990), Havana Club rum is produced under different circumstances, using modern techniques: there are assembly lines, robotics, the forklifts carrying large quantities—all the production equipment necessary for large-scale global-scale production. To maintain the illusion of artisanal craftsmanship, such modern industrial practices must remain hidden.

A link to Cuba's past is also evident in the museum's use of performers. In his discussion of tourism, John Urry (1990) invokes the term "corporeal travel" to describe the embodied nature of travel. According to Urry, the tourists who travel from place to place are composed of vulnerable, aged, gendered, racialized bodies. Over the course of their journeys, these bodies may encounter other bodies, who are performing their gender and racial identities, sometimes for the sake of the tourist.

This kind of interaction becomes most evident during moments that involve what MacCannell (2013) terms a "reconstructed ethnicity" or "staged authenticity." Ethnic performances such as the Hawaiian hula, Mexican folklorico, or Spanish flamenco may appear to be authentic cultural expressions, but they represent a kind of performance created for consumption. However, this kind of interaction is an illusion. Visitors believe that they are witnessing a genuine folk tradition rather than a performance merely undertaken for the visitor.

At the Havana Club Museum of Rum, women have been hired to dress up in *Bata Cubana*, traditional Afro-Cuban dress. This type of bodily display appears to serve several purposes. The first is to reframe the history of sugar and rum production by acknowledging the role that Afro-Cubans have played in building the industry. The second is political. The integration of Afro-Cubans into the story of Cuban rum is consistent with socialist discourses ideals around race. As Ada Ferrer (2021) points out, the long-standing narrative of the revolution is that Cuba is a nation born out of racial unity. Finally, the presence of Afro-Cuban performers makes the experience more exotic and interesting to an audience of primarily white tourists. As bell hooks (1992) argued in *Eating the Other: Desire and Resistance*, the ethnic Other can enhance the consumption experience by engaging the consumer is a kind of colonial fantasy. Black bodies can, in her words, be "the seasoning that can liven up the dull dish that is mainstream, white culture."

Consuming Cuban History

Once the educational aspect of the tour is concluded, the real sales work of the museum begins. Toward the end of the tour, visitors are funneled into the museum's gift shop, which is an essential part of the visit. The ultimate function of the corporate museum, after all, is to promote the product, and here consumers are exposed to Havana Club's full product portfolio, including its super-premium rums and limited-edition rums, such as their "Cuban Smoky" brand as well as their brand of Cuban spiced rum. These products have the aura of scarcity, since they are not readily found in the global marketplace. Also available for purchase are related goods. Visitors can purchase cigars for pairing with the rum, books, items for making authentic Cuban cocktails, and Cuban souvenirs.

According to Charles McIntyre (2010), the purpose of the museum gift shop extends beyond its simple retail function. If done properly, the gift shop can be

MUSEUMS AND MEMORY

Figure 9. Bar at the Havana Club Museum of Rum. Photograph taken by Christoper Chávez.

a seamless extension of the museum by connecting the aesthetic experience to the consumption experience. The gift shop at the Havana Club Museum of Rum certainly serves this function. It has been designed to mimic a colonial storehouse, with dark mahogany shelves and cast-iron screens, thereby maintaining the illusion that the visitor has stepped back in time.

This is particularly evident in the Bar Havana Club, which has been designed to mimic a Republican Era establishment. With a large mahogany counter, the bar is reminiscent of those frequented by Ernest Hemingway, a notable figure in popular imagination (Figure 9). For an additional cost, visitors can participate in rum tastings, take bartending classes, or enjoy special Havana Club cocktails that are unique to the bar. At times, the bar will host live musicians, thereby becoming a wholly immersive experience, in which visitors can link Cuban rum to Cuban cigars, while listening to Cuban music, all the while believing that they are having an authentic Cuban experience. In this way, the brand can be consumed both symbolically and physically. The entire experience serves its overt commercial function by generating revenue for the museum and increasing awareness of the Havana Club brand.

The Museum and High Art

I also found that the museum provides branding value by showcasing the work of Cuban visual artists, albeit to a limited degree. In this way, the Havana Club Museum of Rum is consistent with other corporate museums, particularly those that cater to luxury audiences. For some fashion and lifestyle brands, corporate museums have the potential to build a link to between the brand and art through temporary exhibitions by demonstrating how the product itself can be a work of art, or the embodiment of cultural expression during a specific period and region (Carú, Ostillio, and Leone 2017).

From a commercial perspective, the display of visual arts also helps to position Havana Club as a premium product. All the commissioned artwork displayed in the museum focuses on the product as its primary subject matter. For example, the museum features a painting by Nelson Domínguez. Simply titled *Havana Club Añejo 7 Años*, the painting is of an abstracted bottle of Havana Club rum. Dominguez is one of Cuba's most notable artists, having been awarded the Doyusha prize by Tenri Biennale Japan in 1996 and in 2009 and the National Award of Art by Cuban Ministry of Culture, Cuba. His work is displayed in such diverse places as the Museo Nacional de Bella Artes in Havana, Casa Presidencial Los Pinos in Mexico, and the Imperial Palace of Japan.

The use of prestigious, Cuban artists to showcase the product borrows heavily from a strategy developed by global advertising agency TBWA on behalf of Absolut Vodka. The agency gained notoriety for establishing a connection between the Absolut brand and the urban, cultural vanguard by commissioning the work of notable artists, including Andy Warhol, Gianni Versace, Annie Leibowitz, and Kurt Vonnegut.

Originally, the Havana Club Museum of Rum was meant to showcase Cuban art. As discussed in chapter 2, the museum was meant to be an extension of the Visual Arts Project, a platform for showcasing rising Cuban artists. But I found no evidence that the museum was truly operating in this way. During the 2019 Havana Biennial, the museum was not one of the featured exhibition spaces that showcased Cuban artists. When I returned to the museum in 2023, the experience was somewhat diminished, likely due to the downturn in tourism in the wake of the global pandemic. The original artwork was not curated, but rather appeared to be haphazardly displayed, and the live performances at the cantina were paused. In this way, it became clear that the health of the museum was directly related to the health of Cuba's tourism industry.

Casa Bacardí

Over a thousand miles away, in the small coastal town of Cataño, just outside San Juan, Puerto Rico, there is a different kind of rum museum. Casa Bacardí is first and foremost a working distillery with a small corporate museum attached to its premises. The company may be headquartered in Hamilton, Bermuda, but it is in Puerto Rico where over 80 percent of Bacardí's rum is produced. Beginning in 1936, the brand began a long-standing relationship with the Puerto Rican government, providing employment and revenue in exchange for closer access to the U.S. market (del Rosa 2020).

Given the industrial nature of the property, movement is highly restricted. Tourists purchase tickets in advance, and upon arriving on the Bacardí campus, they announce their presence to a security guard. Visitors are not allowed entry until their designated times, and even when they enter the campus, their movements are highly directed. Tours are led by guides, called "brand ambassadors," who take the visitors on a scripted tour, relying on trams to shuttle visitors to predetermined destinations.

No clear chronology is evident at Casa Bacardí, and the campus itself is a juxtaposition of different buildings and artifacts that reflect different time periods. Scattered between the modern factory buildings are a random collection of props: a small sugarcane patch, a stack of old barrels, and a train car from the Ponce Guayama Railroad Company, the last operating sugarcane railway in Puerto Rico. There are no placards to explain their significance, yet they appear designed to make some connection between the company's modern production values and its past.

The buildings within the campus similarly reflect various time periods. Referred to as the "Cathedral of Rum," several of the distillery's original buildings were influenced by the architectural style of the Works Progress Administration (WPA) of the interwar period. By the early 1960s, new buildings were constructed that reflected modernist Latin American influences as reflected in the work of architect Felix Candela (Schulman 2016).

One of the most striking buildings, however, is the Centennial Pavilion, which currently serves as Casa Bacardí's welcoming center. Designed in 1962 by Enrique Gutierrez and Luis Saenz of SACMAG of Puerto Rico, the pavilion's bat-winged design is said to have been influenced by the corporate logo. It is here where visitors are formally greeted and invited. In a press statement, Ruben Rodriguez, Bacardí's former CEO, described the function of the Casa Bacardí Visitor's Center, which had been recently opened: "The new Casa Bacardí Visitor represents the very spirit and soul of Bacardí, our family history, and our role as the world's leading producer of premium spirits. Through this magnificent attraction, we share the fascinating history of a Family, a Brand, and a Company that have added joy and enjoyment to fun-loving people since 1862" (Dawson, and Argamasilla 2006).

As Rodriguez makes clear, the visitor's center is designed to connect Bacardí's contemporary practices with the family's long-standing history. To evoke a sense of late nineteenth-century Cuba, visitors are given tokens that are fashioned after old currency. One side of the coin depicts the Bacardí logo. On the other side is a coat of arms, with the words *Fortuna, Buena Suerte, Salud,* and *Unidad de Familia* (Fortune, Good Luck, Health, and Family Unity). Visitors can exchange these tokens for a Bacardí cocktail.

After consuming the product, the official guided tour begins, and the first stop is the Foyer Museum, housed in a building designed by Miguel Rosich and Ignacio Carrera-Justiz in 1965. The Foyer Museum, which works like a traditional corporate museum, focuses on company history, underlining the contributions of the founder and other key individuals, and displaying historical documents, photographs, and iconic products.

At the Havana Club Museum of Rum, the story of Cuban rum begins with the arrival of Columbus. But Casa Bacardí serves as a more conventional corporate museum, in which the story of Cuban rum begins with the birth of company's founder, Facundo Bacardí Masso. This is reflected in a mural located in the foyer exhibit. The mural includes the Bacardí family tree painted in 1967 by commercial artist Homer Hill. At the base of the tree is Facundo and his wife, Lucia Victoria Amalia Moreau, as if the family lineage did not exist prior to the creation of the company.

Also included in the mural are depictions of the tools of early rum production: a machete and a stalk of sugarcane, a rudimentary device for pressing the sugarcane, and the original equipment used to distill rum during the late 1800s. There are also depictions of postcards from some of Bacardí's iconic buildings, including the Emilio Moreau Bacardí museum in Santiago and the company's original distillery in San Juan, Puerto Rico.

Spain figures prominently in the Bacardí narrative, and the museum draws upon its vast inventory of advertising to tell its story. Depicted is the company's long-standing tagline, "El Rey De Los Rones, El Ron de Los Reyes" (King of Rum, Rum of the Kings). But there are other nods to Spain, including the Spanish flag and the original medallions won during the expositions. At the same time, the museum also reflects the ethos of globalization. The mural showcases flags for Puerto Rico, Mexico, the United States, Brazil, and Bermuda, places that are of strategic business interest to the company. The entire experience is an exercise in branding. Throughout the property is the ubiquitous presence of the bat logo. The purpose is not necessarily to learn about any given rum-producing region, but to learn more about the product.

The actual consumption of rum is an important part of the museum experience. At this halfway point in the tour, a small tasting of the product is again offered to the guests. After a short tasting, visitors are then shuttled to a separate facility where they are exposed to a flight of Bacardí rums. There, visitors are educated on the process of drinking and appreciating fine Bacardí rum. After tasting the product, visitors are directed into a gift shop, where they have access to the museum's full range of products and Bacardí-branded merchandise, such as t-shirts, totes, and Panama hats. The visitors conclude their trip with one last trip to the bar before exiting the property.

The Art of Storytelling

Brand ambassadors serve an important part in role in maintaining the Bacardí legacy. Essentially playing the role of corporate storytellers, brand ambassadors ensure that the family history is kept cohesive and consistent. While the brand ambassadors I encountered at Casa Bacardí were from Puerto Rico, there is a small army of these storytellers located across the globe, anywhere Bacardí has a business interest.

Job announcements for brand ambassadors across the globe call for specific personal qualities that are desired in a candidate. In addition to professional traits, such as organizational skills and an expertise in communications prospective candidates are informed that a Bacardí brand ambassador must also engage in a kind of cultural brokering by attempting to insert the brand into local culture and customs. As one job posting for a brand ambassador based in Dubai stated, the prospective candidate must "be aware of local drinking culture, tastes, and seasonal ingredients and adapt with appropriate presentation/mixology demonstration accordingly" (Bacardí 2022c).

Once they are hired, Bacardí's brand ambassadors enter into an intensive training program. All are trained with the "Brand Master Story," which is shared with their sales force, as well as distributors, buyers, bartenders, and other important stakeholders. To assist the brand ambassadors in their efforts to tell the Bacardí story, there are plenty of other resources to draw upon. Brand ambassadors turn to social media to connect with other brand ambassadors and share information. Bacardí has also produced a number of books that serve the same function of telling and retelling the story, in a highly consistent and disciplined fashion.

Bacardí: A Tale of Merchants, Family, and Company (2006) is a good example of this. Written by Marí Aixalá Dawson and Pepin Argamasilla, the book is well produced, complete with beautifully restored historic images. Published by Bacardí Global Brands, the book provides one of the most complete histories of the brand by documenting the family's humble beginnings in Sitges, to its time in Santiago de Cuba, and later to its exile. The book also details the global expansion of the company.

This kind of labor is, in part, personal. Bacardí is a family-owned company, and the heirs have taken an active role in curating this history. Dawson herself is a sixth-generation heir who serves on the company's board of directors. She has also cowritten with Facundo L. Bacardí, previously the company's chairman, a book titled *Bacardí Superior Rum Legacy Cocktail Book* (2011). At the same time, Dawson is also part of a community of writers who have developed a specialty in writing about food and spirits.

To help them in their efforts to retell the Bacardí story, the authors have had access to a substantial amount of archival material. In Coral Gables, Florida, the family has established Bacardí Archives, which has over 30,000 cataloged artifacts that includes photographs, advertisements, and the medals and awards that Bacardí has won over the years. All of this contributes to a vast knowledge-generating mechanism that serves as a resource for a variety of stakeholders, including journalists, bartenders, and consumers. The ability for Bacardí to amass this amount of archival material is noteworthy. Significant resources have been invested in reclaiming the family history, which was particularly challenging given that so much material was lost when the company was expropriated.

In addition to their own corporate materials, Bacardí has also collaborated with creative partners who can tell the family story in new and compelling ways. For example, in 2014, Bacardí partnered with writer Warren Ellis and graphic artist Michael Allred to produce an online graphic novel that focuses on Emilio Bacardí's involvement in Cuba's independence movement and his time as the first democratically elected mayor of Santiago de Cuba. The comic serves up a morally unambiguous portrait of Emilio, presenting him as a stoic and reluctant hero. But as a form of marketing, the creators have placed the Bacardí family at the front and center of one of the most significant periods in Cuban history. As Javier Lázaro (2016) points out, countless, unrecognized Cuban entrepreneurs have collectively contributed to the cultivation of a large-scale industry in Cuba. At Casa Bacardí, however, a single family has been privileged above all others. This itself reflects the ethos of capitalism that celebrates the individual rather than the collective.

All of this is a clear reminder that an exercise in memory is also an exercise in forgetting. Certain truths are lost in the practice of corporate storytelling. As Miguel Bonera (2000) astutely notes, Don Facundo Bacardí's success was due not necessarily to his individual resourcefulness but rather to the economic capital to which he had access. Revenue was needed to pay the initial start-up costs and to survive bankruptcy when it occurred in 1855. Facundo's access to economic capital was, in large part, due to his marriage to Lucia Victoria Amalia Moreau, who was born in Haiti and was the granddaughter of Pedro Benjamin Moreau, a French coffee plantation owner. Given the substantial inheritance she received from her grandfather, her marriage to Facundo was seen by some as one of convenience and opportunity.

Also absent from the narrative is the controversy that surrounded the Moreau family. The Moreau family had left France because of their Bonapartist sympathies and had ultimately settled in the Santiago region in 1814. Then there was the family's ambivalent relationship with slavery. Elvira Cape, wife of Emilio Bacardí, was a slave owner, and according to Bonera (2000), Don Facundo passed along to his sons twenty slaves, which were valued at 10,000 pesos. According to Laura Muse (2012), the Bacardí family had slaves in their home until 1886, but in the spirit of the Independence movement, Emilio Bacardí freed all the slaves he had inherited.

Finally, Bacardí promotes the narrative that their family was singularly responsible for building Cuba's rum industry. But as Bonera (2000) argues, it was in fact, a variety of competing distilleries that managed, over time, to create a genuinely Cuban liquor, which was known as "a la Española" (Spanish style). But it is important to remember some of the other individuals who helped Bacardí launch his business. After all, Bacardí's first rums were made with the still of John Munne, a Briton who had established a small distillery in Santiago to compete with rum makers in Jamaica and Martinique. Munne's business was a modest operation, but he was successful enough to have sold his product throughout the island. Then there was León Bouteiller, a French merchant living in Santiago at the time, who became Bacardí's original business partner. It was Boutellier, a distiller and a confectioner, who brought expertise, labor, and some limited capital to the partnership. These are just two individuals who had a direct impact on the fledgling business, which suggests that Bacardí was not alone in his efforts, but rather building on the contributions of other Cuban entrepreneurs.

Havana Club's Counterhistory

The Arechabala family was in the process of curating its own historical narrative in the years before the company was expropriated by the revolutionary government. In 1947, for example, José Arechabala S.A. published a special edition of *Gordejuela*, its corporate publication, which marked a century since the founder's birth. There is a full-page announcement (Figure 10) that positions Don José as a man of clear importance. On the left side of the advertisement, there is an allegorical figure, standing amid stalks of sugarcane. In one hand, she holds up a large cog, a symbol of industry, and with the other, she holds an olive branch, the symbol of peace and eternal life. There is also an illustrated image of La Vizcaya, Arechabala's prized distillery, along with the corporate logo, with its references to Arechabala's native country.

To the right of the advertisement is a portrait of Don José followed by a set of quotes from notable figures, who describe the contributions the man and the company have made to Cuba. Senator José Manuel Casanova describes José Arechabala S.A. as "having contributed to the economic independence of the

Figure 10. "Centenario de Don Jose Arechabala Aldama." From *Gordejuela* (November 1947). Accessed through Liburuklik Digital Library.

country," while Dr. Carlos Prío Socarrás, a politician who would later serve as Cuba's president, described the company as "the supreme aspiration of the responsible men of this country."

The exultation of the company's founder would continue when the company celebrated its diamond jubilee in 1953. To mark that milestone, the company produced a seventy-fifth-anniversary book, which included a biographical history of José Arechabala, and a collection of archival documents, photographs, and the original floor plans for the distilleries. In one excerpt, corporate writers attempted to link the fate of the Arechabala family to the fate of Cuba itself:

> The Arechabala Company can boast three quarters of a century of vigorous life. During that long period, Cuba has suffered some serious difficulties which, quite naturally, have affected business conditions: wars for Cuba's freedom, two world wars, a terrible economic crisis, political upheavals, frequent deep disturbances in the most vital element of the national economy, sugar; and moral tribulations which have smitten the firm with sorrow. (Sainz 1954)

After their business was nationalized, the Arechabala family essentially lost the capacity to tell its own history. Instead, maintaining the family memory has been taken on by two competing organizations. As discussed in Chapter 3, Bacardí Ltd. has taken on responsibility for telling the Arechabala family's story in a way that sheds a favorable light on the Bacardí family. However, the Cuban State, in partnership with Pernod Ricard, has also assumed the role of retelling the brand story but places the Arechabala family at the margins.

Pernod Ricard has access to its own army of corporate storytellers who specialize in writing about food and spirits. A good example of this is *Cuba: The Legend of Rum*, cowritten by Anistatia Miller and Jared Brown, the owners of Mixellany Books, a publishing house that focuses on the spirits industry. Miller and Brown have made a successful career writing about various distilled spirits. Other books in their portfolio include *Shaken Not Stirred: A Celebration of the Martini* (Miller and Brown 2013), *The Mixellany Guide to Vermouth and Other Aperitifs* (Brown and Miller 2011), and *Champagne Cocktails* (Miller and Brown 2010). They also have written several books on Cuban spirits, including *Cuban Cocktails* (Miller and Brown 2012) and *The Spirit of Cane: The Story of Cuban Rum* (Miller and Brown 2017).

Cuba: The Legend of Rum is branded as a Havana Club publication, and there are similarities with the Havana Club Museum of Rum as to how the Havana Club story is told. The book also begins with Columbus and the first planting of sugarcane on the island. It follows with the development of a thriving rum industry in Cuba, but one in which the Arechabala family only plays a nominal role. The book positions Havana Club rum as a national product, not a private one. And like the museum, the true purpose is to promote the product, and to promote consumption. The authors discuss the unique qualities of Cuban rum and provide cocktail recipes that call for the product.

This kind of book is a necessary part of the marketing process. Published in 2009, the couple was approached by Yves Schladenhaufen, Havana Club International Global Marketing director, to write a trade book on Cuban rum that would showcase the brand. The intended audience was bartenders, who needed to be educated on the singularity of Cuban rum, and in particular, the Havana Club brand. According to Miller:

> If you don't educate both the key decision makers (beverage managers) and the people who make the drinks and sell them through to the consumers (bartenders) about your products, you will never gain market share. It's the reason why brand ambassadors became a key part of the marketing strategy for many brands. They go in and educate these key people to deliver the history and quality of the brand; educate bartenders on 'perfect pour' strategies for cocktail development; stimulate bartender loyalty through cocktail competitions.

As Miller points out, accuracy is not necessarily the true purpose of these kinds of histories. The real point is to sell the product, and both museums serve up a well-produced and immersive experience that will appeal to consumers who crave an authentic experience. Both museums are similar in that they attempt sincerity through the avowal of commitments to traditions (including production methods, product styling, firm values, and/or location), passion for craft and production excellence, and the public disavowal of the role of modern industrial attributes and commercial motivations (Beverland 2005).

Havana Club's authentic credentials have been bolstered after the announcement, in 2022, that UNESCO was adding the distillation of Cuban light rum to its List of Intangible Heritages, a recognition that is meant to safeguard historical cultural practices. When describing the rum making process, UNESCO confirmed that the Cuban light rum, for which Havana Club is known, is made through a unique process that has been uninterrupted since 1862. They also stated that Cuban rum masters form a guild-type community, in which its members follow an ethical code that is centered on respect for culture, quality, and sustainability (UNESCO 2022).

Havana Club executives were quick to leverage UNESCO's designation. A delegation that included Maestro Roneros Juan Carlos Gonzales and Asbel Morales was dispatched to Rabat, Morocco, to attend a formal ceremony as part of the final step in the process. Havana Club followed with a number of congratulatory online posts. "Today we celebrate Cuba's Maestros del Ron Cubano, the island's resident rum Masters, who've just gotten their know-how officially recognized by UNESCO as World Intangible Heritage," is how they put it on social media. "As el ron de Cuba, Havana Club is proud to be part of this journey and to share this incredible achievement" (Havana Club International 2022).

This kind of legacy has become an important asset for the brand, and the Havana Club Museum of Rum makes effective use of history. The museum is housed in a building that was built three centuries ago and is located in La Habana Vieja, far away from the modern factory that actually produces the rum. The interior design, the building, and the neighborhood all collude to create the perception that guests are stepping back in time. As Erving Goffman (1959) notes, this a kind of social performance that includes a back region, which is closed to audiences and outsiders, and allows concealment of props and activities that might discredit the performance out front, what he calls "mystification."

At the Casa Bacardí, it is harder for the company to maintain the illusion. The campus is clearly a working factory, and while tourists are kept at a distance, it is difficult to ignore the modern mechanisms by which rum is produced. But rather than deny the large scale and transnational nature of modern production, transnationalism has become a talking point in the tour. Facundo Bacardí is described as a man who embodied globalization itself. As a man, he immigrated Spain and prospered in Cuba. In corporate form, he built networks that extended globally.

A global sensibility extends to how the product itself is characterized. Visitors are told about the sugarcane that is brought from Mexico and India and then distilled in Puerto Rico. They are also told about the corporate headquarters located in Bermuda but also the family's ties to southern Florida. I asked one of Bacardí's brand ambassadors about how he reconciles Bacardí's claim to Cuban authenticity with the global nature of the company. In other words, given how Bacardí's rum is produced, what makes the product uniquely Cuban? According to the brand ambassador, it is not the extract ingredients that make the product Cuban. According to the ambassador, sugarcane is sugarcane, whether it was grown in Cuba, Mexico, or India. What truly makes the rum unique are both the unique formula and the process by which it is made. These processes predate the family's exile from Cuba and are said to be unique to Bacardí.

Because the fundamental purpose of the museum is to place the brand in a positive light, tourists are only exposed to a sanitized version of Cuban history. This was evident in how the museum ignores the virulent racism that was inherent in rum production. Given the museum's focus on the Bacardí family, the museum's history of Cuba is one of whiteness. Yet visitors hear little about the transatlantic slave trade and the countless Afro-Cubans who harvested and distilled Cuban rum under oppressive conditions. Bacardí's approach to racial politics is evident in a large painting that hangs in the Foyer Museum at Casa Bacardí in Puerto Rico. Titled *Fiesta en el Cobre, 8 de Septiembre en Santiago de Cuba*, the painting depicts a crowd of Afro-Cubans celebrating the Our Lady of Charity, the patron saint of Cuba. Despite the painting's theme of religious devotion, the mood is celebratory. Set in what appears to be a colonial setting, the painting depicts a carnival celebration with fireworks, musicians, and costumed performers. But the painting could also be an advertisement for Bacardí. Branded bottles of rum are clearly visible amid all the celebration, as the bat logo adorns the light fixtures that are depicted in the painting.

A positive reading of the painting would be that Bacardí is paying homage to the Afro-Cuban laborers who were essential to the business. In this light, the painting can be seen as an effort to reclaim the role of Afro-Cubans in Cuba's rum industry. A more cynical reading, however, is that the painting reflects the ways in which corporations continue to use Black bodies for marketing purposes. The depiction of preindustrial Black laborers in rapt celebration lends the brand historical authenticity, but it also places the product at the center of what is in essence a religious celebration.

In either case, the painting must be read as a form of what Renato Rosaldo (1989) calls "imperialist nostalgia," in which people mourn the loss of what they themselves have destroyed. What are not reflected in the painting, or acknowledged during the tour, are the actual racist practices of that time. Spanish colonialism was a brutal project, and things did not get better when Cuba gained its independence from Spain. As Roberto Nodal (1986) points out, after the Cuban Republic was established in 1902, there were attempts to suppress any African vestiges in Cuban culture. Members of Black religions were persecuted, and the use of African drums was forbidden. Cuban authorities went as far as banning the celebration of the annual carnivals under the pretension that these were things of a "savage and uncivilized nature." These realities have been suppressed in order to tell a more favorable story.

The Havana Club Museum of Rum was no different. The use of Afro-Cuban performers dressed in period costumes was a kind of performance meant to transport visitors into another time. But one in which slavery is only implicitly acknowledged in this kind of performance. It is colonization without the oppression. However, these kinds of curatorial decisions distort rather than illuminate reality, but a meaningful reflection of Cuban culture, politics, and history is not really the goal anyway. The goal is to brand the company, and both companies seem to be astutely aware that such ugly realities impede the sale of rum. As I will discuss in chapter 5, these practices are not limited to the corporate museum. Havana Club and other rum marketers have used various strategies to navigate shifting racial politics and to reconcile their relationship with Cuba's racist past.

CHAPTER 5

Rum, Race, and Representation

I became intrigued after discovering real-life adverts from the era that were in bewilderingly poor taste. So, I set myself the grimly amusing task of collecting as many examples of them as possible. They show that marketing men—and they were mostly men—in the middle of the last century had few qualms about creating brutally sexist and racist adverts that would never see the light of day today, and which most of us now would find offensive to the point of callousness. —Charles Saatchi, co-founder of M&C Saatchi

The very first newspaper advertisement for Bacardí was placed on January 4, 1892, in *La Ilustración Artística*, an illustrated weekly magazine that was published in Barcelona in the late nineteenth century.[1] The focal point of the advertisement is an illustrated bottle of Bacardí Ron Superior, along with some important details about the product. The advertisement is clearly branded, informing the reader that the rum is a product of Bacardí y Compañia. The copy further indicates that the rum is an internationally renowned product, having been awarded two gold medals at international competitions, one in Barcelona in 1888 and the other in Paris in 1889. Finally, the advertisement provides details about where Bacardí rum can be found—in cafés, restaurants, and corner stores.

The placement of the advertisement in *La Ilustración Artística* also suggests that Bacardí was attempting to position the rum as a premium spirit. The reader of this publication would have been a Spaniard with cosmopolitan taste sensibilities. Published by the Montanar y Simón publishing house, *La Ilustración Artística* catered to the bourgeoisie with its focus on literature, art, and science. The magazine included literary essays, art reviews, and elegantly produced engravings of museum pieces or original works by salon artists (Charnon-Deutsch 2008). Together with its sister publication, *La Ilustración Ibérica*, the magazine reflected an ethos of la ética realista (a realist ethic), which included highly detailed depictions of exotic and faraway places, such as a marketplace in Shanghai or a narrow street in Jerusalem.

This reader would also have had the economic resources to buy the goods that were being advertised. In the same January 4 issue, there were advertisements for high-end, specialty products that were made and sold in Spain—a chocolatier in Madrid, who also sold tea and coffee, a store that sold organs and pianos; and a boutique in Barcelona that specialized in children's clothing. There were advertisements for tonics of all kinds, promising cures for various ailments, including fatigue, anemia, epilepsy, heart conditions, asthma, and other breathing disorders. In limited cases, the advertiser would use illustrations to represent the prospective consumer, such as a stately gentleman consulting with a pharmacist, or a trio of Spanish children wearing fashionable clothing.

However, the Bacardí advertisement is remarkable because of its blatant use of racist, visual tropes (Figure 11). Next to the bottle of Bacardí rum is an

Figure 11. Bacardí's first advertisement, placed in *La Ilustración Artística* (January 4, 1892). Accessed through the Biblioteca Virtual de Prensa Histórica.

illustration of two primitive Black figures, presumably Afro-Cuban, who are pointing to the product. Compared with the bottle, the figures are rendered disproportionately small, as if they were engaging with a religious artifact. The figures are dressed in loincloths and are drawn in distorted, exaggerated ways, with dark skin and excessively protruding lips.

Strategically, the inclusion of such imagery may have been intended to signal the product's country of origin. In a Spanish publication filled almost exclusively with advertisements for Spanish businesses, a Cuban rum would have been a novelty. By contrast, the Bacardí rum is clearly marked as Cuban, in both its copywriting and its art direction. The advertisement makes mention that the rum is produced in Santiago de Cuba, but the imagery itself seems to tap into preconceived notions of Cuba, which had become linked with African identity (Pérez 2008).

In this way, the Bacardí advertisement reflects the ways in which advertisers perpetuated notions of Black servitude during this time. As Livia Gershon (2019) notes, marketers at the end of the nineteenth century often defined an ideal, white consumer in relationship to a preindustrial Black laborer. As commodities began to flood late-century homes, advertising became important vehicles for racial and capitalist ideologies. In the course of selling products, advertising reflected larger discourses that were circulated within Cuba, in which white civilization was held in opposition to black savagery.

But the advertisement is also insightful for what it conceals about the complex nature of Cuba's racial politics during the late nineteenth century. For example, Bacardí's depiction of an infantilized slave class concealed the actual fears that many Cubans had of a "Black threat." After the massive uprising that took place in Haiti in 1791, many white Cubans lived in fear of the island's large population of enslaved African-descended laborers. Certainly, Afro-Cubans were not passive participants in Cuban society. By the time this advertisement ran, Black and mestizo Cubans were actively involved in planning and executing Cuba's War for Independence, which was in part fought to upend racial hierarchies.

The advertisement also obscures the Bacardí family's own contradictory role in these systems of inequality. As a large-scale rum manufacturer and exporter, the Bacardí family would have maintained strong relationships both with the sugar plantation owners, who supplied the sugarcane, and with Spanish officials, who helped facilitate the entry of the product into Spain. Yet Emilio Moreau Bacardí, who would go on to helm the Bacardí company, was himself an abolitionist who engaged in pro-independence activities, which landed him twice in prison in the Chafarine Islands and briefly exiled in Jamaica (Gjelten 2009).

In this chapter, I explore how advertising for Cuban rum has, over the past 150 years, reflected shifting notions of race. According to Devyn Spence Benson (2016), conceptions of race and Cuban national identity have been centered around two competing discourses. The first perspective reflected those of the Spanish elite, which was later embodied by writer and social critic José Antonio Saco, who envisioned Cuba as a white, space. Blacks and mestizos were not considered part of Cuba's national project. The second perspective is reflected by José Martí, who envisioned a postracial, revolutionary society. One of the key figures in Cuba's fight for independence, Martí injected the movement with a unifying rhetoric of "racelessness"—the idea that the country was not composed of whites or Blacks, only Cubans.

But such discourses have been reconceptualized according to the logic of advertising in which race takes on an exchange value. In his essay "Making Sense of Advertisements," historian Daniel Pope (2003) argues that advertisements can reveal tremendous insight about the economic and political conditions of a given time. But although advertisements may be seen as historical artifacts, we must account for the fact that they are highly selective in their depiction of the world. How advertisers represent a given society will be shaped by their notions of race, class, and gender. To fully ascertain the full meaning of an advertisement, it is essential to consider a variety of factors, including ad's ultimate purpose, the intended audience, its persuasive strategies, and the larger cultural context.

Over the course of the island's history, representations of Cuba's multiracial society were taken up by different kinds of cultural intermediaries based in Europe. I begin with an analysis of how Cuba's mixed-race society was represented by European painters and illustrators toward the end of Spanish colonial rule. During this time, German, French, and Spanish artists depicted Afro- and mestizo Cubans in ways that reflected the perspective of the Spanish elite. European artists would simply ignore the Afro-Cuban perspective, limiting their gaze to the white, wealthy patrons who subsidized their work. In some cases, depictions of Black servitude were meant to uphold the social hierarchies that were established during Spanish colonial rule.

I follow with a discussion of how advertisers extended these racialized ideologies during Cuba's Republican era, which ushered in an era of social, economic, and technological change. Advertising in Cuba reflected the racist ideologies endemic to Spanish colonialization, but it also reflected American sensibilities. As American products and advertising agencies entered the Cuban economy, they brought with them U.S. sensibilities of racial difference.

It was during this time that Havana Club was first launched, and for over twenty years the brand would advance a version of Cuba as an almost exclusively white space. Through its advertising, the brand advanced a version of Cuba that was genteel and white, a strategy that served them until their expropriation by the Cuban State. Havana Club advertising would disappear for close to forty years, only to be reemerge after Cuba's Special Period. The campaigns produced by M&C Saatchi have taken an alternative approach by featuring, almost exclusively, Cubans of color. Like many spirits brands, Havana benefits from racial difference. In the consumer marketplace, authenticity is believed to reside in the bodies of racial and ethnic Others (bell hooks 1992). By casting its advertising strategically, brand managers and their creative partners hope to secure Havana Club's position as a subcultural product.

Race and Representation in Cuba's Colonial Era

In 1935, the Arechabala family opened the Havana Club Bara Privada, located in Havana's Cathedral Square. A photograph of the bar from the time shows that there once hung a painting by noted Cuban artist Enrique García Cabrera, titled *Zafras de Antaño* (Harvest of the Past), which depicts a scene in what appears to be an *ingenio*, a small-scale, water-driven sugar mill. In the mill, two Afro-Cuban laborers are tending to the boiling of sugarcane while three others observe.

Cabrera's painting is set in an unspecified past and presents sugar production as an artisanal process, in which Black craftsmen work peacefully without the supervision of white slavers. The mural's pastoral sensibility is essential to how the Arechabala company could imagined itself, not only because it softens the uncomfortable reality that forced labor that was involved in sugar processing, but it also suggests that the company was built on humble beginnings. Furthermore, the Arechabala family believed that its fortunes were essential to the future of Cuba itself. The family was so pleased with this depiction of sugar production that it decided to include the image in a commemorative book, celebrating its seventy-fifth anniversary. The image included the following caption: "Sugar crops of the past . . . beginnings of the sugar industry. In primitive mills, at the slow pace of oxen, the future of Cuba was forged. The day was still far off when the slogan would be coined, 'No sugar, no country'" (Sainz 1954).

This idealized vision of sugar production obscures the rum industry's violent history. In a profound act of forgetting, rum manufacturers have, over time, erased the role of the transatlantic slave trade in sugar production, and by extension, the emergence of the rum industry. It is important to remember, however, that sugar production would not have been possible without the use of slave laborers, who were forced to engage in backbreaking and dangerous work. The difficult process of making sugar was originally a barrier to its production, but the establishment of a large-scale international market for the product required a labor force that could produce it in mass scale.

The working conditions within the sugar mill were inhumane. Children and adults labored under the constant threat of injury from boiling-hot kettles, open furnaces, and grinding rollers. To achieve the highest output, plantation owners operated their sugarhouses both night and day. Enslaved persons would often lose an arm to the grinding rollers or were punished for falling behind. Those who resisted were often cruelly punished (Muhammad 2019).

If the conditions of slavery were not bad enough, sugar plantation owners also created a system of dependence. Slave owners originally used rum as an important tool of control, in part because of its addictive properties. Even after the abolition of slavery in the Caribbean, many former slaves continued to work on sugar plantations for meager pay, since they had few other options. Rum was instrumental in keeping them there. Rum shops were present on nearly all estates, and they were usually located near pay offices that remained open all night (Smith 2005). Workers were often sold rum on credit, which could be an additional source of profit for the plantation owners. According to John Gust and Jennifer Matthews (2020), plantation owners would sometimes give young boys crude rum, encouraging them to develop a taste for it. By the time they grew into adulthood, they would already be addicted.

Slavery was instituted by all the colonial powers, but as Esteban Morales Domínguez (2012) points out, there were significant differences between the Spanish and British colonies that fundamentally shaped Cuban society. In the British colonies, social interaction between whites and Blacks was highly discouraged, and there was an apartheid-like system where slaves were forbidden from speaking their language or practicing the culture and religious beliefs they had brought from Africa. By contrast, in the Spanish colonies there was a greater degree of mixing between white Spaniards, white Creoles, and Afro-Cubans. By the early nineteenth century, a significant portion of the population on the island was Black, a reality that prompted the Spanish government to pass laws encouraging European immigration to the island. Although they existed within a racist system, a limited number of Black and mestizo Cubans enjoyed some social mobility and some even became economically independent. Under Spanish rule, some Black slaves in Cuba could buy their freedom and thus mixed more with whites. Some established themselves as merchants, artisans, and other craftsmen.

The task of depicting Cuba's mixed-race society was largely taken up by Spanish, French, and German authors, painters, and journalists, who served as the primary cultural brokers with European audiences. For example, European painters Ludwig Friedrich Emil Piani (Germany) and Miguel Arias Bardou (Spain) made names for themselves by traveling to Cuba and documenting the island's tropical landscape, as well as its social and economic life. French artist Eduardo Laplante's *Ingenios de la Isla de Cuba* (1857), printed in Havana, showed the conditions in the sugar mills of Havana, Cárdenas, Trinidad, Matanzas, and Santiago de Cuba, which documented the social relationships within the island's sugar mills.

Such depictions purported to objectively represent life in Cuba, yet any work of art involves some degree of subjective choice through the neutral gaze it assumes. Consider the painting by Frédéric Mialhe, a French painter who arrived in Cuba on an invitation from the Real Sociedad Patriótica. His painting *Vista de Una Casa de Calderas* (View of a Sugar Boiling House) in 1855 depicts three Black slaves boiling sugar in a large cauldron, under the supervision of a white supervisor. In the foreground, there are two white Cubans, presumably the owners of the mill, engaged in conversation. To the left side of the painting are two finely dressed women seated, while a young Afro-Cuban boy serves them tea.

The artist passes no judgment by depicting a well-ordered and productive factory, in which Black slaves passively accepted their role in the social hierarchy. Other artists, however, were much more overt in their racial biases. The most infamous of these was Spanish painter and caricaturist Víctor Patricio de Landaluze, who arrived in Havana around 1850. Much of Landaluze's work documented scenes from Cuban social life with an emphasis on free and enslaved Afro-Cubans. However, Landaluze's depictions clearly reflect a distinct political orientation.

Smithsonian curator Carmen Ramos (2019) points to two works by Landaluze that reflect his position on Cuba's racial hierarchy. Both were painted during Cuba's Ten Years' War, which ultimately set the stage for the abolition of slavery. The first of these is *Corte de Caña* (Cutting Sugarcane), a pastoral scene that depicts the various figures involved in sugar cultivation. Afro-Cuban slaves are engaged in the peaceful act of cutting and gathering of sugarcane. An elderly woman is tending to a Black child. In the background there is a sugar mill, where the sugarcane is cut, ground, and processed. The only sign of threat is a Black slave engaging in conversation with a white slaver on horseback, holding a whip.

Landaluze's choice of subject may be partially explained by the preferences of his clientele, which was primarily composed of the white bourgeoisie. Elizabeth Morán (2012) notes that Landaluze was very popular with affluent white Cubans, who were not inclined to purchase scenes that reflected the cruelty and inequality of poverty and slavery. Nor were they interested in being reminded of the potential threat that Afro-Cubans posed to the current system. But these depictions of peaceful harvesting were deeply incongruent with the reality of Cuba at the time. Painted during the insurrection in 1874, *Corte de Caña* was an effort to portray passive slaves during a time when Afro-Cubans were directly involved in their own emancipation efforts. The revolutionary army made no racial distinctions in its ranks, and Afro-Cubans were appointed to the municipal councils of the towns occupied by the revolutionary army (Nodal 1986).

The second piece represents one of Landaluze's caricatures in the staunchly conservative journal, *Don Junípero*, which supported Spanish occupation and the upholding of the slave system. The illustration ran in October 1869, which marked the one-year anniversary of the "Grito de Yara," in which Carlos Manuel de Céspedes granted freedom to all of the slaves who worked on his large sugar estate of La Demajagua, which in effect launched the Ten Years' War. In this reimagining of his painting, *Fiesta de Carnaval*, Landaluze depicts Manuel Céspedes as the leader of an absurd, mixed-race group in drunken celebration.

The scene is racially charged. A Black gentleman makes unwanted advances on a white woman, who is clearly distressed. A mestizo man drunkenly approaches a Black woman. A member of his party is depicted as a crude, barbaric character donning a raffia skirt. Céspedes himself is dancing, not with a woman but with a bull dressed in women's clothing, suggesting a link between miscegenation and bestiality. The caption to the image reads, "The General Céspedes celebrating the anniversary of Yara in the middle of his court." A subhead reads, "The great General Quesada remembers his good times, and Minister Mendocita flirts with the ladies. The field is filled with perfumed Mambises." The term *mambises* was used as a derogatory term used to describe an army composed of indigenous, Afro-Cuban, Asian Cuban, and Spanish descendants. The Cuban fighters adopted the name with pride.

In some of Landaluze's paintings, commodities play an important role in distinguishing the unruly, mixed-race Cubans from the elite white Cubans. It is significant that in the illustration, which ran in *Don Junípero*, a man holds up two unmarked bottles of rum. This form of consumption would have been a marker of incivility at the time when Spanish wine and sherry denoted sophistication.

Images like these were exported back to Spain, where they found an audience that was primed to see Cubans as subservient. For example, Landaluze was also a contributor to *Ilustración España y Americana*, a publication that routinely advanced colonial ideologies. The presumption of Spanish superiority over its racialized subjects is evident in the publication's masthead, which features three of Spain's architectural jewels: the Alhambra in Granada, the Giralda in Seville, and the Plaza Mayor of Madrid (Sánchez 2017). There are also symbols of European Enlightenment thinking: a globe and other instruments that symbolize the sciences and the arts. Then there are the colonized, who literally lie at the margins of the masthead. To the right is small group of native Americans, sitting in front of a conical skin tent. To the left is an Afro-Cuban slave cutting sugarcane under the watchful eye of a white master.

The publication advanced a second discourse, which was that Cuba's racial integration was a violent threat to Spanish (read white) dominance. Consider an illustration that ran as part of an editorial in *Ilustración España y Americana* on March 16, 1872. Titled "La Isla de Cuba—Combate en la Manigua" (Combat in the Jungle), the image was created by Spanish artists Ramon Padrón y José Severini. The illustration depicts a fierce battle being fought in a dense jungle. In the foreground, there is a troop of Spanish soldiers, and their Cuban allies are surrounded and suffering casualties. They are firing at an enemy they cannot see. Meanwhile, the rebel soldiers are using the dense foliage to their advantage, attacking the Spaniards while perched atop or hidden behind trees.

The editors of *Ilustración España y Americana* clearly frowned upon the rebels' style of guerrilla warfare, which was characterized by ambushes, surprise raids, and irregular methods of combat. The Spanish, and their Cuban allies are described as loyal sons to their mother country. By contrast, the independence fighters are described as "insurrectionists" who lack the discipline and honor of combat. According to the editors, "They do not fight hand to hand. They flee before our guerrillas, and they hide in the treetops, behind a rock, at the bottom of a ditch. They stalk the staunch defender of the honor of Spain and tend to murder him villainously" (*Ilustración España y Americana* 1872). It is hard not to notice the racial makeup of the "insurrectionists" compared with the Spanish soldiers, who are rendered faceless. The decision by Padrón and Severini to depict the rebels as a multiracial unit may have been meant to minimize any sympathies a Spanish reader might have with Cuba's independence fighters. As Louis Pérez (2008) notes, European aversion to Cuban independence was based on a moral objection, which had a racialized component. The Spanish saw a white Cuba as a pathway toward civilization and progress. An independent Cuba was one associated with racial mixing, which meant incivility and barbarism.

The Rum Industry's Uneasy Relationship with Race

During Cuba's fight for independence, the racial politics of the Cuban rum industry was ambivalent at best. Distillers needed a steady flow of molasses from Cuban sugar plantation owners, some of whom continued to rely on slave labor. At the same time, they found a ready consumer base in the soldiers who occupied the island. The sale of Cuban rum to Spanish soldiers was enough to cause concern amongst the revolutionaries, and so the Spanish Cuban Liberation Army ordered production to be brought to a halt (Lázaro 2016). This was complicated by the fact that rum producers were at the mercy of the Spanish government, which continued to levy taxes and control their access to markets domestically and abroad.

The political and economic instability in Cuba motivated some businesses to take their operations elsewhere in the Caribbean. Cuba's rum industry would regain stability during U.S. occupation. During this time, U.S. soldiers acquired a taste for Cuban cocktails and then brought their taste preferences back to the United States, where Americans began to acquire an appreciation for the drink. Soon Cuban rum became popular among cosmopolitan consumers, but to exploit this new market, Cuban distillers attempted to reposition rum from a common product to a refined spirt that would be appealing to white, upscale consumers. Race would be used, in different ways, to advance this strategy.

To elevate rum, distillers felt compelled to divest the product of its Blackness. For much of Cuba's colonial history, rum was seen as a common product, because it was originally concentrated among slaves, servants, and Caribs. Consuming rum led to stereotyping of these groups as disorderly or drunken (Smith 2005). At times, rum was also associated with paganism and other illicit activities, that ranged from conspiracies to undermine Spanish rule to slave uprisings. These concerns led to continuous efforts to ban the consumption of rum in public spaces.

Marketing played an important role in repositioning rum in the minds of prospective consumers. To elevate the perception of rum, Cuban distillers employed a variety of strategies for legitimizing their products through branding. One strategy was to associate Cuban rum with its European heritage. This was the strategy employed by José Arechabala S.A., whose prolific use of the Vizcaya coat of arms was a way of establishing its Basque credentials. Ron Castillo similarly used icons that referenced old Spain. Others embraced images associated with early Spanish colonialism. La Niña Rum, for example, produced by the Havana Rum Company, depicted one of the first ships to arrive in the New World.

A second strategy was to endow the product with international legitimacy through the awards circuit. Matusalem Rum featured the awards it had won in international competitions, but it was Bacardí, which was by far the most prolific advertiser in the category, that made use of this strategy. Smith (2008) speculates that Bacardí's strategy of focusing on its international awards was a way to deemphasize its Caribbean origins in order to promote itself as a more universal spirit.

A final strategy was to appropriate the image of the Black and brown bodies in order to mark their products as Cuban or to promote them as exotic. For example, Ron Viejo Palau, distilled in Santiago de Cuba, and Ron Tutankamen, distilled in Havana, used imagery of ancient Egypt, possibly to capitalize on Orientalist sensibilities that had become fashionable at the time. However, other rum brands chose to distinctly mark themselves as Caribbean products, and the use of Black and mestizo characters was an easy heuristic. Rhum Vieux, which was produced by Compañia Nacional de Vinos in Havana, depicted four Afro-Cuban slaves loading barrels onto a ship under the watch of an overseer. Ron de las Tres Negritas employed an image of three Afro-Cuban domestics. Aguardiente Compuesto El Negrito Libre featured the image of a stately Afro-Cuban dandy, flawlessly dressed in a fine suit with cane.

The Republican Era and the Rise of Advertising

Cuba's wars for independence were based on the promise of racial equality. However, José Martí's promise of a raceless, Cuban revolutionary nation would not materialize during the Republican era. Instead, there were a number of stunning reversals. Cuban Blacks and mestizos were excluded from the massive sectors of the economy, including the most desirable jobs. The Partido Independiente de Color (PIC), founded by Veterans of the War for Independence, was designed to promote the integration of Afro-Cubans into social and political spheres, but racial tensions escalated into violence. In May of 1912, PIC organizers launched an armed demonstration seeking legal rights. In response, the government retaliated against the party, massacring an estimated 3,000 Afro-Cubans.

During this same period, Cuba saw the emergence of lifestyle magazines, such as *Bohemia* and *Carteles*, that presented a much more harmonious view of Cuban life. As they did in other Westernized countries, lifestyle magazines were instrumental in promoting a consumer society by converting readers into buyers. However, publishers were primarily interested in consumers who had the means to purchase the products and services being promoted. Because the imagined consumer was believed to be affluent and white, advertisers either rendered Afro-Cubans invisible in advertising or depicted them in ways that legitimized white superiority.

These lifestyle magazines reflect Cuba's transition toward becoming a consumer society during the Republican Era. As Pope (1983) notes, advances in production, packaging, labeling, and physical distribution and an increase in personal salesmanship ultimately led to the development of global markets for branded, standardized products. These developments had a profound impact on the Cuban economy and culture. It is a time when American products start to flood the Cuban marketplace, bringing with them American notions of modernity (Pérez 1999). Consequently, advertising practitioners emerged as important cultural brokers in Cuba by connecting corporations with middle-class Cuban consumers. Selling quantities of goods to millions of consumers required intensive advertising, and so a burgeoning industry began to emerge. In addition to Cuban-owned agencies, many of the large U.S. agencies established offices in Havana, including Grant, A. B. Ayers, McCann-Erickson, and J. Walter Thompson.

These advertisers would benefit from technological innovations that were occurring at the time, which allow for richer, more vivid art direction. The emergence of color rotogravure printing and the halftone press, and later photography, enabled art directors to move beyond black-and-white line drawings (Pope 1983) and represent the human body in more sophisticated ways. The circulation of these images allowed consumers to more clearly imagine their aspirational selves. Within advertising during the early twentieth century, Black and brown bodies were commonly used to uphold the privileged positions of white Cubans.

When it first launched in 1910, *Bohemia* was a modest publication with just a few local advertisers. However, early signs of a commodity culture in Cuba began to appear. There are listings for local doctors, dentists, photographers, and other small businesses. Due to the technological limitations of the time, these advertisements were primarily copy driven, which was common at the time. Newspaper and magazine advertisements of the period enlisted almost exclusively written appeals, with the exception of a few illustrations printed in black and white (Mehaffy 1997). The few exceptions were fashion and lifestyle brands, which included some line drawings. Fashion and cosmetic businesses such as *La Louvre*, *La Oriental*, and *Floreine* all featured a illustrations of fashionable and affluent white Cuban women.

It appears as if Bacardí was the only rum brand to advertise in those early years. Its advertisements during this time contained no art direction with the exception of a specialized typeface and a decorative border. The copy was primarily informative, with its details on where to acquire the rum. The only persuasive language was a tagline that reads, "El mejor del mundo" (Best in the world). By the end of the decade, however, illustrations had become much more sophisticated. There were advertisements for commodities that would signal modernity. There were advertisements for typewriters and high-end furniture. There is an advertisement for White Frost, a company that sold ice boxes. There are advertisements for Frank Robinson Co. in Havana, which sold town cars and roadsters. Those cars needed tires, and so there are advertisements for Goodyear.

By the 1930s, both *Bohemia* and *Carteles* had evolved into longer, more sophisticated publications, and the role of advertising appears to have become more integral to their business models. Advertisements for local businesses gave way to large national organizations, including Cuban Electric and the Credit Bank of Cuba. But we also begin to see the increasing presence of American products, such as Quaker Oats, RCA, and Philadelphia Cream Cheese. Some of the advertisements were for transportation and record players (technology), but a majority were for products that reflected what Jackson Lears (2000) called a "therapeutic ethos," marking perfumes, cosmetics, and tonics of all kinds.

There were also a limited number of advertisements for alcohol brands, including Sidra El Gaitero champagne, Moscatel Quincarne, and Cerveza Tropical. However, Bacardí stands out for both its consistent presence and the quality of its advertising. The brand's advertising in the 1930s reflects its overall strategy to position the rum for affluent consumers, and Black and mestizo Cubans were largely absent from Bacardí's advertising. Instead, the brand focused on white Cubans as the embodiment of luxury: a gentleman wearing a tuxedo or a businessman at his desk daydreaming about Bacardí rum.

To a lesser degree, Bacardí would employ creative concepts that reified the notion of white superiority. As Gershon (2019) points out, the creation of an ideal white, female consumer was dependent on the inclusion of women of other races, particularly Black domestics, as a foil. Consider the following advertisement for Bacardí (Figure 12), which ran in *Bohemia* on February 30, 1930. The advertise-

Figure 12. Advertisement for Bacardí. From *Bohemia* (September 21, 1930). Courtesy of the Cuban Heritage Collection. University of Miami.

ment features the silhouette of a woman lounging on a Turkish-inspired sofa. The accoutrements of the room suggest that the woman is wealthy, a notion that is reinforced by the presence of an Afro-Cuban domestic servant, who is serving her a clearly branded bottle of Bacardí. The asymmetrical relationship between the mistress and her domestic servant is evident in the art direction. The mistress is the dominant figure, taking up much of advertisement, while the figure of the domestic is rendered disproportionately small.

This Bacardí advertisement is consistent with Benson's (2016) observation that a number of the advertisements published in *Bohemia* were designed for consumers who aspired to upper-middle-class lifestyles. Because domestic servants in white, middle-class homes were predominantly Afro-Cuban, marketers often included Black bodies in their advertising to signify white luxury.

Advertising for Hatuey, Bacardí's brand of beer, was targeted primarily to men, and invoked race through the use of caricature and humor. Bacardí named its beer Hatuey after the Taíno cacique chief who organized a rebellion against the Spanish conquerors, what may be a nod to Cuba's own independence movement. The campaign's story is told over the course of four different comic strips, which communicated the idea that Hatuey beer is a product that can bring people together.

The first execution is a cartoon that depicts Chief Hatuey and Christopher Columbus engaged in a poker game, along with Taíno and Spanish soldiers. The Taíno are dressed in grass skirts, and Chief Hatuey is recognizable by his headband with two feathers, as it is depicted in the brand's logo. A bucket of beer lies at the left side of the table, and in the horizon, we see the famed Spanish galleons, the *Niña*, *Pinta*, and *Santa Maria*. The second execution continues the camaraderie, with the Spaniards and Taíno engaged in a friendly game of soccer.

By the third execution, the Spanish soldiers are returning to their homeland. A Taíno warrior is resting peacefully in a hammock perched between two trees. In the background, we see the Spanish galleons returning to Spain. It is only in the final execution that we find out that Hatuey is accompanying Columbus back to Spain. The two are sharing a beer on the Spanish galleon, taking with them a stock of Hatuey beer.

By making light of the Taíno genocide, the sponsors of the advertisement appear unreflective about the island's own history of Spanish exploitation. But within the logic of advertising, the creative execution is entirely appropriate. This retelling of the Hatuey story would have been humorous to an ideal, white reader. The Hatuey brand may have been created to honor the spirit of resistance, but the notion of rebellion has been rearticulated in order to meet the needs of the marketplace. Advertising is optimistic and always assumes progress. Conquest and enslavement are not conducive to selling beer, so instead, the message becomes about unity, in which the product plays an instrumental role.

Havana Club Advertising as a White Public Space

In 1939, Havana Club placed a one-page advertisement in a book of cocktail recipes, produced on behalf of Bar La Florida, more popularly known to American consumers as La Floridita. The bar, which was a favorite of Ernest Hemingway, had become a popular destination for American tourists, and to capitalize on this notoriety the bar published a small booklet of its recipes for would-be mixologists. The book includes recipes for drinks with names like the "Flying Tiger," the "Golden Glove," and the "Havana Special." To reach this upscale, cosmopolitan reader, there were advertisements for H. Upmann Cigars and Tabu Dana perfume, as well for spirits brands including Fundador Brandy, Haig Whisky, and Osborne Cognac. Bacardí was a prolific advertiser in these books.

The Havana Club advertisement features an illustration of a smiling white, Cuban bartender who is extending a cocktail toward the imagined reader (Figure 13). Based on his white jacket, the bartender is presumed to work at La Floridita. It's a simple ad with the headline "Pruebalo, Ahora" (Try It, Now). The body copy informs the reader that Havana Club is a fine rum, best served in Cuban cocktails. The depiction of Cuba as essentially a white, public space would become a hallmark of Havana Club advertising during the Republican era.

When Havana Club launched in 1934, the brand was primarily focused on the U.S. market, and from its inception, Arechabala's strategy was to appeal to affluent male consumers by positioning Havana Club as an authentic, but upscale, Cuban product. In collaboration with its U.S. distributor, W. A. Taylor and Co., and its advertising agency Charles Hoyte, the brand placed advertisements in U.S. publications, such as the *New York Times*, the *New Yorker*, and *Esquire*.

Figure 13. "Pruebelo Ahora!," print advertisement. From *Floridita Cocktails* (1939). Accessed through EUVS Digital Collection.

To establish its Cuban credentials, Havana Club chose to invoke a white genteel Cuba. The following quarter-page advertisement (Figure 14) gives an indication of Havana Club's advertising strategy shortly after its launch. Placed in 1935 in the *New York Times*, the advertisement clearly positions the product as an authentic Cuban rum. American readers are advised as to how to correctly

Figure 14. "Put Them Together and They Spell Havana Club Rum Cocktail," print advertisement. From the *New York Times* (April 18, 1935). Accessed through the *New York Times* digital archive.

drink Cuban rum: begin by smelling the rum, tilt the glass, and then to swallow it to ascertain its smoothness. But the embodiment of the brand in this advertisement is a stately white creole gentleman wearing a white suite and canotier hat. The body copy reads, "It is the rum of Cubans, and Cubans know rum."

Havana Club's advertising was consistent with that of other Cuban advertisers that had chosen to focus on the island's Spanish heritage while ignoring the island's Afro-Cuban population (Mogul 2019). There is a notable absence of

Afro-Cubans from almost all of Havana Club U.S. advertising, an ethos that would extend to later campaigns. For example, Havana Club's "Now That I've Been to Cuba" campaign, which includes several different executions. The campaign is told from the point of view of a white American tourist who has just returned from a visit to Cuba.

Havana Club's focus on whiteness was not necessarily indicative of the category. In the advertising landscape, Cuba was characterized as a place that was both local and exotic. For some advertisers, Black bodies became central to this purpose. For example, Rum Negrita from Martinique ran a series of advertisements in *Esquire* magazine that depicted a tropical island lit by an active volcano. The bottle itself features the image of an Afro-Caribbean woman. Ron Marno Imported Cuban Rum signifies its location by featuring an inset image two barrels placed on a tropical beach next to a small distillery. Similarly, Bandana rum positions itself as a "Tantalizing Tropical Treat" and features the words, "Imported from Havana. In the background of the advertisement is a rendering of Castillo de la Real Fuerzal located in Havana Harbor.

The Early Revolutionary Period

It is not entirely accurate to say that advertising ended when the new revolutionary government took control in 1959. Rather, there was a short period of transition when the new government was honoring the commitments made by Cuban publications to advertisers who had placed media while figuring out how to manage an entirely new kind of economic system. The sanctions imposed by the United States in 1962 would fundamentally end relationships between Cuba and U.S. businesses, but between 1959 and 1961, advertising continued to be placed in Cuban publications. *Bohemia* and *Carteles* carried advertisements for American companies, including Nescafé, Esso, BF Goodrich, and Max Factor cosmetics.

During this time, there was a stark contrast between how Cuban society was presented in advertising and the actual lived experiences of Cubans. Alongside features about revolutionary heroes and messaging about collective struggle, there were advertisements for lifestyle brands, which continued to feature white, bourgeois culture. Most of these advertisements were direct holdovers from the Republican era. Advertisements for rum brands Matusalem and Tres Cepas, for example, consistently depicted elegantly dressed, middle-class couples, drinking rum in well-adorned homes. For example, advertisements were placed for Bacardí and Hatuey, even though the company was in the process of reorganizing abroad.

There is one notable exception. There is an advertisement for Cristal beer, which had been expropriated from the Blanco Herrera family. Unlike other spirits ads of the time, which focused on Cuba's most affluent consumers, this advertisement focuses on the laborers who make the rum, which is consistent with the ideals of the revolution. The illustrated print advertisement shows the beer-making process over the course of several images. There is an image of workers cutting the grain, the extract ingredients traveling by train to the brewery, workers tending to the beer, and so forth. The headline reads, "Hay Ambiente, Mi Gente?" (Is There a Change in the Atmosphere, My People?). The body copy promotes the notion of collective effort, which reads, "The mill is grinding, and my people are happy . . . and in all of Cuba there is atmosphere and joy with Cristal."

The advertisement demonstrates how marketing could be used to promote revolutionary ideals while simultaneously selling product. The laborers depicted in the advertisement are a multiracial ensemble, and the image of white, mestizo, and Black Cubans working alongside for the collective good would become more representative of the official discourse coming from the state. As Benson (2016) notes, when the revolutionary government took control, it passed over 1,500 pieces of legislation during its first thirty months in power, including laws delivering land redistribution, free health care, and educational scholarship programs. In an antidiscrimination campaign during a public rally on Palm Sunday, March 22, 1959, Castro outlined plans for Black and white Cubans to work and go to school together.

Advertising would eventually disappear from the island, but the project of a raceless, unified Cuba would be taken up by artists, musicians, journalists, and public intellectuals. For example, the promise of a new, revolutionary racial sensibility is evident in Miguel Barnet's essay "The Culture That Sugar Created" (1980), in which he describes the figure of the "mulatto," as the embodiment of Cuba's unique multiracial identity. Barnet writes:

> On the plantation, white and Black came together for the first time. The first night a Black woman and white man spent together marked a turning-point for our country, and a day aglow with light dawned for the culture of the Caribbean. Thanks to this union, two factors were conjoined for the first time, later to play the definitive role in the shaping of Cuban nationality. The union, which first occurred to the rhythm of sugar farming, created the Cuban in all his complexity and richness.

Similar messages of racial unity were delivered through multiple forms of persuasive communication. In this way, Black and brown bodies began to perform new kinds of labor in the form of state propaganda. As Benson (2016) argues, the new revolutionary government had hoped to invoke Martí's unifying rhetoric of "racelessness," or the idea that the country was not composed of whites or Blacks, only Cubans. The state's strategy of linking to the revolutionary struggle was necessary to quell the unrest by Afro-Cubans over their continued marginalization. If Afro-Cubans were to assert their racial identity, they would be seen as undermining the collective struggle of the revolution.

Havana Club in a Colorblind World

When Havana Club reemerged from its advertising hiatus, it entered into a very different advertising landscape. Racial minorities were no longer excluded in advertising but were suddenly welcomed with open arms. Believing that Black and brown bodies could advance their strategic objectives, rum brands increasingly featured multiracial ensembles in their advertisements. Casting actors and models of color was a way to target ethnic consumers, but the practice also invested brands with subcultural capital (Thornton 1996).

Much of the advertising in this category reflected a colorblind approach, in which models and actors used in advertising are presumed to operate in a world in which racial difference simply does not exist. Images of young people of diverse races, socially interacting with one another, often present a "progressive" image for the brand, while upholding racial hierarchies. But here, Havana Club could point to a true point of difference. Given many of the reforms instituted by the revolutionary regime, Cuba's society is more racially integrated than other Western countries. In the execution of the campaign, however, M&C Saatchi relied simply on the practice of colorblind casting, which was not seen as particularly unique or authentic. Let us, then, reconsider the campaigns that M&C Saatchi has produced for Havana Club through the prism of race. The first campaign that M&C Saatchi produced was *La Culta de Vida*, which centered on young, stylish, attractive models. They were notably models of color, but as the agency noted, there was nothing distinctly "Cuban" about the campaign, and so it blended in with other advertising in the category.

The failure of this campaign suggests that is does not matter if claims the authenticity are true. It only matters that consumers believe them to be true. And so the agency regrouped and developed its highly successful "Nothing Compares to Havana" campaign, which reflected more directly on the revolution's promise of racial equality. This was accomplished through art direction. The campaign is notable for its racially mixed characters across various spectrums. This approach was a stark contrast to the highly stylized approach of most spirits advertising. Aroch's photos for the campaign feature a racially diverse cohort of Cubans in serendipitous moments. A group of older men, playing chess in a public park, a pair of ballerinas stretching in front of a bus stop, and a jazz band riding in a 1950s-era convertible.

Similarly, Harmony Korine's video work depicted the same kind of racial unity. In a spot titled "Kitchen," we see four men of varying skin tones, sitting at a kitchen table in a modest apartment, simply creating music. Because of the campaign's verité approach to photography, the consumer is led to believe that these four men are longtime friends. There is no music, the scene is not overedited, and there is no voice-over. Just a glimpse into a particular world. It is the realistic nature of the campaign that lends credibility to this message of equality compared with campaigns that are highly staged and feature paid models. The "Nothing Compares to Havana" campaign has been designed to convince consumers they are bearing witness to real Cubans interacting with one another.

By the time we get to M&C Saatchi's "From the Heart" campaign, however, the fantasy of a racially integrated Cuba begins to fade. The campaign focuses on rum's division of labor, but the campaign's simultaneous focus on "real people" inadvertently reveals hierarchies that persist in Cuba. It is meaningful that Asbel Morales, who is white, has been elevated to the role of *maestro ronero* and has served as the public face of the company, often speaking to the international press. By contrast, Claudio, who is Black, does the manual labor of cutting sugarcane.

When M&C Saatchi launched its "Cuba Made Me" campaign, any sense of realism disappears, and the campaigns become more conventional. Rather than taking on a realistic approach, the advertisement invokes the visual grammar of music videos, which is heavily stylized and orchestrated to a clear music track. There is a noticeable shift in focus onto young Afro-Cuban culture (Figure 15), which certainly was certainly a strategic choice. The architects of the campaign had intended to maintain the brand's authenticity by focusing on urban subcultures, and within popular imagination, the hallmark of any exotic urban space is the prevalence of racial and ethnic Others.

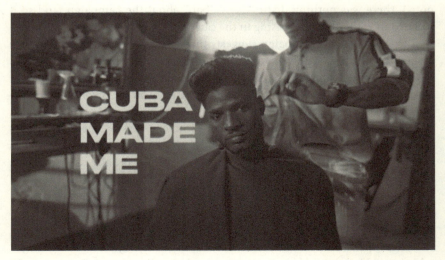

Figure 15. Scene from "Cuba Made Me—Street Style." Directed by Courtney Phillips, 2021.

The use of actors who are clearly marked as Other is essential to the campaign's reliance on urban authenticity. Urban culture is often conflated with ethnic culture, and it precisely the marginalization of ethnic residents that is believed to produce rich cultural expression, including new forms of fashion, music, and art. Thus, Havana Club follows in the tradition of other advertisers who have come to realize that the exploitation of Otherness can be good for business. Given Havana Club's attempts to associate itself with Afro-Cuban culture, however, it is easy to forget that rum marketers originally saw Blackness as a deficiency, rather an asset.

Advertising as Postracial Fantasy

In *Tobacco and Sugar*, Cuban essayist and anthropologist Fernando Ortiz (1995) describes the relationship between national identity, race, and the marketplace. According to Ortiz, Cuba's two most infamous export products are marked by the island's African heritage. Yet they must be invested with whiteness in order to find acceptance in markets outside the island. He writes:

> Tobacco is dark, ranging from Black to mulatto; sugar is light, ranging from mulatto to white. Tobacco does not change its color; it is born dark and dies the color of its race. Sugar changes its coloring; it is brown and whitens itself; at first it is a syrupy mulatto and in this state pleases the common taste. Then it is bleached and refined until it can pass for white, travel all over the world, reach all mouths, and bring a better price, climbing to the top of the social ladder.

In some ways, the same can be said of Cuban rum during the island's Republican period. What started out as a product consumed mostly by Afro-Cubans needed to be whitened in order to appeal to white, middle-class audiences The inclusion of Black bodies in in the role of domestics and laborers was necessary for white consumers to envision their aspirational selves.

These advertisements, in many ways, were extensions of larger discourses about Cuba's racial identity, which is embodied by José Antonio Saco, who dreamed of a white, Cuban society. One that was devoid of Cubans of African descent. "Whiten, whiten, whiten" is how Saco put it. "And then make ourselves respected" (as quoted in Domínguez 2012). During the Republican era, advertisers articulated this sentiment through a new kind of discourse, in which the consumption of products could be a way to achieve white status.

In some cases, these racial ideologies were expressed quite literally. "Ahora usted puede blanquear su cutis" (Now you can whiten your skin) reads the copy for a 1950 advertisement for Crema la Bella whitening cream. "Su cara, su cuello, sus brazos y sus manos se iluminará con una clara belleza (Now you can whiten your skin. . . . Your face, your neck, your arms and your hands will illuminate with a clear beauty). To ensure that the message that beauty is equated with whiteness, there is an illustration of a single woman's face transforming from black to brown, and then white.

When Havana Club launched its "Nothing Compares to Havana" campaign in 2010, it drew heavily on the island's multiracial identity in order to assert its authenticity. By then they were navigating a very different racial politics, in which marketers routinely attempted to distinguish themselves by invoking race. Today, there are numerous rum brands that routinely employ racialized images without any reflection of their sociohistorical contexts. Consider the label for Ron Legendario, a Cuban rum which was founded in Havana in 1946. The logo depicts a shipyard scene, complete with Black slaves loading barrels of rum onto a ship set for sail. There's Ron Mulatta, which depicts Osun, a Yoruban deity often associated with purity, love, and sensuality. And then there's Santero rum, whose logo features an Afro-Cuban shaman playing the drums.

Today, colonial images in advertising exist alongside contemporary images of diverse, fashionable, beautiful consumers. A hodgepodge of symbols circulating within the marketplace, collectively suggesting that racism is something that exists in another place or time. But of course, the problem of racism has not been solved in Cuba. This reality would become clear when the Soviet Union collapsed and Cuba entered the Special Period in a Time of Peace. Black and mestizo Cubans suffered more than their white counterparts because they were shut out of economic opportunities. Because the Cubans living in the diaspora are predominantly white, Afro-Cubans did not have the same access to family remittances, which had become an economic lifeline during the time (Morales and Scarpaci 2011). But Afro-Cubans also faced racial discrimination in the employment sector. As Domínguez (2012) points out, one's "buena presencia" (good appearance) frequently meant that you needed to have fair or white skin to qualify for lucrative hotel positions in the tourism industry.

Cuba's racial project is ongoing, and there is a need to examine issues of equality in nuanced ways. When discussing the need for more thoughtful dialogue, Domínguez (2012) rightly points out that racial issues on the island need to be addressed by Cubans themselves and not by actors living outside the island. However, advertising that has been created by Western advertisers does not allow for this kind of thoughtful discussion. Instead, they are motivated to depict the world favorably so that they can go about the business of selling rum. There is a consequence to this. Advertising's continuous depiction of racial harmony in Cuba, inadvertently obscures the unfortunate reality for many Afro-Cubans, who continue to face exclusion.

CHAPTER 6

The Losing Game of Authenticity

> Across Cuba there is a sense that a bold new future is imminent. It's a future where trade with the United States reaches $13 billion almost overnight, and a new surge of Cuban entrepreneurialism finds a way to coexist with the country's existing values.
> —Lucie Green, J. Walter Thompson

In 2019, Norwegian spirits marketer Island Rum Co. S.A. entered into a partnership with Azcuba, one of Cuba's largest sugar producers. The 50–50 joint venture resulted in the creation of Ron Vigía S.A., Cuba's first fully integrated rum production center since Havana Club International (Kiely 2019). Drawing on stocks of rum produced in Ciego de Ávila, in central Cuba, Ron Vigía offers a portfolio of products that includes Black Tears, a spiced rum; La Progresiva 13, a dry sipping rum; and La Progresiva 500, a limited-edition rum that was developed in celebration of Havana's 500th anniversary.

History is essential to La Progresiva's branding. Beautifully packaged in an embossed glass bottle, the product positions itself as an authentic Cuban rum by emphasizing the unique properties of Cuban soil and the age-old methods by which it is produced. According to its press materials, La Progresiva rum is crafted by Bodega Vigía's women rum maestros, using ingredients grown in Ciego de Ávila, where rum has been produced since 1577. But the producers make sure to communicate that the rum is also contemporary, and therefore viable for the international marketplace. "As the world falls in love with Cuba and Cuba opens up to the world," their website reads. "La Progresiva remains anchored in the island's rich traditions yet looks forward to its bright, international future" (Ron La Progresiva 2023).

Ron Vigía's more widely promoted product, however, is Black Tears, a brand of spiced rum made with notes of coffee, cocoa, and aji dulce, a sweet chili pepper. According to its press materials, the name Black Tears was inspired by the 1931 song *Lágrimas Negras*, written by Miguel Matamoras, which tells the story of a young woman who weeps inconsolably after her lover abandons her. As the company tells the story, the jilted lover sobbed into a vat of rum, filling it with her sorrow (Black Tears Rum 2023).

The brand plays heavily into the idea of Cuban pathos. The website features the words *amor* (love) and *pena* (suffering), and the advertisements for the product include the words "Love + Loss." But ultimately, Black Tears is a lifestyle brand, and to generate cultural cachet, the brand has showcased Afro-Cuban artists, including Kercia, a singer, actress and model, and Yosvel Alvarez Sosa, the lead singer of New World, a band that mixes hip-hop with funk, jazz, and reggae. The website includes interviews with graffiti artists, other local musicians, and dancers.

With its focus on Cuba's rich cultural art scene and the extract ingredients native to Cuba, the upstart brand appears to be drawing inspiration from Havana Club's marketing strategy. A significant difference, however, is the specific way in which Cuban authenticity is defined. If the Havana Club represents the cultural and political center of Cuba, then Black Tears represents the periphery. Furthermore, the brand appears to be establishing its authentic credentials based on Cuba's Afro-Cuban culture. The rum is produced in a region of Cuba that has been culturally influenced by immigrants from Haiti, Jamaica, and the Dominican Republic.

To communicate this particular kind of authenticity, the marketing for Black Tears includes copy that describes the product as "exotic" and "using centuries-old distillation methods and indigenous flavors." The packaging is meant to evoke premodern forms of cultural expression, with a typeface that simulates hand-painted imagery and iconography that implies a connection to Santeria. The logo itself consists of two interlocking tears. A print advertisement builds on this theme. On the right side of the panel, there is an Afro-Cuban model adorned in white body paint. To the left is the bottle of Black Tears rum with the headline "Let Black Tears Flow."

The creative approach, however, seems unreflective of the Black experience in Cuba, and the name Black Tears seems disconnected from the long-standing suffering Afro-Cubans have faced, beginning with Spanish colonial rule. Celebrating Cuban pathos to sell rum may seem tone-deaf, but advertisers have proven deft at reconstructing meaning. In a cultural context in which advertisers routinely unhinge signifiers from their referents, new meanings are fashioned. In a globalized world, Third World locales and racialized bodies are now the new markers of authenticity.

This reframing of history goes unnoticed because the targeted consumer is a Western European, not a Cuban, and therefore lacks a deep historical understanding of the island. Authenticity, at least in the historical sense, is not relevant, since the producer and consumer are sharing a fantasy, not a reality. But this is not necessarily unique. Other Cuban rum brands such as Santero, Ron Mulatta, and Ron Legendario are also targeting international consumers and are all drawing, to varying degrees, on the Afro-Cuban experience. In doing so, they are encoding their products with historical referents and touting their proprietary relationship with Cuban soil. As more and more brands claim Cuban authenticity, Havana Club loses its unique competitive advantage.

All this is to say that authenticity is a losing game. As Potter (2010) astutely points out, marketers frequently invoke the "jargon of authenticity" to distinguish their products in a crowded marketplace. Yet advertisers have defined authenticity in such varied ways that it has lost any sense of meaning. It is fluid and elusive. Authenticity has become a floating signifier that has different meanings at different times to different consumers.

That consumers would look to corporations to provide genuine emotions and experiences is itself a self-defeating move. Therein lies the paradox. Consumers long for authenticity but struggle with how to gain it. Businesses long to fulfill that need by selling authenticity but cannot really provide it (Molleda and Roberts 2008). The concept itself remains allusive, and more often is a designation that is defined in terms of what it is not. To be authentic is to not be mass-produced, Westernized, manufactured, artificial. But assertions of what is and what is not authentic distort how things really are, since everything is genuine and real. Therefore, the "real" Cuba, as mediated by cultural brokers, will always be more appealing than the real Cuba with all its inherent contradictions.

There is some hope that advertising might serve as a kind of dialectic in the marketplace of ideas. As more Cuban brands enter the global marketplace, marketers may bring with them different iterations of Cuban authenticity: Cuba as a Black nation; Cuba as a postracial society, Cuba as a repository of creativity, Cuba as an alternative economic and social model. Or simply Cuba as a functioning society. The more competing claims that circulate in the marketplace, the more complex a picture of Cuba we get.

But it is important to remember that these expressions of Cuban authenticity are not articulated by Cuban intellectuals, or state officials, or even by the "Cuban people." Rather, claims to authenticity are asserted and amplified by cultural intermediaries who are beholden to a system that abides by its own internal logic: Christian Barré, CEO of Havana Club International; advertising magnates Maurice and Charles Saatchi; music producer Gilles Peterson; art curator Flora Fairbairn; photographer Guy Aroch; filmmakers Nick Rutter and Harmony Korine; and the countless others who promote the Havana Club brand throughout Europe. None of them are Cuban, and none of them have a personal investment in the long-term future of the island. They do not participate substantially in Cuban political life, nor are they personally impacted by Cuban domestic policy.

Furthermore, because these various actors grew up in Western, capitalist societies, their depictions of Cuban authenticity will be subject to particular racial, political, and capitalist ideologies. This is generally true of most advertising, but Havana Club represents a singular kind of discourse. As the country's flagship rum brand, Havana Club represents the Cuban State, which carries with it several inherent contradictions: the tension between state discourses and commercial discourses, the tension between the ideals of the revolution and marketing's economic mandate, and finally, the tension between global flows and the local values.

The Ongoing Practice of (Mis)Representing Cuba

The practice of representing Cuba for economic gain is not new. Ever since the Spaniards landed on the island, foreigners have touted the island's rich resources that were available for exploitation. But creative professionals were needed to make these imperial designs intelligible to the masses. Cuba came to the attention of the Western world largely through representations created by foreign artists, journalists, and writers, who collectively projected their colonial perspectives and desires. As early as the sixteenth century, Cuba was described in terms of its access to resources, as "key to the New World," or "Bulwark of the West Indies." By the nineteenth century, Cuba was described in terms of the resources it provided to Spain, "the Pearl of the Antilles," and "the richest jewel in the royal crown" (Pérez 2008).

By the time that Havana Club launched in 1934, the project of authenticity was well underway. The emergence of the market economy, the rise of liberal individualism, and a growing disenchantment with the world left consumers feeling disaffected with modernity and mass culture. In the modern landscape, Cuba came to be seen as the antidote to hypercapitalist countries, even though that is precisely what Cuba sought to become during the Republican era. The proliferation of mass media brought with it a new set of cultural intermediaries, including photographers, journalists, magazine editors, filmmakers, and of course, advertising executives, who articulated Cuban authenticity in new and vivid ways. As James Kent (2019) argues, Havana has historically been depicted as an exotic city, locked in the past.

Businesses quickly learned to capitalize on the American consumer's hunger for the authentic, and Cuban products gained currency in the marketplace because they were somehow seen as more real and genuine than those being produced within the system of mass production. Travel books, hotels, and alcohol companies offered images of tropical landscapes and "native" Cubans dressed in traditional apparel. These images offered Americans a fantasy of escape from the unrewarding, fast-paced, modern, urban life in the United States (Mogul 2019).

Cuban rum brands have historically been able to build inroads with Western consumers by touting their Cuban identity, and thereby have benefitted from the country-of-origin effect. However, the meanings of nations are not fixed.

They are subject to political, cultural, and economic changes that shift how they are perceived by outsiders. This is particularly true in the case of Cuba, which carries ambivalent, sometimes contradictory, political meaning. Because of the political upheavals that have occurred over the past century, it is better to think about Cuba as having layers and layers of meaning, all of which can be exploited for marketing purposes. As Kent (2019) notes, the brand has leveraged modern-day conceptions of Havana drawn from Cuba's colonial past, the excesses of the Republican era, the Cuban Revolution, and the post–Special Period, characterized by the city's decay. This historical sense of place has been an asset as Cuba reenters the global marketplace and has been particularly helpful in the development of Cuba's tourism sector.

Certainly, the brand has done its part to promote Cuban tourism, and marketers have made sure to leverage these many layers of meaning. The Havana Club Museum is a featured tourist destination, located in La Habana Vieja and housed in a centuries-old building, making a connection to Cuba's colonial past. Travel to downtown Havana or Trinidad, or any popular tourist destination, and you will find that the Havana Club logo can be seen on t-shirts, on tote bags, on refrigerator magnets. On many of these commodities, the Havana Club logo sits alongside images of Che Guevara, the Cuban flag, cobblestone streets, and 1950s-era cars, all of which visually signify the island (Figure 16).

A cynical point of view is that Che Guevara's portrait placed alongside a corporate logo is a betrayal of revolutionary ideals. However, critiques of the revolutionary project are largely based on the notion that the socialist project was inherently antithetical to commerce. However, this point of view does not fully represent Cuba's history. Che Guevara may have been a guerrilla, but he was also the economic mind of the revolution. It was Guevera who envisioned a new kind of Cuban industry, in which brands would function for the good of the people rather than for private interests (Guevera 1968).

From this perspective, the image of "El Che" conjoined with an image of the Havana Club logo takes on an alternative reading: a brand in service of the revolution—at least that was the vision when the brand was expropriated in 1960. But over the years, the Havana Club brand has evolved as the economic needs of the state have evolved. The current articulation of the brand as a transnational product is reflective of Cuba's more current economic policies, which increasingly rely on corporate partners from Western capitalist countries. The natural product of this marriage is a campaign that reflects the contradictions involved in reconciling socialist values with capitalist measures.

A Different Kind of Advertising

Despite its transnational structure, Havana Club has become the face of Cuba, so there is the assumption that Havana Club's marketing might be congruent,

Figure 16. Souvenir from tourist shop in Havana. Photograph taken by Christopher Chávez.

to some degree, with the socialist ideals of the state. The degree to which Havana Club performs various kinds of labor on behalf of the Cuban government has been a key question of this book. Advertising is, after all, a powerful form of public discourse, which can shape how consumers make sense of the world, or at least an aspect of it.

Teun van Dijk (2001) argues that there are inherent power dynamics that are evident in public discourse. In an unequal society, dominant groups have control or influence over public discourse. Members of powerful groups may decide on the kinds of topics that will be addressed publicly, and they control the ways in which these topics can be addressed. These efforts are not purely symbolic.

According to van Dijk, public discourses can have material consequences by shaping the beliefs and actions of less powerful groups.

Advertising represents a unique kind of public discourse, since it is generally controlled by large corporations with the help of advertising executives and their creative partners. What makes advertising a particularly powerful form of discourse, however, is the share of voice that marketers command. With enough economic resources, advertisers have ready access to mass media, thereby allowing them to expand their potential reach. Advertisers can run television spots or place ads in magazines and on social media platforms, or they target consumers in more personal ways through event marketing.

In the process of selling products, however, advertisers give us workable ideas of how society is organized. John Sherry (1987) calls on us to look at advertising as a cultural system, a way of apprehending our world, in much the way that science, religion, and art represent ways of knowing. By teaching us the meaning of commodities, their supposed origins, and their use, advertisers help make the categories of culture stable and visible.

Given its inherently commercial function, advertising will ultimately reflect capitalist ideologies. Material objects are fetishized, and audiences are hailed not as citizens but as consumers. The people depicted in advertising are not meant to represent real people but rather to typify larger consumer categories (Schudson 1984). Instead of offering a critical lens to social life, advertising depicts an optimistic view of the world and that whatever problems might exist are problems that can be solved with the product.

Havana Club's prolific use of marketing reflects the Cuban State's willingness to engage in some of the practices of capitalism, but Cuba is not alone in negotiating this transition. Other socialist-oriented countries, including China, Vietnam, and Russia have similarly turned to the private sector to deliver strong economic growth (Corrales 2004). Advertising has played a significant role in facilitating this transition. In their study of Chinese advertising during the transition from communism to consumerism, for example, Xin Zhao and Russell Belk (2008) found that marketers have appropriated anti-consumerist ideology to justify their promotion of consumption, thereby bridging the apparent ideological tensions between communism and consumerism.

Zhao and Belk found that this task was accomplished semiotically, and the tensions between capitalism and socialism can be seen within a single advertisement, where political symbols have been reconfigured for marketing purposes. Images that were once used to celebrate the once-dominant ideology of anti-consumerism have been reconfigured to naturalize China's transition to global capitalism. For example, the image of "the worker" was frequently celebrated in communist myths, but Chinese advertisers have utilized this image in the service of selling goods.

The findings of this research suggest that the Havana Club campaigns work in a similar way. Images of "the people" and "the worker" have been reappropriated for marketing purposes. In its execution, the focus on the proletariat rather than the bourgeoisie was consistent with state propaganda. Depictions of joy, unrelated to material wealth, were in and of themselves political. But a review of the agency's strategic documents indicates that advertising executives were explicitly attempting to tap into socialist ideals in order to give Havana Club a competitive advantage in the global marketplace. The was particularly evident in M&C Saatchi's "Nothing Compares to Havana" campaign, which was designed to sell rum by tapping into consumers' disaffection with the capitalist system.

But a second key finding of this research is that it does not take long for marketplace logic to overwhelm socialist ideals. In just a decade, M&C Saatchi's campaigns have become increasingly more conventional in response to market imperatives, which has compelled the agency to focus more and more on the product. To ensure that the rum sells, more attention has been paid to individual fulfillment rather than collective struggle. Marketplace logic also determines which Cubans are worthy of being represented in advertising. The original "Nothing Compares to Havana" campaign depicted a broader cross-section of Havana residents, while later campaigns focused on young, fashionable Cubans who are believed to represent an idealized version of the targeted consumer.

Havana Club and Its Diplomatic Labor

In several ways, the campaign serves as a form of corporate diplomacy, which is an attempt to ensure that companies can conduct business smoothly in the various nations in which they operate. Referred to as "private sector" diplomacy, corporate diplomacy is the process by which corporations engage local publics to achieve a variety of strategic objectives, such as ensuring the reputation of the company and shaping policy that will impact the business (Marschlich 2022). When Havana Club promotes a positive image of Cuba to publics abroad, it is creating the conditions that will facilitate the sale of rum in those markets.

Then there are ways in which Havana Club engages in cultural diplomacy, which was most evident in the Havana Cultura platform. This project has successfully converted Cuban artists into successful brands. Their artwork hangs in Western museums and in private collections. Their films are screened in international film festivals, and their songs are carried on local radio stations and listed on streaming platforms. The artists go on tour and give interviews about Cuban music. In the course of doing this work, these artists generate favorable attitudes toward the island that are needed to facilitate diplomatic relations.

Finally, these marketing efforts serve as a form of public diplomacy, or official government efforts aimed at communicating directly with publics abroad.

Furthermore, public diplomacy and corporate diplomacy are closely linked as the reputation of a nation helps a company to sell its products the world over. Likewise, the organization's products and services reinforce the nation's reputation and heritage. If one sees Havana Club as an extension of Cuba itself, the brand helps Cuba in its larger goal of enhancing its image and reputation abroad (Kochhar and Molleda 2015).

According to Michael Bustamante and Julia Sweig (2008), Cuba's effective use of diplomacy has enabled it to advance its strategic objectives in the global landscape. Furthermore, the state has proven to be highly sophisticated at employing cultural products to support diverse political, diplomatic, and economic ends—many of which arguably serve a market-oriented purpose rather than a strictly anti-imperialist or anti-globalization agenda. In the global landscape, commodities including Cuban rum and cigars have come to signify Cuba, allowing consumers to appreciate the island while shying away from explicitly political themes.

Similarly, Cuba has been effective at utilizing its cultural products to advance its strategic objectives (Bustamante and Sweig 2008). After Cuba's Special Period, the promotion abroad of Cuban art, music, and film has helped the island fulfill other, equally important national interests, including the attraction of tourists and hard currency. Although nearly all Cuban cultural products that are sold or promoted abroad are, to varying degrees, brokered through state-run cultural institutions, their connection to state actors is less visible.

To what degree does Havana Club complement the state's discourse in the global landscape, and to what degree does it diverge from it? On one hand, the campaign advances the ideals of the revolution simply by representing Cuba as a sovereign and functional nation. This is a stark difference to how Cuba has been imagined by Western journalists, activists, and politicians, who have advanced an image of Cuba as an island that is impoverished, unstable, and unable to meet the basic needs of its citizens.

The campaigns may also be seen as political, since they decenter the role of the United States. Throughout its history, Cuba was understood through its subordinate relationship, first to Spain, then to the United States. In fact, as Pérez (2008) notes, Americans are taught that Cuban independence and indeed the very existence of the Cuban republic were achieved through the sacrifice of the United States, a narrative that continues to be told by Bacardí. Advertising campaigns produced during the Republican era were created from the Western point of view. They were centered on the experiences of American travelers, who were seeking an exotic experience.

Havana Club's contemporary campaigns may be written from the point of view of Cubans living on the island, but the product and the logo will always be the focal point of the advertising. And so there are contradictions involved using capitalist means to market Cuban rum. Critics might argue that the prolific use of advertising undermines state rhetoric, which for the most part has been disciplined. For internal publics, the increasingly commercial nature of Havana Club advertising must be seen as the antithesis of revolutionary ideals. After all, in *Socialism and Man in Cuba* (1968), Guevara warned Cuba's citizens about the corrupting influence of capitalism, which prevented individuals from expressing their true interests, or to see themselves as part of a greater whole.

Increasingly, the advertising for Havana Club promotes the product as the path toward self-fulfillment, and over the course of several campaigns, the company has positioned the rum as the pathway toward joy, happiness, community, and even rebellion. This kind of commodity fetishism may be violation of revolutionary values, but it is a necessary strategy. As scholar Hope Bastian (2019) argues, the state position is that advertising and marketing are a "necessary evil" to ensure the nation's economic stability and the survival of the revolution.

How does the Cuban State reconcile these two competing points of view? Sujatha Fernandes (2006) distinguishes between the needs of the "pragmatic state" and those of the "populist state." On one hand, the pragmatic state negotiates and deals in the international market and the local tourist trade, appropriating the language of efficiency and austerity. On the other hand, the populist state assures the people that market values are not virtues in and of themselves but rather means by which to achieve the goals of true communism. Therefore, political leadership tries to assure the Cuban people that it is committed to preserving the socialist model of development for the Cuban economy, in contrast to the "market socialism" of China and Vietnam.

However, a dual messaging strategy is based on the assumption that there are two parallel but mutually exclusive sets of discourses, one for the Cuban people and the other for Western consumers. In today's media landscape, however, the way in which audiences actually consume media is much more fluid and borderless. Social media has made it more difficult for Cuba to be a closed society, and its citizens are becoming businesses in their own right. There is a growing awareness of the how the island is impacted by the global economy, and of its evolving relationship with the United States.

The Americans Are Coming

In her research on the shifting nature of the Cuban economy, Bastian (2019) argues that there are several "befores" that exist within the Cuban imaginary. The first "before" is "Before the Revolution." According to this narrative, Cuba was once a profoundly unequal place marked by racial segregation under the Batista regime. Class and geography mostly limited access to quality health care and education to Havana. The population lived under a dictatorship that brutally repressed those fighting to make the country a more just and equal country.

The second "before" is "Before the Special Period," or the time before the economic crisis that is associated with the fall of the Soviet Union. This was the "before" that photographer Alejandro González had attempted to invoke in his installation for the Havana Club Visual Arts Project. According to Bastian, Cubans characterize life before the Special Period as one in which there was enough food and people had access to consumer goods. The transportation system was more reliable, and prices were controlled and subsidized by the state. Cubans had enough not only to survive, but to indulge from time to time.

Bastian argues that Cubans are confronting a new kind of "before," which is before the Americans come. During the Obama administration, there was widespread anticipation that the embargo would soon be lifted and that American visitors would come to the island in droves. But in coming to Cuba, it was believed that the Americans would transform the island into another tropical playground, ruining the socialist authenticity of the country.

And for a short while, this seemed like a very real prospect. President Barack Obama demonstrated an openness to resuming relations with Cuba. What started with the revision of a few regulations had soon evolved into an orchestrated effort to reopen relations (Anderson 2016). On December 17, 2014, Obama announced that he would reassess diplomatic relations between the two countries and examine pathways for normalizing relationships (White House 2016). Both the U.S. and Cuban embassies were reopened, and an agreement was reached to restore air services between the United States and Cuba.

It seemed all but inevitable that the Americans would come to Cuba. In 2016, Obama gave a speech in Havana, where he described a possible new relationship between the two countries. "I have come here to bury the last remnant of the Cold War in the Americas," Obama stated in a speech delivered in Havana. "I have come here to extend the hand of friendship to the Cuban people." In his case for improving relations, Obama spoke to the resourcefulness of the Cuban, invoking the phrase "El Cubano inventa del aire," the Cuban invents out of air (White House 2016). In the speech, Obama walked a fine line between touting the benefits of capitalism and respecting socialist ideals. He framed economic opportunity as good for the Cuban people, focusing on those Cuban entrepreneurs who had started small businesses.

While it was not explicitly stated, one underlying message of Obama's speech was that normalizing relationships could be good for businesses as well as citizens, and it seems that both Cuban and American entrepreneurs were eager to develop new relationships. American business would have access to a sizable new market. In turn, Cuban products would now be more readily available to American consumers. For executives at Havana Club, there was tremendous optimism that the brand would gain access to U.S. markets, which consume 40 percent of rum worldwide. "Of course, we have great hopes now that there's a new situation between the two countries. If the blockade is lifted someday, we'll enjoy significant growth" stated Jérôme Cottin-Bizonne, CEO of Havana Club at the time.

In anticipation, Havana Club had already been preparing for an entryway into the U.S. market. According to Cottin-Bizonne, the company could potentially sell 1.7 million cases of Cuban rum annually in the United States (Pineau and Vidalon 2015). If they were to enter the U.S. market, Havana Club would simply continue its current strategy, stating "we'd have to do what we did in other countries: build up the brand, concentrate on our points of differentiation, on the quality of our rum, of Cuban rum in general, on its brand recognition among bartenders worldwide, and on its ties to Cuban culture." Certainly, the company would have to resolve its ongoing trademark with Bacardí for use of the Havana Club name in the United States. But this too had been considered. Corporación Cuba Ron had created the new brand, Havanista, which would be sold to U.S. customers. In 2011 Havana Club International registered the trademark in anticipation of embargo's end.

J. Walter Thompson's Cuban Adventure

It did not take long for advertisers to take notice of these developments. When it appeared that relations between Cuba and the United States were on the brink of normalization, emissaries were sent to Cuba by J. Walter Thompson, one of the largest advertising agencies in the world.[1] The goal of the visit was to serve as a sort of reconnaissance mission, surveying the Cuban consumer landscape and then reporting on the potential opportunities for advertisers.

According to the agency, a team of five market researchers spent a total of ten days on the island in January of 2016. During that time, they interviewed more than forty Cubans about their lives, the economy, and the opportunities that would become available as relations with the United States improve. To purport to understand the Cuban people with just a small sample is a lofty claim, but not unexpected. As I have previously argued (Chávez 2015), market research is only loosely based on practices of anthropology, which is not without its own problems. Even at its best, anthropology is what Michael Agar (1996) calls an "arrogant exercise" in which researchers attempt to ingratiate themselves into a group of strangers, document their social lives, and describe their beliefs and practices, all within a relatively short period of time. All the while, they struggle with the legacy of colonialism, which continues to shape their perspective. Further complicating matters is the fact that agencies are engaging in a form of sponsored research, in which they are motivated to uncover findings in which they stand to benefit economically.

The product of this exploratory visit was a report titled *The Promise of Cuba* (Thompson 2016), which was shared widely throughout the agency's global network. In the report, the agency methodically lays out the argument for American companies to enter the Cuban market once the embargo is lifted. The underlying argument for entering the Cuban market was not based on political or moral reasons but on economic ones. The reader was told that U.S. companies have been limited by the embargo, providing a competitive advantage to other multinationals. British-Dutch multinational Unilever and Richmeat de Mexico had already established a strong presence, and if American companies did not move quickly, they argued, they would be watching from the sidelines. "First movers in Cuba get the lobster," William Lane from Caterpillar Inc. was quoted as saying.

The city of Havana, of course, would be the focal point of any effort, and the authors of the report describe the city in detail. Unlike Havana Club, which depicts the capital city as protected from consumerism, J. Walter Thompson frames it as a consumer society in waiting. The city is characterized as a vacation paradise for millennials, with such alluring ideas as organic foods and a DIY spirit. But most important, it has what J. Walter Thompson refers to as a brandless character: "With not a Starbucks in sight, Havana appears barely touched by mass consumerism. This appeals to jaded millennials who have been marketed to relentlessly since birth" (Thompson 2016). However, the authors of the report also note presence of known luxury brands, which they see as a sign of Cuba's progress:

> A few years ago, commercial activities in this area were largely limited to official hotels and kitschy destinations like the Havana Club Rum Museum or the Museum of Chocolate, interspersed with shops selling tourist trinkets. But now, upscale restaurants and tastefully decorated private tourist accommodations are mixed in. Shops from non-U.S. brands like Pepe Jeans, Lacoste, Adidas, and United Colors of Benetton can already be found dotted throughout the area.

By relegating the Havana Club Museum of Rum to the realm of kitsch, J. Walter Thompson is suggesting that "authentic" is equal to "premium," something the Cuban State is purportedly not able to provide. Therefore, "inauthentic" spaces like the Museum of Rum are contrasted with "real" places like Adidas and Pepe Jeans. These brands are seen as markers of quality but also evidence that there is a market of Cubans who have the potential to be citizens in the global economy.

Once a society has been conceptualized as a market, the next logical step is to categorize that society according to their consumer preferences. In Thompson's *The Promise of Cuba* report, the agency engages in the practice of market segmentation where we begin to see the logic of advertising take form. The Cuban society is massified and then reorganized according to its consumption patterns, and its openness to consumption. The oldest consumer segment that J. Walter Thompson defines is the "Revolutionary Generation." According to the report, these Cubans were young adults when the Cuban Revolution took place. Cubans that belong in this generation remain influential in state leadership, but the agency argues that their cultural influence has been diminished.

Then there are the "Cuban Boomers," those who were born from around 1945 to around 1970. The agency states that this generation grew up during the early years of the revolution and was shaped by the influence of the Soviet Union. The authors of the report warn the reader that Cuban Boomers may be resistant to American advertising, having committed to an ideal of a prosperous revolutionary Cuba. This generation also came of age during a time of intense political conflict with the United States.

The authors of the report appear to suggest that these first two segments are not ideal target audiences, because of their age and because they may be ideologically resistant to consumer values. However, J. Walter Thompson sees promise in the younger generation of Cubans who can be persuaded by capitalist measures. For example, the agency identifies "Cuba's Generation Y," who are in their thirties and forties but negatively impacted by the economic collapse of the 1990s and the measures taken during the Special Period in a Time of Peace. The name for this segment was taken from Yoani Sánchez, who coined the term *Generación Y* in reference to a generation whose names were influenced by the Soviet Union (Yulexis, Yasael, Yurisbel, and so forth).

Then there is the "Upstart Generation," which is where the agency finds true promise. Members of this generation are said to be true entrepreneurs. Cubans of this generation have created their own businesses, and rather than relying on the state, this generation is committed to determining its own destiny. This is a younger generation, under the age of thirty, which has a strong memory of the Special Period, and seek a better way. According to J. Walter Thompson, this consumer segment is open to American brands and American culture, making its members ideal consumers.

In addition to identifying the most promising Cuban consumers, the authors of the report also made sure to report that there is a viable media system that could carry the advertising messages of prospective businesses. There are magazines such as *Vista*, a lifestyle magazine focusing on the arts; *Garbos*, a women's magazine focusing on fashion; and *Novisima*, described as a youth culture magazine. In addition to legacy media, the authors note that Cubans are prolific users of digital platforms, which allow them to engage in business activities and consume culture from outside the island. Having made a successful case to American businesses, J. Walter Thompson would, of course, be there to create the advertising.

But this transformation never happened. Any steps toward normalization were reversed when the Trump administration took office in 2017. In a reassertion of nationalism, Trump began reversing crucial pieces of what he called a "terrible and misguided deal" with Cuba. In a speech delivered in Miami's Little

Havana, the epicenter of a Cuban exile community, Trump argued that normalizing relationships with the communist government in Cuba would only embolden its oppressive military system (Davis 2017).

We can only assume that if markets had opened up to American businesses, J. Walter Thompson would have conducted business as usual. It would have used its vast resources to create advertising that would target Cuban consumers relentlessly. The agency has grown into one of the largest international advertising agencies in the world, largely through a combination of expansion, mergers, and acquisitions and by centralizing its resources. It is a large, heavy mechanism that operates according to its own internal logic and produces a highly consistent product.

Regardless of client or cultural context, marketers engage in a similar set of practices within the advertising industry. Agencies seek out opportunities for their clients by surveying the financial landscape, using quasi-scientific methods. In the process, account executives identify the intended consumer, agency strategists describe their consumer practices, and media planners identify the appropriate outlets for carrying advertising messages. Art directors and copywriters develop creative ideas that will best sell the product, and they enlist filmmakers, musicians, editors, and so forth, who can develop a polished, well-produced advertisement. The same essential process for making advertising has not changed over the course of the past century.

Brokers Who Break

J. Walter Thompson's *The Promise of Cuba* reflects the totalizing impact of capitalism. The ideals and practices of advertising practitioners are heavily shaped by marketplace logic, which in turn limits their perspective. In the process of showcasing the economic opportunities that are to be exploited in Cuba, the executives at J. Walter Thompson are unable to see an alternative point of view. That the impact that the revolution has had on Cuban society has been totalizing in its own way. Therefore, it is not entirely accurate to conceptualize Cubans simply as consumers in waiting, but rather as citizens with a different consciousness.

Conceptualizing Cuban citizens, first and foremost, according to their economic value is itself ideological. To account for the mindset of cultural producers, Bourdieu invokes the concept of doxa, which he describes as conventions we do not question. They are the deeply rooted, tacit understandings of the world that become so naturalized that we no longer see them. According to Bourdieu, cultural producers possess two overall forms of doxa. First, there is a general doxa, or general beliefs that seem commonsense yet have historically been created by social, cultural, economic, and political institutions. In many Western societies, for example, there is an unquestioning belief in capitalism.

Then there is a specific doxa, which is unique to a given profession. This is the doxa of a certain field that can be understood as a system of presuppositions inherent in the membership of a field. Consider the routine practice of market segmentation, which J. Walter Thompson used to create their typology of the consumer landscape in Cuba. According to Pamela Odih (1999), a central idea behind market segmentation is the precise classification of groups to facilitate the marketing of goods through the efficient channeling of resources.

However, what is often presented as objective, irrefutable discovery is, in fact, the product of a given social orientation. Historically, advertising practices have reflected the positivist sensibilities that evolved out of the Enlightenment and the Scientific Revolution. These intellectual movements emphasized empirical knowledge and the use of scientific methods for understanding human experience. Despite the pretense that advertising practices are based on objective rationale, they are in fact quite subjective. Decisions about who gets to be included in the target market, which target audiences will be prioritized, and which messages are deemed relevant to the target audience are all decisions that reflect the biases of marketers.

Then there are the larger ideological implications. As Bourdieu notes, to succeed within a given field of cultural production, producers must learn to play the game. But to play the game, producers first need an unquestionable belief that the game is worth playing. For advertising executives, there is the normative idea that products and corporations serve an important role in stabilizing the economy, creating new jobs, or making product choices visible to consumers. At their best, brands might even serve as good corporate citizens.

Thus, it is likely that executives at J. Walter Thompson were uncritical of their work. *The Promise of Cuba* expresses the optimistic viewpoint that by facilitating economic opportunities between the United States and Cuba, they might be able to improve the everyday lives of Cuban citizens. Or that Cuba's public institutions might become more stable as more income flows into the island. Or that entrepreneurial, young Cubans might simply grow into their ideal selves. Perhaps there was even the belief that if the agency played a small role in promoting capitalism, it may have done its part to prompt regime change.

These beliefs, however, belie the fact that capitalism is itself antagonistic in nature, which is reflected in the professional jargon used by marketers. Advertising professionals routinely invoke the language of war. They develop campaigns and target audiences and use guerrilla tactics, all with the goal of capturing market share (Behrends 2023). The marketing enterprise is, in essence, a zero-sum game, in which competing entities vie for dominance in a competitive and unforgiving marketplace.

In short, there are winners and losers in capitalism, and the J. Walter Thompson report gives some insight into this reality. The ultimate goal of the report is to encourage U.S. businesses to exploit the economic opportunities in Cuba as they had during the Republican era. Such practices illustrate the ways in which dynamics within fields of cultural production are never independent of the larger field of power. Whether consciously or unconsciously, there is an effort to promote the exploitation of the Cuban people by American corporations.

It is unlikely that Cuba would win in this relationship. History tells us that the island has been subject to continuous exploitation from foreign actors throughout its history, which has cost the nation dearly. Thus, efforts to deliver Cuban consumers to American businesses seem like a form of neocolonialism, which represents the new system of exploitation in contemporary society. According to Aimé Césaire (2001), neocolonialism has adopted the same main working principles as colonialism: uneven social and economic relations based on the extraction of resources. It is a system in which resources flow toward more powerful, richer nations and where local industries are reduced to positions of dependence. Since 1959, Cuba has been able to maintain its political sovereignty and assert its economic independence, but it is difficult to thrive the global marketplace, when the landscape remains highly uneven.

Cárdenas, the Global City

In 2023, I visited Cárdenas, in the province of Matanzas. The city has historical significance in Cuban history. It is where the Cuban flag was flown for the very first time in 1850, and it served as an important military destination during Cuba's wars for independence. This is also the city where José Arechabala y Aldama built his rum-making empire. Once called the "Pearl of the North," Cárdenas had tremendous economic importance. The port and sugar mills made the city an important economic center in the nineteenth century, while the railroad enabled Cárdenas to actively stay connected with other economic centers throughout Cuba.

Since its establishment in 1828, Cárdenas has been a global city. Ships from different parts of the world arrive to the port of the city delivering commodities from far off places. It is also where Cuban sugar and rum were loaded onto ships and exported to foreign nations. These operations required labor, and as one of Cuba's principal sugar-exporting towns, Cárdenas demanded a workforce that was composed of slaves brought in from West Africa, Chinese contract workers, and Spanish immigrants.

José Arechabala himself embodied the global nature of the city. At the age of fifteen, Arechabala boarded a ship in northern Spain and sailed to Cárdenas, where he joined an enclave of Basque immigrants who had come to the area seeking their fortunes in trade and commerce (Knight 1977). These Basque entrepreneurs were negotiating a difficult relationship with the Spanish crown. Later, during U.S. occupation, these businessmen began to build business relations with U.S. business and consumers.

In their marketing materials, the Arechabala family would reflect an ethos of transnationalism by fixating on two locales. The first is Spain's Basque region, where Arechabala was born. The Vizcaya coat of arms was present on every bottle the produced, and Arechabala named his prized distillery La Vizcaya in reference to his homeland. And when the company developed a publication to report on economic affairs related to Cárdenas, he titled it *Gordejuela*, after his birthplace. This connection to the homeland was so ingrained that when the company produced a book to celebrate its seventy-fifth anniversary, it made sure to mention Arechabala's connections to Spain:

> This book would be incomplete, indeed, if we did not give our readers some facts about two widely separated spots, which mean so much in the history of our Company. One is the Valley of Gordejuela, in far off Spain, the birthplace of our Founder; the other the City of Cárdenas, where our Company grew and developed. To us at Arechabala, Gordejuela is a symbol, and Cárdenas, a bright reality to which we are lovingly bound.

As the company states, Arechabala may have had symbolic connections to Basque country, but his material resources were invested in Cárdenas, and when business was good, the Arechabala family began to invest heavily in the city that it adopted as its new home. Arechabala Industries grew to become Cárdenas's largest employer and invested in public works, including the Arechabala Theater, which was inaugurated in 1910, and a number of port improvements. José Arechabala S.A. also deepened the harbor and modernized the port facility, and constructed the pier in 1939. The family's business had become so important to the city that it was honored with the designation of "Benefactora Eminente" (Eminent Benefactor) of Cárdenas (Sainz 1954).

Havana Club—The People's Rum

Today, it is hard to imagine that Cárdenas had once been a thriving port city. Many of its public buildings have fallen into disrepair, and the horse and buggy remains a common form of public transportation. La Vizcaya, Arechabala's prized distillery, is still standing, but it is no longer the model example of technological innovation in Cuba. The eroding building is now home to the offices of Corporación Cuba Ron, the joint venture between the Cuban State and Pernod Ricard (Figure 17). Yet the factory no longer produces Havana Club rum. The scale and efficiency needed for global output require a more modern operation, and so production has shifted to Santa Cruz del Norte, which was built in 1970. The other distillery is in San José, which was built in 2007.

This is not to say that Cárdenas has been relegated to the past. Instead, it has simply transformed into something different. Despite its age, the distillery is still operating and open to tourists, who visit from the nearby resorts travel to see a

Figure 17. Arechabala's prized La Vizcaya distillery, now home to Cuba Ron S.A. Photograph taken by Christoper Chávez.

historic Cuban distillery that dates back to the late nineteenth century. Today, the distillery produces Ron Perla de Norte, which has been described as "the little sister of Havana Club" (Ron Perla del Norte 2024) If you look closely, there are still references to place, yet they are signifiers that have been disconnected from their original referents. The distillery still bears the name La Vizcaya and features a slight variation of the coat of arms that José Arechabala had once included on his products.

Aside from these few references, traces of the Arechabala family can no longer be found, either on the product he created or in the city he once called home. In Cárdenas, one is likely to encounter a number of memorials dedicated to revolutionary heroes, but evidence of the once-prominent family in Cárdenas is hard to find. The once-grand Arechabala Theater, which was unveiled in 1919, is no longer there, and the former Arechabala home has been turned into a public library. It is uncertain what these erasures mean. Perhaps these erasures simply signaled a shift away from private enterprise. Or perhaps the new revolutionary government resented the Arechabalas for leaving Cuba after the revolution. The family would have been among the first wave of white, wealthy Cubans who left for the United States after the revolution. Those who Castro pejoratively referred to as "gusanos."

But while the family name has gradually disappeared in Cuba, it is Arechabala's product that has become an omnipresent part of Cuban life. Havana Club has in essence become the "people's rum," and its presence on the island is unrivaled. It is the rum that many Cubans consume when they celebrate special occasions, or when they want to escape their troubles. It is the rum that some Cubans place before their Catholic saints or Yoruban orishas, as part of their religious rituals (Figure 18). It is the rum that is commonly served to tourists at restaurants, bars, and *paladores* across the island.

Figure 18. Havana Club rum placed at an altar in a home in Trinidad, Cuba. Photograph taken by Christoper Chávez.

That Arechabala's legacy would continue to exist in commodity form is not surprising, given the logic of global capitalism. Havana Club's evolution from a family-run business, to a state-owned product, to a transnational partnership is testament to the resiliency of the brand. In the face of severe political and economic disruptions over the past century, the brand continuously reinvented itself to maintain its identity and its relevance. This kind of reinvention in some ways represents the resiliency of the revolution itself. The revolution has existed for over sixty years defying impossible odds. As Jacqueline Loss and Manuel Prieto (2012) argue, the U.S. administration's use of economic sanctions combined with both implicit and outright military intervention against Castro's regime had given the Cuban revolutionaries only one acceptable alternative. They had to throw in their lot with the Soviets.

And when its relationship with the Soviet Union collapsed, Cuba had to reinvent itself again by seeking foreign investments, developing the tourism industry and taking other measures meant to improve economic efficiency. As Yuri Pavlov (2012) notes, the Cuban government introduced its equivalent of Lenin's New Economic Policy, a temporary tactical retreat from socialism. However, this economic policy stopped short of instituting reforms that would undermine the foundations of the Communist Party.

"We do not want to sell our country" is how Castro put it (Vásquez Raña 1995). "We are doing business to jumpstart factories that are paralyzed, factories with no raw materials, factories that could be improved with new technology, or factories that need to be built because it is advisable to do it in a specific time." At the time, the entire enterprise seemed highly tentative. The Cuban State was not receiving many offers of capital investment, and so Castro dispatched emissaries to seek out investors. Eventually, these efforts paid off. Mexican firms were early partners, participating in joint ventures in developing such various sectors as telecommunications, cement production, and tourism. Businesses from Spain, France, Britain, and Canada invested in developing oil production and nickel mining (*Los Angeles Times* 1995). Pernod Ricard, of course, was among these first investor, helping to reinvigorate Cuba's declining rum industry.

But it is hard to stop this momentum once the door to capitalism has been opened, which is evident in Havana Club's logic of expansion. No longer satisfied with having made inroads in Western Europe, Canada, and Mexico, Havana Club now seeks new opportunities in other parts of the world. The Cuban News Agency (2022) reported that steps were currently being taken to launch Havana Club in Asia and Africa. Conceptualizing these regions as markets, rather than publics, is a notable shift in logic. In the early days of the revolution, there was interest in bringing revolutionary ideals to the "developing world," thereby expanding its influence beyond the Soviet bloc. But the United States remains the most coveted market of all. According to the Distilled Spirits Council of the United States, 24.1 million cases of rum were sold in the United States in 2019, generating over $2.3 billion in revenue for distillers (2019). But before the rum can flow, the political conditions must be right. Today, Cuba remains excluded from this market, but Havana Club International has expressed its interest in engaging U.S. consumers if the embargo is ever lifted.

In the meantime, Havana Club international will continue to affirm its position in the global marketplace by positioning itself as an authentic Cuban product. Given the proliferation of marketing materials, which are shot in Havana and feature Cuban citizens, it is easy to forget that this is only half true. Havana Club International is, after all, half-owned by a French company, working in collaboration with creative partners that are based in Europe and the United States. Thus, it is Western brokers who have taken on responsibility for articulating what it means to be authentically Cuban. And in the process of selling rum, they are enacting the logic of advertising, which places the product at the center of a fulfilling and productive life.

But this optimistic view of the world can also obfuscate the complex reality on the island. Despite the promise of new global partnerships, it has become increasingly apparent that the Cuban State has not been able to serve its citizens' basic needs. On July 11, 2021, thousands of Cubans took to the streets in the largest nationwide demonstrations against the government since the 1959 Cuban Revolution. These protests were a response to long-standing restrictions on rights, food and medicine scarcity, and the government's response to the COVID-19 pandemic. As it has done in the past, the state responded aggressively by detaining and arresting hundreds of protesters.

For Cuban scholars like Rafael Hernández and Esteban Morales Domínguez, domestic issues require thoughtful debates by Cubans who are invested in the fate of the nation. However, narratives about Cuba and Cubans have, for too long, been shaped by people living outside the island. "We have, in effect, handed over the task of analyzing a problem of vital importance in this country's life," Domínguez (2012) writes. "The resultant danger is that we find ourselves having to clarify matters about which we still have not been able to have a scientific discussion of our own."

Both scholars were referring to dissidents, journalists, intellectuals, and government officials who are living outside the island. They did not adequately account for the profound influence of corporate executives, advertising practitioners, music producers, visual artists, filmmakers, and other kinds of cultural producers, who benefit economically by circulating their own narratives about Cuba. These cultural producers, too, are enacting a pernicious form of symbolic violence by advancing a specific notion of what it means to be Cuban while simultaneously rendering the Cuban people voiceless.

Acknowledgments

I began this research during the Obama administration, when it appeared all but certain that relations with Cuba would be restored. At the time, there were questions about what exactly this would mean. How aggressively would American corporations pursue their interests on the island? How would Cuban society be transformed? Such questions, of course, were premature. Cold War politics reemerged during the Trump administration, and by the time I completed this book, President Biden seemed to have little interest in investing the political equity needed to normalize relations. And so Cuba remains out of reach for most Americans. It is perhaps its unattainability, however, that continues to make Cuba so appealing for U.S. consumers.

A political history of Cuba through its rum industry would not have been possible without the help of several journalists, marketers, and academics. I want to thank Dr. Ricardo Valencia, who began this journey with me. I also want to thank my colleagues in the School of Journalism and Communication, who were extremely generous with their time and insight, including Charlie Butler, Dr. Peter Laufer, Tom McDonald, and Dr. Leslie Steeves. I would also like to thank the journalists and advertising practitioners who lent their perspectives, contacts, and materials, including Tom Gjelten, Doreen Hemlock, Dave Leroi, Noah Rothbaum, and Johannes Werner. None of this would have been possible without their knowledge about this industry and about Cuba. Finally, I want to thank the administration at the University of Oregon for their continued support of my research.

Notes

INTRODUCTION

Epigraph: Entire interview published in *El Sol de Mexico*, January 1995.

1. The name Gordejuéxa is a Basque word, with different spellings in the public record (Gordejuela and Gordexola). When describing the city, I use Gordejuéxa. When describing the publication, I use Gordejuela, which was employed by Arechabala S.A.

CHAPTER 1 — ADVERTISING AND AUTHENTICITY

Epigraph: From the case study submitted for the Cannes Creative Lions award show, 2013.

CHAPTER 3 — LONG-DISTANCE NATIONALISM AND THE LOGIC OF CAPITALISM

Epigraph: Testimony given to the Senate Judiciary Committee on July 13, 2004.

CHAPTER 5 — RUM, RACE, AND REPRESENTATION

Epigraph: As quoted in "Racist, Sexist, Rude and Crude: The Worst of 20th Century Advertising," *The Guardian*, November 18, 2015.

1. *Bacardí: A Tale of Merchants, Family and Company* (Dawson and Argamasilla 2006) identifies this as the company's first advertisement, taken from the periodical *Ilustración*, circa 1891. I found that ad ran three years earlier in *La Ilustración Artística*.

CHAPTER 6 — THE LOSING GAME OF AUTHENTICITY

Epigraph: From *The Promise of Cuba* by J. Walter Thompson.

1. In 2018, J. Walter Thompson merged with Wunderman to form Wunderman Thompson.

References

Agar, Michael. 1996. *The Professional Stranger: An Informal Introduction to Ethnography*, 2nd ed. San Diego: Academic Press.

Álvarez, Pedro Castelló. 2008. *The Signs Pile Up: Paintings by Pedro Álvarez*. Los Angeles, CA: Smart Art.

Anderson, Benedict. 1983. *Imagined Communities: Reflections on the Origin and Spread of Nationalism*. London: Verso.

———. 1998. *The Spectre of Comparisons: Nationalism, Southeast Asia, and the World*. London: Verso.

Anderson, Jon Lee. 2016. "A New Cuba: President Obama's Plan Normalized Relations. It May Also Transform the Nation." *New Yorker*, October 3. https://www.newyorker.com/magazine/2016/10/03/a-new-cuba.

Assaf, Katya. 2009. "Trademark Law: A Semiotic Perspective." *Journal of Intellectual Property Law and Practice* 4, no. 9: 643–657.

Bacardí. 2012. "150 Years of the Bacardí Archive Revealed." Bacardí. https://www.bacardilimited.com/media/news-archive/150-years-of-the-bacardi-archive-revealed/.

———. 2016. "Havana Club Puerto Rican Rum Rolls Out National Market Expansion with the Unveiling of Añejo Clasico and 'The Golden Age, Aged Well' Campaign." Bacardí, June 1. https://www.bacardilimited.com/havana-club-puerto-ricanrum- rolls-out-national-market-expansion-with-the-unveiling-of-anejo-clasico-andthe-golden-age-aged-well-campaign/.

———. 2022a. "About Us." Bacardí. https://www.bacardilimited.com/our-company/about-us/.

———. 2022b. "Welcome to the World's Largest-Privately Held International Spirits Company." Bacardí. https://www.bacardilimited.com.

———. 2022c. Job posting. https://careers.bacardilimited.com/careers/JobDetail/Brand-Ambassador-Gulf/5934.

———. 2024. "The World's Most Awarded Rum." Bacardí. https://www.bacardi.com/culture/the-worlds-most-awarded-rum/#:~:text=%27%20BACARDÍ%20rum%20was%20just%20fourteen,day%2C%20alongside%20Don%20Facundo%27s%20signature.

Banet-Weiser, Sarah. 2012. *Authentic: The Politics of Ambivalence in a Brand Culture*. New York: New York University Press.

Barber, Benjamin. 1996. *Jihad vs. McWorld: Terrorism's Challenge to Democracy*. New York: Ballantine Books.

Barnet, Miguel. 1980. "The Culture That Sugar Created." *Latin American Literary Review* 8, no. 16: 38–46.

Barty-King, Hugh. 1983. *Rum: Yesterday and Today*. London: Heinemann.

Bastian, Hope. 2019. *Everyday Adjustments in Havana: Economic Reforms, Mobility, and Emerging Inequalities*. Lanham, MD: Lexington Books.

Behrends, Michael. 2023. "Agency War Rooms: Why Violent Language Is Ruining the Fun in Our Jobs." *Ad Age*, March 20. https://adage.com/article/opinion/agency-war-rooms-why-violent-language-ruining-fun-our-jobs/2480016.

Benson, Devyn Spence. 2016. *Antiracism in Cuba: The Unfinished Revolution*. Chapel Hill: University of North Carolina Press.

Beverland, Michael. 2005. "Crafting Brand Authenticity: The Case of Luxury Wines." *Journal of Management Studies* 42, no. 5: 1003–1029.

Black Tears Rum. 2023. Home page. https://www.blacktears.com.

Blake, Meredith. 2015. "Conan O'Brien's History-Making Cuba Mission: 'Make Them Laugh.'" *Los Angeles Times*, March 3. https://www.latimes.com/entertainment/tv/showtracker/la-et-st-conan-obrien-cuba-20150303-story.html.

Bonera, Miguel. 2000. *Oro Blanco: Una Historia Empresarial del Ron Cubano*. Toronto: Lugus.

Booth, Charles, Peter Clark, Stephen Procter, and Michael Rowlinson. 2007. "Accounting for the Dark Side of Corporate History: Organizational Culture Perspectives and the Bertelsmann Case." *Critical Perspectives on Accounting* 18, no. 6: 625–644.

Bourdieu, Pierre. 1986. *Distinction: A Social Critique of the Judgement of Taste*. New York: Routledge.

———. 1993. *The Field of Cultural Production: Essays on Art and Literature*. New York: Columbia University Press.

Brooker, Alice. 2022. "Havana Club Collaborates with Bad Gyal." *The Spirits Business*, March 23. https://www.thespiritsbusiness.com/2022/03/havana-club-collaborates-with-bad-gyal/.

Brown, Jared M., and Anistatia R. Miller. 2011. *The Mixellany Guide to Vermouth and Other Apéritifs*. London: Mixellany Books.

Buren, Daniel. 1970. "The Function of a Museum." Statement produced for Museum of Modern Art, Oxford, England.

Bustamante, Michael J., and Julia Sweig. 2008. "Buena Vista Solidarity and the Axis of Aid: Cuban and Venezuelan Public Diplomacy." *Annals of the American Academy of Political and Social Science* 616, no. 1: 223–256.

Campaign UK. 2005. "M&C's French Office Lands Havana Club." October 14. https://www.campaignlive.co.uk/article/m-cs-french-office-lands-havana-club/522345.

Cannes. 2013. Case study, Havana Club: Nothing Compares to Havana. WARC. https://www.warc.com/content/article/cannes/havana_club_nothing_compares_to_havana/99604.

Cantor-Navas, Judy. 2015. "Giles Peterson Explains Cuba's Music Scene: Where He's Been Working since '08." *Billboard*, May 14. https://www.billboard.com/pro/gilles-peterson-cuban-music-havana-cultura-qa/.

REFERENCES

Carú, Antonella, Maria Carmela Ostillio, and Giuseppe Leone. 2017. "Corporate Museums to Enhance Brand Authenticity in Luxury Goods Companies: The Case of Salvatore Ferragamo." *International Journal of Arts Management* 19, no. 2: 32–45.

Center for a Free Cuba. 2019. "Cubabrief: What is the Difference between an Immigrant and an Exile." September 20. https://www.cubacenter.org/archives/2019/9/20/cubabrief-what-is-the-difference-between-an-immigrant-and-an-exile.

Césaire, Aimé. 2001. *Discourses on Colonialism*. New York: Monthly Review Press.

Cetino, Melissa, Johanna Karlsson, Meiru Lu, and Xinyi Yao. 2018. "Artistic Brand or Brand with Art: Brand and Art Collaborations in the Alcohol Industry." Strategic Brand Management Master Papers. https://lup.lub.lu.se/luur/download?func=downloadFile&recordOId=8966483&fileOId=8967032.

Charnon-Deutsch, Lou. 2008. *Hold That Pose: Visual Culture in the Late Nineteenth Century Spanish Periodical*. University Park, PA: Penn State University Press.

Chávez, Christopher. 2015. "Re-Thinking the Hispanic Market: A Call for Reflexivity in Advertising Practice." In *Routledge Companion to Ethnic Marketing*, edited by Ahmad Jamal, Lisa Peñaloza, and Michel Laroche, 295–308. New York: Routledge.

Chávez, Christopher, and Ricardo Valencia. 2018. "Branding the Revolution: Havana Club Advertising and the Fight for Cuban Authenticity." *Journal of Communication Inquiry* 43, no. 3: 293–312.

Congressional Research Services. 2021. "Cuba: US Policy Overview." *In Focus*, November 17. https://sgp.fas.org/crs/row/IF10045.pdf.

Contreras, Felix. 2017. "Review: Daymé Arocena, 'Cubafonía.'" NPR, March 2. https://www.npr.org/2017/03/02/517785441/first-listen-daym-arocena-cubafon-a.

Corona, Ignacio. 2017. "The Cultural Location/s of (US) Latin Rock." In *The Routledge Companion to Latina/o Media*, edited by María Elena Cepeda and Delores Inés Casillas, 241–258. New York: Routledge.

Corrales, Javier. 2004. "The Gatekeeper State: Limited Economic Reforms and Regime Survival in Cuba, 1989–2002." *Latin American Research Review* 39, no. 2: 35–65.

Cronin, Anne. 2007. "Regimes of Mediation: Advertising Practitioners as Cultural Intermediaries?" *Consumption, Markets & Culture* 7, no. 4: 349–369.

Cuban Art News. 2019. "In Havana, Personal Museums and the Bittersweet Influence of Sugar." August 21. https://cubanartnewsarchive.org/2019/08/21/havana-personal-museums-cuban-art-influence-of-sugar/.

Cuban News Agency. 2022. "Havana Club Expands around the World, Despite the US Blockade." *ACN*, November 7. http://www.cubanews.acn.cu/cuba/19349-havana-club-expands-around-the-world-despite-the-u-s-blockade.

Cuban Research Institute. 2020. "The Amparo Experience." YouTube. https://www.youtube.com/watch?v=Zivo1HZLuho.

Curtis, Wayne. 2006. *And a Bottle of Rum: A History of the New World in Ten Cocktails*. New York: Broadway Books.

Danilov, Victor. 1991. *Corporate Museums, Galleries and Visitor Centers: A Directory*. Westport, CT: Greenwood.

Davis, Julie Hirshfield. 2017. "Trump Reverses Pieces of Obama-Era Policies." *New York Times*, June 16. https://www.nytimes.com/2017/06/16/us/politics/cuba-trump-engagement-restrictions.html.

Davison, Hubie. 2012. "Mala in Cuba." *Inverted Audio*, August 29. https://inverted-audio.com/feature/mala-in-cuba/https://inverted-audio.com/feature/mala-in-cuba/.

Dawson, Marí Aixalá, and Pepin Argamasilla. 2006. *Bacardi: A Tale of Merchants, Family and Company.* Hamilton, Bermuda: Bacardi Global Brands.

Dawson, Marí Aixalá, and Facundo L. Bacardí. 2011. *Bacard Superior Rum Legacy Cocktail Book.* Kent, UK: Westerham Press.

del Rosal, Jorge. 2020. *The Rise of Bacardi: From Cuban Rum to Global Empire.* London: LID.

Denis, Richard. 2016. *Una Revista al Servicio de la Nación: Bohemia and the Evolution of Cuban Journalism (1908–1960).* Master's thesis, University of Florida.

Deutschmann, David, and Maria del Carmen Ari García. 2022. *The Che Guevara Reader: Writings on Politics and Revolution.* New York: Seven Stories.

Dickey, Jennifer. 2016. "Reviewed Work(s): Museo de la Revolución." *Public Historian* 38, no. 3: 155–161.

DiMaggio, Paul. 1982. "Cultural Entrepreneurship in Nineteenth-Century Boston: The Creation of an Organizational Base for High Culture." *Media, Culture & Society* 4, no. 1: 33–50.

Dinan, Donald. 2002. "An Analysis of the United States-Cuba 'Havana Club' Rum Case before the World Trade Organization." *Fordham International Law Journal* 26, no. 2: 337–376.

Domínguez, Esteban Morales. 2012. *Race in Cuba: Essays on the Revolution and Racial Inequality.* New York: Monthly Review Press.

Eads, Lauren. 2018. "Bacardí Hits Back at Pernod over 'Misleading' Forever Cuban Campaign." *The Drinks Business,* January 10. https://www.thedrinksbusiness.com/2018/01/bacardi-hits-back-at-pernod-over-misleading-havana-club-campaign/.

Effies. 2012. "Havana Club: Nothing Compares to Havana" Case Study. https://www.warc.com/content/paywall/article/euro-effies/havana_club_nothing_compares_to_havana/97818.

English, John F. 2002. "Winning the Culture Game: Prizes, Awards, and the Rules of Art." *New Literary History* 33, no. 1: 109–135.

Featherstone, Mike. 1991. *Consumer Culture and Postmodernism.* London: Sage.

Feld, Steven. 2000. "A Sweet Lullaby for World Music." *Public Culture* 12, no. 1: 145–171.

Fernandes, Sujatha. 2006. *Cuba Represent! Cuban Arts, State Power, and the Making of New Revolutionary Cultures.* Durham, NC: Duke University Press.

Ferrer, Ada. 2021. *Cuba: An American History.* New York: Scribner.

García Canclini, Néstor. 2001. *Consumers and Citizens: Globalization and Multicultural Conflicts.* Minneapolis: University of Minnesota Press.

Gaytán, Marie Sarita. 2014. *Tequila! Distilling the Spirit of Mexico.* Palo Alto, CA: Stanford University Press.

Gershon, Livia. 2019. "Racism of 19th Century Advertisements." *JSTOR Daily,* January 28. https://daily.jstor.org/the-racism-of-19th-century-advertisements/.

Gilmore, James, and Joseph Pine. 2007. *Authenticity: What Consumers Really Want.* Cambridge, MA: Harvard University Press.

Gjelten, Tom. 2009. *Bacardi and the Long Fight for Cuba.* New York: Penguin Books.

Gleadell, Colin. 2021. "Why Cuban Artists Are Leading the Political Revolt in Their Country." *The Telegraph,* June 2. https://www.telegraph.co.uk/luxury/art/cuban-artists-leading-political-revolt-country/.

Goffman, Erving. 1959. *The Presentation of Self in Everyday Life.* New York: Anchor Books.

REFERENCES

Goldman, Robert, and Stephen Papson. 1996. *Sign Wars: The Cluttered Landscape of Advertising*. New York: Guilford.

González, Pablo Alonso. 2014. "Museums in Revolution: Changing National Narratives in Revolutionary Cuba between 1959 and 1990." *International Journal of Heritage Studies* 21, no. 3: 264–279.

———. 2018. *Cuban Cultural Heritage: A Rebel Past for a Revolutionary Nation*. Gainesville: University Press of Florida.

Green, Alex. 2016. "Gilles Peterson's Havana Cultura Club—Havana Club Rumba Sessions." *Clash Music*, March 23. https://www.clashmusic.com/reviews/gilles-petersons-havana-cultura-club-havana-club-rumba-sessions/.

Grenier, Yvon. 2017. *Culture and the Cuban State: Participation, Recognition, and Dissonance under Communism*. Lanham, MD: Rowman & Littlefield.

Grosvenor, Melville. 1947. "Cuba, American Sugar Bowl." *National Geographic* [pamphlet].

The Guardian. 2010. "Havana Club Case Study." http://image.guardian.co.uk/sys-files/Guardian/logos/2010/08/27/HavanaClub.pdf.

———. 2015. "Racist, Sexist, Rude and Crude: The Worst of 20th Century Advertising." November 18. https://www.theguardian.com/media/gallery/2015/nov/18/racist-sexist-rude-crude-worst-20th-century-advertising-in-pictures.

Guevara, Ernesto. 1968. *Socialism and Man in Cuba*. Atlanta, GA: Pathfinder.

Gust, John, and Jennifer Mathews. 2020. *Sugar Cane and Rum: The Bittersweet History of Labor and Life on the Yucatan Peninsula*. Tucson: University of Arizona Press.

Hassan, Marcos. 2015. "Danay Suarez Speaks Out about Cuba-US Relations and Gender Hip Hop Politics." *Remezcla*, January 9. https://remezcla.com/features/music/interview-danay-suarez-cuba/.

Havana Club. 2012a. Visual Arts Project [Havana Cultura]. YouTube. https://www.youtube.com/watch?app=desktop&v=BIAKlNYjzMs.

Havana Club International. 2012b. "Cuba Año Cero." Alejandro González, YouTube. https://www.youtube.com/watch?v=xc4_2TphTbo.

———. 2014. *Havana Cultura Mix—The SoundClash!—The Film*. YouTube. https://www.youtube.com/watch?v=MjdgTFXXnvg.

———. 2015. "Havana Club Launches New Advertising Campaign, From the Heart." Press Release.

———. 2021. "Havana Club X Skepta 2.0." May 5. https://havana-club.com/en-ca/project/havana-club-x-skepta-2-0/.

———. 2022. "Havana Club X Bad Gyal." March 17. https://havana-club.com/en/project/havana-club-x-bad-gyal/.

———. 2023. "Today we celebrate Cuba's Maestros del Ron Cubano." LinkedIn. https://www.linkedin.com/posts/havana-club-international-s.a._cuban-rum-masters-tradition-declared-unesco-activity-7003775641397395456-WTQV/.

Hernández, Deborah P. 1998. "Dancing with the Enemy: Cuban Popular Music, Race, Authenticity, and the World-Music Landscape." *Latin American Perspectives* 25, no. 3: 110–125.

Hernández, Rafael. 2003. *Looking at Cuba: Essays on Culture and Civil Society*. Gainesville: University Press of Florida.

Hernández-Reguant, Ariana. 2012. "The Inventor, the Machine, and the New Man." In *Caviar with Rum: Cuba-USSR and the Post-Soviet Experience*, edited by Jacqueline Loss and José Manuel Prieto, 199–210. New York: Palgrave Macmillan.

hooks, bell. 1992. "Eating the Other: Desire and Resistance." In *Black Looks: Race and Representation*, edited by bell hooks, 21–40. Boston: South End Press.

Hopkins, Amy. 2017. "Havana Club Feud Heats Up." *The Spirits Business*, December 7. https://www.thespiritsbusiness.com/2017/12/pernod-hits-out-at-bacardis-forever-cuban-campaign/.

Hypebeast. 2020. "Havana Club and Skepta Pay Homage to Yoruba Culture." https://hypebeast.com/2020/7/havana-club-skepta-bottle-collaboration

Immigrant Archive Project. 2019. "Vanessa Garcia & Victoria Collado Discuss 'The Amparo Experience.'" https://immigrantarchiveproject.org/vanessa-garcia-victoria-collado-discuss-amparo-experience/.

Irish Times. 2009. "Man on a Cuban Mission: Gilles Peterson Was Sent to Seek Out Young, Urban Sounds of Cuba, and the Result Is a Record Featuring Some of the Finest." December 8. https://www.irishtimes.com/culture/music/roots-world-jazz/man-on-a-cuban-mission-1.786162.

Kent, James Clifford. 2019. *Aesthetics and the Revolutionary City: Real and Imagined Havana*. London: Palgrave Macmillan.

Kiely, Melita. 2019. "First Cuban Rum Production Joint Venture in 20 Years Agreed." *The Spirits Business*, November 12. https://www.thespiritsbusiness.com/2019/11/first-cuban-rum-production-joint-venture-in-20-years-agreed/.

Kiely, Melita. 2022. "Havana Club Collaborates with Rapper Frenna." *The Spirits Business*, May 4. https://www.thespiritsbusiness.com/2022/05/havana-club-collaborates-with-rapper-frenna/.

Knight, Franklin W. 1977. "Origins of Wealth and the Sugar Revolution in Cuba, 1750–1850." *Hispanic American Historical Review* 57, no. 2: 231–253.

Kochhar, Sarabdeep, and Juan Carlos Molleda. 2015. "The Evolving Links between International Public Relations and Corporate Diplomacy." In *International Public Relations and Public Diplomacy*, edited by Guy J. Golan, Sung Un Yang, and F. Dennis Kinsey, 51–72. New York: Peter Lang Publishing, Inc.

Laplante, Eduardo. 1857. *Ingenios de la Isla de Cuba*. Havana: Luis Marquier and Eduardo Laplante.

Lázaro, Javier. 2016. "Rum, Business, and Society in Cuba, 1832–1965." *Revista de Historia Industrial* 25, no. 63: 13–48.

Lears, Jackson. 2000. "From Salvation to Self-Realization: Advertising and the Therapeutic Ethos of Consumer Culture (1880–1930)." *Advertising and Society* 1, no. 1: 1–38.

León, Dermis P. 2001. "Havana, Biennial, Tourism: The Spectacle of Utopia." *Art Journal* 60, no. 4: 68–73.

Lepore, Jill. 2010. "Untimely: What Was at Stake in the Spat between Henry Luce and Harold Ross." *New Yorker*, April 12. https://www.newyorker.com/magazine/2010/04/19/untimely-jill-lepore.

L'Etang, Jacquie. 2009. "Public Relations and Diplomacy in a Globalized World: An Issue of Public Communication." *American Behavioral Scientist* 53, no. 4: 607–626.

Levinson, Sandra. 2015. "Nationhood and Identity in Contemporary Cuban Art." In *A Contemporary Cuban Reader: The Revolution Under Raúl Castro*, edited by Phillip Brenner, Marguerite Rose Jiménez, John Kirk, and William Leo Grande, 335–341. London: Rowman & Littlefield.

Lipsitz, George. 1994. *Dangerous Crossroads: Popular Culture, Postmodernism, and the Politics of Place*. London: Verso Books.

REFERENCES

Little Black Book. 2018. "M&C Saatchi and Havana Club Take to the Streets." May 14. https://lbbonline.com/news/mc-saatchi-and-havana-club-take-to-the-streets.

López, Antonio. 2010. "Cosa de Blancos: Cuban American Whiteness and the Afro-Cuban Occupied House." *Latino Studies* 8, no. 2: 220–243.

Los Angeles Times. 1995. "Foreign Investing Helping, Castro Says: He Calls the Change One of the Most Important Made to His Nation's Economy." February 9, 1995. https://www.latimes.com/archives/la-xpm-1995-02-09-fi-30127-story.html.

Loss, Jacqueline, and José Manuel Prieto. 2012. *Caviar with Rum: Cuba-USSR and the Post-Soviet Experience*. New York: Palgrave Macmillan.

MacCannell, Dean. 2013. *The Tourist: A New Theory of the Leisure Class*. Berkeley: University of California Press.

Maguire, Jennifer. 2014. "Bourdieu on Cultural Intermediaries." In *The Cultural Intermediaries Reader*, edited by Jennifer Maguire and Julian Matthews, 15–24. London: Sage.

M&C Saatchi. 2022. https://mcsaatchi.com.

Marschlich, Sarah. 2022. *Corporate Diplomacy: How Multinational Corporations Gain Organizational Legitimacy*. Wiesbaden: Springer.

Martínez, Juan A. 1994. *Cuban Art & National Identity: The Vanguardia Painters, 1927–1950*. Gainesville: University Press of Florida.

Matusalem. 2022. "The Origins of Matusalem Rum." https://www.matusalem.com/brand-facts/.

McAllister, Matthew. 2010. "But Wait, There's More! Advertising, the Recession, and the Future of Commercial Culture." *Journal of Popular Communication* 8, no. 3: 189–193.

McCracken, Grant. 1986. "Culture and Consumption: A Theoretical Account of the Structure and Movement of the Cultural Meaning of Consumer Goods." *Journal of Consumer Research* 13, no. 1: 71–84.

———. 1989. "Who Is the Celebrity Endorser? Cultural Foundations of Endorsement Process." *Journal of Consumer Research* 16, no. 3: 310–321.

McIntyre, Charles. 2010. "Designing Museum and Gallery Shops as Integral, Co-Creative Retail Spaces within the Overall Visitor Experience." *Museum Management and Curatorship* 25, no. 2: 181–198.

Mehaffy, Marilyn. "Advertising Race/Raceing Advertising: The Feminine Consumer-(-Nation): 1876–1900." *Signs* 23, no. 1: 131–174.

Miller, Anistatia R., and Jared M. Brown. 2010. *Champagne Cocktails*. London: Mixellany Books.

———. 2012. *Cuban Cocktails*. London: Mixellany Books.

———. 2013. *Shaken Not Stirred: A Celebration of the Martini*. New York: HarperCollins.

———. 2017. *The Spirit of Cane: The Story of Cuban Rum*. London: Mixellany Books.

Miller, Anistatia, Jared McDaniel Brown, Dave Broom, and Nick Strangeway. 2009. *Cuba: The Legend of Rum*. London: Mixellany Books.

Miller, Nicola. 2008. "A Revolutionary Modernity: The Cultural Policy of the Cuban Revolution." *Journal of Latin American Studies* 40, no. 4: 675–696.

Mintz, Sidney. 1985. *Sweetness and Power: The Place of Sugar in Modern History*. New York: Penguin Books.

Mistral Productions. 2022. Homepage. http://www.mistralproductions.com.

Mogul, John. 2019. *Promising Paradise: Cuban Allure, American Seduction*. Miami: The Wolfsonian–Florida International University.

Molleda, Juan-Carlos, and Marilyn Roberts. 2008. "The Value of 'Authenticity' in 'Glocal' Strategic Communication: The New Juan Valdez Campaign." *International Journal of Strategic Communication* 2, no. 3: 154–174.

Montgomery, David. 2016. "Havana Club vs. Havana Club: Inside the Rum War between Bacardi and Cuba." *Washington Post*, July 23. https://www.washingtonpost.com/business/havana-club-v-havana-club-inside-the-rum-war-between-bacardi-and-cuba/2016/07/22/57c32a06-2cb4-11e6-9b37-42985f6a265c_story.html.

Moore, Robin. 2006. *Music and Revolution: Cultural Change in Socialist Cuba*. Berkeley: University of California Press.

Morales, Emilio, and Joseph Scarpaci. 2011. *Marketing without Advertising: Brand Preference and Consumer Choice in Cuba*. New York: Routledge.

Morán, Elizabeth. 2012. "Visions of 19th-Century Cuba: Images of Blacks in the Work of Victor Patricio de Landaluze." In *Comparative Perspectives on Afro-Latin America*, edited by Kwame Dixon and John Burdick, 114–133. Gainesville: University Press of Florida.

Muhammad, Kahlil Gibran. 2019. "The Barbaric History of Sugar in America." *New York Times Magazine*, August 14. https://www.nytimes.com/interactive/2019/08/14/magazine/sugar-slave-trade-slavery.html.

Muse, Laura. 2012. "Ron y Rebelión: 'Phociona' or the History of the Cape Sisters and Their Fight for Nineteenth Century Cuban Independence." *International Journal of Cuban Studies* 4, no. 2: 179–199.

New York Times. 1936. "Cocktails Must Live up to Name: Court Decides Bacardi Drink Should Contain Product Implied by Label." April 29, 1936.

New York Times. 1937. "Advertising News and Notes: Bacardi to Gumbinner." September 17, 1937.

New York Times. 1940. "Advertising News and Notes." September 9, 1940.

Nodal, Roberto. 1986. "The Black Man in Cuban Society: From Colonial Times to the Revolution." *Journal of Black Studies* 16, no. 3: 251–267.

Numéro. 2022. "Havana Club and Frenna Launch 'A Toast to the Culture' Campaign." April 1. https://www.numeromag.nl/havana-club-and-frenna-launch-a-toast-to-the-culture-campaign/.

Odih, Pamela. 1999. *Advertising in Modern & Postmodern Times*. Thousand Oaks, CA: Sage.

Ortiz, Fernando. 1995. *Cuban Counterpoint: Tobacco and Sugar*. Durham, NC: Duke University Press.

Ortiz, Ricardo. 2007. *Cultural Erotics in Cuban America*. Minneapolis: University of Minnesota Press.

Otero, Lisandro, and Francisco Martinez Hinojosa. 1972. *Cultural Policy in Cuba*. Paris: UNESCO.

Pavlov, Yuri. 2012. "Socialism as the Main Soviet Legacy in Cuba." In *Caviar with Rum: Cuba-USSR and the Post-Soviet Experience*, edited by Jacqueline Loss and José Manuel Prieto, 229–238. New York: Palgrave Macmillan.

Pedraza, Silvia. 1996. "Cuba's Refugees: Manifold Migrants." In *Cuban Communism, 1959–2003*, edited by Irving Louis Horwitz and Jaime Suchliki, 308–328. Belmont, CA: Wadsworth.

Pérez, Louis. 2008. *Cuba in the American Imagination: Metaphor and the Imperial Ethos*. Chapel Hill: University of North Carolina Press.

REFERENCES

———. 1999. *On Becoming Cuban: Identity, Nationality, and Culture.* Chapel Hill: University of North Carolina Press.

Pernod Ricard. 1994. *1994 Annual Report.* https://assets.pernod-ricard.com/pr_ra_1994_fr.pdf.

———. 2003. *2003 Annual Report.* https://assets.pernod-ricard.com/pr_ar_2003_en.pdf.

———. 2006. *Annual Report: 2005/2006.* https://pernod-ricard.com/en/download/file/fid/8113/.

———. 2016. "Gilles Peterson and Havana Club Present: 'Havana Cultura Anthology, 2009–2017.'" August 12, 2016. https://www.pernod-ricard.com/en/media/gilles-peterson-and-havana-club-present-havana-cultura-anthology-2009-2017.

———. 2018. "A Message from Asbel Morales, Maestro Ronero del Ron Cubano Havana Club." January 31, 2018. https://www.pernod-ricard.com/en/media/message-asbel-morales-maestro-del-ron-cubano-havana-club.

Pertierra, Anna Cristina. 2011. *Cuba: The Struggle for Consumption.* Coconut Creek, FL: Caribbean Studies Press.

Peterson, Gilles. 2009. "From Our Correspondent: Gilles Peterson's Havana." *The Guardian*, December 19. https://www.theguardian.com/travel/2009/dec/20/havana-from-our-correspondent-peterson.

———. 2012. "How We Met: Mala and Gilles Peterson." *The Independent*, August 30. https://www.independent.co.uk/news/people/profiles/how-we-met-mala-gilles-peterson-8092750.html.

———. 2018. "Havana Cultura: Subelo Cuba." https://www.gillespetersonworldwide.com/blog/2018/5/21/havana-cultura-sbelo-cuba.

Phillips, Courtney. 2021. "Cuba Made Me." Vimeo. https://vimeo.com/432972101.

Pineau, Elizabeth, and Dominique Vidalon. 2015. "Pernod Prepares to Take Cuban-Made Rum to the United States." *Reuters*, May 19. https://www.reuters.com/article/cuba-havana-club/pernod-prepares-to-take-cuban-made-rum-to-the-united-states-idINL5N0Y93S320150519.

Pope, Daniel. 1983. *The Making of Modern Advertising.* New York: Basic Books.

———. 2003. "Making Sense of Advertisements." History Matters: The US Survey Course. http://historymatters.gmu.edu/mse/Ads/.

Potter, Andrew. 2010. *The Authenticity Hoax: How We Get Lost Finding Ourselves.* New York: Harper.

Purdom, Tim. 2012. "Havana Meets South London: The Story of Mala in Cuba." *Fact Magazine*, June 10. https://www.factmag.com/2012/06/10/havana-meets-south-london-the-story-of-mala-in-cuba/.

Ramos, Carmen. 2019. "Between Civilization and Barbarism: Víctor Patricio de Landaluze's Paintings during the Ten Year's War in Cuba (1868–1878)." In *Picturing Cuba: Art, Culture, and Identity on the Island and in the Diaspora*, edited by Jorge Duany, 30–50. Gainesville: University Press of Florida.

Rathbone, John Paul. 2010. *The Sugar King of Havana: The Rise and Fall of Julio Lobo, Cuba's Last Tycoon.* New York: Penguin Books.

Resident Advisor. 2022. "Gilles Peterson, Biography." https://ra.co/dj/gillespeterson/biography.

Rivero, Yeidy. 2009. "Havana as a 1940s–1950s Latin American Media Capital." *Critical Studies in Media Communication* 26, no. 3: 275–293.

Roderick, Leonie. 2016. "Havana Club Looks to Transform Rum's Image from Cheap to Premium." *Marketing Week*, December 9. https://www.marketingweek.com/havana-club-looks-transform-image-rum/.

Ron La Progresiva. 2023. "Forward Looking yet Anchored in Tradition." https://ronlaprogresiva.com/#:~:text=As%20the%20world%20falls%20in,to%20its%20bright%2C%20international%20future.&text=and%20Cuba%20opens%20up%20to%20the%20world.

Ron Perla del Norte. 2024. "The Pearl of the North." https://www.ron-perla-del-norte.com.

Rosaldo, Renato. 1989. "Imperialist Nostalgia." *Representations* 26: 107–122.

Rutter, Nick. 2015a. "Claudio." https://nick-rutter.com/havana-club-claudio.

———. 2015b. "Maestro Ronero." Ads of the World. https://www.adsoftheworld.com/campaigns/the-maestro-ronero.

Sainz, Juan de Dios. 1954. *Jose Arechabala, S.A. On Its 75th Anniversary, 1878–1953.* Cuba: N.P., 1954.

Sánchez, Lilia Vieyra. 2017. "*La Ilustración Española y Americana* (1869–1921): Producto Mercantil y Cultural." *Caleidescopio* 35/36: 15–42.

Sanger, J. W. *Advertising Methods in Cuba.* Washington, DC: U.S. Government Printing Office.

Saruski, Jaime, and Gerardo Mosquera. 1979. *The Cultural Policy of Cuba.* UNESCO. https://unesdoc.unesco.org/ark:/48223/pf0000032827.

Scarpaci, Joseph, Roberto Segre, and Mario Coyula. 2002. *Havana: Two Faces of the Antillean Metropolis.* Chapel Hill: University of North Carolina Press.

Schneider, Cynthia. 2006. "Cultural Diplomacy: Hard to Define, but You'd Know It if You Saw It." *Brown Journal of World Affairs* 13, no. 1: 191–203.

Schubert, N. 2018. "Bacardi Rum Takes Over Miami with New Campaign Art Collaboration." *Ocean Drive*, May 25. https://oceandrive.com/bacardi-rum-takes-over-miami-with-new-campaign-art-collaboration.

Schudson, Michael. 1984. *Advertising, the Uneasy Persuasion: Its Dubious Impact on American Society.* New York: Basic Books.

Schulman, Allan. 2016. *Building Bacardi: Architecture, Art, and Identity.* New York: Rizzoli.

Schwall, Elizabeth. 2012. *Dancing with the Revolution: Power, Politics, and Privilege in Cuba.* Chapel Hill: University of North Carolina Press.

Scott, Linda. 1994. "Images in Advertising: The Need for a Theory of Visual Rhetoric." *Journal of Consumer Research* 21, no. 2: 252–273.

Senate Judiciary Committee. 2004. "Testimony of Mr. Ramon Arechabala." U.S. Senate Committee on the Judiciary, July 13. https://www.judiciary.senate.gov/imo/media/doc/arechabala_testimony_07_13_04.pdf.

Sherry, John. 1987. "Advertising as a Cultural System." In *Marketing and Semiotics: New Directions in the Study of Signs for Sale*, edited by Jean Umiker-Sebeok, 441–462. Berlin, Boston: De Gruyter Mouton.

Slanted. 2013. *Cuba: The New Generation.* Karlsruhe, Germany: Slanted Publishers.

Slater, Russ. 2014. "Brazilian Love Affair: An Interview with Gilles Peterson." *Sounds and Colours*, May 26. https://soundsandcolours.com/articles/brazil/gilles-peterson-sonzeira-brazilian-music-24092/.

———. 2016. "Mala's Latest Album Takes Inspiration from Peru." *Sounds and Colours*, April 26. https://soundsandcolours.com/articles/peru/malas-latest-album-takes-inspiration-from-peru-32068/.

REFERENCES

Smith, Frederik. 2005. *Caribbean Rum: A Social and Economic History*. Gainesville: University Press of Florida.

Spencer, Neil. 2009. "Gilles Peterson Presents Havana Cultura." *The Guardian*, October 31. https://www.theguardian.com/music/2009/nov/01/gilles-peterson-havana-cultura.

Stempel, Jonathan. 2011. "Pernod Loses US Appeal on Bacardi Havana Club Rum." Reuters, August 4. https://www.reuters.com/article/bacardi-pernod-havanaclub-idAF N1E7731KP20110804.

Team Enterprises. 2022. "Taste the Real Havana Club and Become Part of the Story." https://teamenterprises.com/case_study/cs-havana-club-amparo-immersive/.

Tertz, Abram. 1960. *On Socialist Realism*. New York: Pantheon Books.

The Real Havana Club U.S. 2023. "Our Story." https://www.therealhavanaclub.com/us/en/our-story/.

Thompson, J. Walter. 2016. *The Promise of Cuba*. https://www.wundermanthompson.com/insight/the-promise-of-cuba.

Thornton, Sarah. 1996. *Club Cultures: Music, Media, and Sub-Cultural Capital*. Middletown, CT: Wesleyan University Press.

Thrift, Nigel. 1987. "The Fixers: The Urban Geography of International Commercial Capital." In *Global Restructuring and Territorial Development*, edited by Jeffrey Henderson and Manuel Castells, 203–233. London: Sage.

Tuch, Hans. 1990. *Communicating with the World: US Public Diplomacy Overseas*. London: Palgrave Macmillan.

UNESCO. 2022. "Knowledge of the Light Rum Masters." https://www.unesco.org/archives/multimedia/document-6013.

Urry, John. 1990. *The Tourist Gaze: Leisure and Travel in Contemporary Societies*. Thousand Oaks, CA: Sage.

Van Dijk, Teun. 2001. "Critical Discourse Analysis." In *Handbook of Discourse Analysis*, edited by Deborah Tannen, Heidi E. Hamilton, and Deborah Schiffrin, 352–371. Oxford: Blackwell.

Vásquez Raña, Mario. 1995. "Don Mario Vásquez Raña Entrevistó al Líder Revolucionario. *El Sol de Mexico*, January 30, sec. A, 20.

White House. 2016. "Remarks by President Obama to the People of Cuba." Office of the Press Secretary, March 22. https://obamawhitehouse.archives.gov/the-press-office/2016/03/22/remarks-president-obama-people-Cuba.

Williams, Alex. 2017. "The 'Esquire Man' Is Dead. Love Live the 'Esquire Man.'" *New York Times*, February 4. https://www.nytimes.com/2017/02/04/fashion/esquire-magazine-jay-fielden.html.

Williams, Raymond. 1980. "Advertising: The Magic System." In *Problems in Materialism and Culture*, edited by Raymond Williams, 170–195. London: Verso.

Wong, Steven. 2018. "With Interactive Theater Experience, Bacardi Stakes Claim to Authenticity." *A.List Daily*, April 12. https://www.alistdaily.com/lifestyle/bacardi-interactive-experience-amparo/.

Zhao, Xin, and Russell Belk. 2008. "Politicizing Consumer Culture: Advertising's Appropriation of Political Ideology in China's Social Transition." *Journal of Consumer Research* 35, no. 2: 231–244.

Index

Abdala Studios, 1–2
Absolut Vodka, 61, 102
advertising: as a cultural system, 141; economic function, 21, 46; history in Cuba, 28, 49, 74, 115, 123–24, 128; and ideology, 26, 37, 45, 70, 126, 138, 180; and marketplace logic, 17, 147–50; as post-racial fantasy, 131, 133–34; as public discourse, 90, 137, 140–41; and racism, 116, 123–28, 134; during Republican era, 9, 21, 25, 28, 143; restriction of, 14–15, 130; as rhetorical exchange, 35
advertising agencies: as brokers of authenticity, 16, 25; creative partners, 54, 56; in Cuba, 116, 123, 128; as cultural intermediaries, 19, 25, 20–21, 53, 123; new business pitch, 34; practices, 149–50; structure of, 35
Afro-Cubans: discrimination and oppression, 49–50, 111, 123, 130–31, 134; inclusion in Havana Club marketing, 24–25, 100, 128–29, 132–37; music, art, and culture, 1–2, 49–52, 55–56, 136; representation in art, 6, 76, 111–12, 116–117, 120; representation in early advertising, 43–44, 76, 115, 122, 125; rights and emancipation, 115, 118–20
"Aged Well" (advertising campaign), 83–84
aguardiente, 7
Álvarez, Pedro Castelló, 6. *See* also *Canción del Amor, La*
Amparo Experience, The, 69–70, 89–90
Anderson, Benedict, 22, 71, 90, 95
Appleton Estate, 13, 15

Archabala, José: commemoration of, 98, 107–9; early life, 9, 21, 107; founding of company, 9, 151–52; image and likeness, 87–88
Arechabala, Amparo, 69
Arechabala, Ramón, 11–12, 69, 85, 89
Arechabala family: business practices, 11, 81; expropriation and exile, 10–12, 21, 69–70, 72, 83, 85–87; importance to Cuba, 9, 72, 117, 153–54; partnership with Bacardí, 70, 83, 91; representation and erasure, 33, 82, 107, 109, 117, 153–54
Arocena, Daymé, 2, 65
Aroch, Guy, 24, 38–39, 131, 137
authenticity: historical, 112; jargon of, 137; and the marketplace, 4, 15–16, 147; natural, 40, 99; and race, 117, 132–34; referential, 38; staged, 100; urban, 133; western desire for, 17

Bacardí, Elvira. *See* Cape, Elvira
Bacardí, Emilio, 75, 95, 106–7, 115
Bacardí, Facundo: access to capital, 73, 106; distillation process, 27; early history, 73–74; representation of, 104, 111
Bacardí Ltd.: archives, 106; awards, 74–75, 122; as category leader, 17, 19, 36, 72; corporate memory, 71–73, 102–6; critiques of Cuba, 17, 71, 79–89, 93; early advertising, 74, 76–79, 113–15, 122, 124–26; economic importance to Cuba, 9, 71–72; exile, 70–71, 83, 91, 105; global structure, 21, 72, 78, 90, 103; Havana Club (Bacardí version), 69–71, 81–89; logo and packaging, 28, 74, 80; product positioning,

173

Bacardí Ltd (Cont)
  36, 124; public relations, 43, 70, 83–84, 103; and race, 111–16, 124–25; symbolic ties to Spain, 74–75, 104; trademark, 79–82, 146
Bad Gyal (Farelo I Solé), 68
Bar La Florida, 126–27. *See also* Floridita, La
Barré, Christian, 137
bartenders: representation in advertising, 2, 32, 42, 44, 76, 126; role in trademark dispute, 80; as target market, 35–36, 72, 89, 106, 109–10, 146
Basque country, 9, 152
Basque diaspora, 9
Batista, Fulgencio, 8, 84, 96
BBDO, 79, 83, 86
Black Tears Rum, 135–36
blurring, 80
Bohemia, 11, 76, 123–25, 129
Bosch, José (Pepin), 81
Bourdieu, Pierre: circuits of legitimation, 75; distinction, 18; doxa, 149–50; of power, 19, 151; theory of practice, 18–19
Bouteiller, León, 107
brand ambassadors, 103, 105, 110, 111
branding, 27, 64–65, 104, 122
brandy, 8, 26–27, 32
Brown, Jared, 109
Brownswood Records, 2, 21, 57, 60, 65
Buena Vista Social Club, 54–56, 58–59, 65

Canción del Amor, La (Álvarez), 6
Cape, Elvira, 95, 107
capital: cultural, 61, 63; economic, 20, 49, 61, 73, 75, 106; objectified, 75; social, 61, 73; subcultural, 131
capitalist realism, 45
Cárdenas, 9–11, 21, 29, 87, 118, 151–53
Carteles, 76, 123–24, 129
Casa Bacardí, 22, 94, 102–6, 111
Castelló, Pedro Álvarez, 6. *See* Álvarez, Pedro Castelló
Castro, Fidel: critiques of, 17, 84; and the Cuban Revolution, 15, 32, 51, 97, 130; and economic reform, 1, 3–4, 155; as embodiment of Cuba, 25; and nationalization, 69, 72, 98
Catalonian diaspora, 73
Cataño, 22, 102
Céspedes, Carlos Manuel de, 119–20
Charles W. Hoyte Advertising, 30, 126

Ciego de Ávila, 135
Cienfuegos, Camilo, 65, 96
Claudio, 40–41, 132
Coca-Cola, 6, 24, 78
Collado, Victoria, 69, 89
colonialism, 7–8, 112, 122, 146, 151
colorblind casting, 131–32
Columbus, Christopher, 7, 125–26
commodity fetishism, 40, 144
commodity sign, 79–80, 89
communism, 13, 24, 38, 141, 144
consumer culture, 16, 38
consumerism, 6, 141, 147
consumer society, 16, 123, 147
Cooder, Ry, 55, 65
Corporación Cuba Ron, 4, 13, 91, 146, 152–53. *See also* Cuba Ron, S.A.
corporate diplomacy, 142–43
corporeal travel, 99–100
Corte de Caña, 119
Cottin-Bizonne, Jérôme, 146
country-of-origin effect, 34, 76, 138
COVID-19 pandemic, 21, 64, 89, 102, 156
Cristal beer, 129–30
Cuba Libre, 8, 79
"Cuba Made Me" (advertising campaign), 43–46, 132
Cuban authenticity: Bacardí's claim to, 36, 70–71, 81, 85, 111; in the competitive landscape, 25, 136–37; and cultural intermediaries, 20, 137–38; and the diaspora, 70–71, 91; Havana Club's claim to, 14, 17, 26, 36, 39, 43, 46, 68; in Western imagination, 21–22
Cuban diaspora, 21–22, 70–71, 78, 85, 90–91, 134
Cuba Ron, S.A., 4, 13, 91, 146, 152–53. *See also* Corporación Cuba Ron
Cuba's wars for independence: and race, 112, 115–16, 121–22; references in art and advertising, 11, 78; and rum and sugar production, 8, 10, 75, 95, 121; U.S. participation in, 143
"Culto a La Vida, El" (advertising campaign), 36–37
cultural brokering, 28, 56, 105, 118, 123, 137, 156
cultural diplomacy, 3–4, 48, 51, 64, 142
cultural intermediaries, 18, 20, 25, 53, 116, 137–38
cultural policy in Cuba, 14, 50, 96
"Culture That Sugar Created, The," 130

INDEX

daiquiri, 8, 28, 76, 78, 84
Domínguez, Esteban Morales, 118, 133–34, 156
Domínguez, Nelson, 102
Dominican Republic, 17, 136
Don Junípero, 119–20
"Don't Tell Us We're Not Cuban" (advertising campaign), 85–87
Duggan, Ned, 90–91

EGREM studios, 55, 58–59
embargo: lifting of, 81, 145–47, 156; negative impact on Cuba, 55, 64; and US politics, 33, 81
Emilio Moreau Bacardí Municipal Museum, 95–96
Esquire, 30–32, 126, 129
exiles, 69–70, 83, 84–87, 149
expropriation, 11, 72, 80, 87, 89, 116

Fairbairn, Flora: background, 61–62; critiques of Havana Cultura, 63–64; goals for Visual Arts project, 21–22, 48, 62; partnership with M&C Saatchi, 49, 54; "Weight of an Island, Love of a People," 64
fields: cultural production, 18–21, 46, 48–49, 50–53, 150–51; of large-scale production, 53; of restricted production, 20
Fiesta en el Cobre, 8 de Septiembre en Santiago de Cuba, 111–12
Floridita, La, 126–27. See Bar La Florida
Fonseca, Roberto, 58–59
"Forever Cuban" (advertising campaign), 85–87, 91, 93
forgetting, 106, 117
Frenna (Francis Junior Edusei), 67
"From the Heart" (advertising campaign), 39–43, 46, 132

García, Vanessa, 69–70, 89
Generation Y, 148
Gilded Age, 84–85
Gilles Peterson Presents: Havana Cultura, the New Cuba Sound, 58
Gilles Peterson Presents: Havana Cultura Anthology, 58
Gilles Peterson Presents . . . Sonzeria: Brazil Bam Bam Bam, 57
Giraldilla, La, 13, 25, 33, 82, 98
globalization, 9, 36, 67, 91, 104, 111
González, Alejandro, 47, 62–63, 145

Gordejuela (city), *also* Gordejuexa and Gordexola, 9, 21, 152
Gordejuela (publication), 29, 88, 107–8, 152
Grito de Yara, 119
Guardian, The (UK), 35, 54–55, 58, 64–65
Guevara, Ernesto (Che): economic vision, 33, 130, 139; image and likeness, 65, 139; Museo de la Revolución, 96–97; socialist ideals, 41, 51, 96, 144

Habana Vieja, La, 21–22, 92, 97, 110, 139
Haiti, 106, 136
Haitian Revolution, 73
Hatuey, 125–26
Hatuey Beer, 125–26, 129
Havana: as economic center, 49, 97, 147; historic district, 21–22, 92, 97, 110, 139 (*see also* Habana Vieja, La); in popular imagination, 2, 38, 43, 45, 97, 138–39
Havana Biennial, 14, 20, 48, 55, 61, 63, 102
Havana Club Bara Privada, 117
Havana Club International: corporate history, 10–11, 107–10, 155; creative collaborations, 4, 13, 23, 67, 136; Cuban authenticity, 17, 19, 24, 34, 37–39, 48; economic importance to Cuba, 3–4, 20, 23, 107–8; global markets, 3, 34, 155–56; joint-partnership, 4, 13, 91, 145, 156; launch, 9–10, 30, 138; logo, 13, 25, 37, 82, 107, 139, 143; original recipe, 69, 81–85, 87; product line, 43–44, 92, 100, 102; product positioning, 13, 28, 30–32, 34, 36, 102, 126, 156; as state owned product, 33; target audience, 30–32, 35–36, 43, 125, 136; trademark, 17, 75, 81
Havana Club Museum of Rum: bar, 92, 101; *Conan in Cuba*, 92; critique of, 147; as exhibition space, 61, 63, 94, 102; gift shop and bar, 100–101; history, 98, 110; location, 22, 94, 110; and the press, 58, 93–94; tour experience, 98–100, 104, 112
Havana Cultura: contemporary focus, 56; as cultural diplomacy, 11, 64, 142; global turn, 67–68; launch, 61; promotion of, 58, 60, 65; selection process, 54; strategic purpose, 4, 7, 47
Havana Cultura Mix—The SoundClash!, 1–5
Havana Cultura: The Search Continues, 65
Havanista, 146
Havanización, 3
Helman, David M., 44

Hemingway, Ernest, 32, 101, 126
Hemmings, Jeremy, 43
Hernández, Rafael, 19–20, 25, 37, 47, 90, 156
Hernández, Sachie, 48, 61, 64
Hinton, Adam, 42

ideologies: capitalist, 19, 26, 53, 71, 115, 138, 141; colonial, 120; racial, 53, 115–16, 133, 138; socialist, 5, 19, 22, 45–46, 50
Ilustración Artística, La (Spain), 76, 113–14
Ilustración España y Americana (Spain), 120–21
imperialist nostalgia, 56, 112
Ingenio La Esperanza, 99
ingenios, 5, 117–18
Ingenios de Cuba, Los, 5. See also Laplante, Eduardo
"Isla de Azúcar" art exhibit, 5–6
Island Rum Co. S.A., 134

Jamaican rum, 13, 15, 17, 28, 32, 107, 136
Jameson Whiskey, 34
jimador, 16
José Arechabala S.A.: business strategies, 10–11, 152; corporate memory, 10, 88, 107; corporate motto, 10; expropriation, 11; importance to Cuba, 9, 11, 107–8; marketing and branding, 27, 29, 122; product line, 10, 30
J. Walter Thompson, 123, 135, 146–50

Kaspen, 17
Kennedy, John F., 33
Korine, Harmony, 24, 38–39, 131, 137

Lagrimas Negras, 137–38
Landaluze, Victor Patricio de, 119–20
Laplante, Eduardo, 118
Lawrence, Mark (Mala), 59–60, 67
Lawrence C.B. Gumbinner Advertising, 76
long distance nationalism, 22, 71, 90

M&C Saatchi: organizational structure, 4, 34; partnerships, 48, 53, 56; and race, 116–17, 131–32; strategy, 3, 13, 24, 35–36, 38
M&C SaatchiGAD, 34
maestro roneros, 40–42, 93, 110, 132
Mala in Cuba, 59–60
mambises, 120
marketplace logic, 14, 16, 22, 51–52, 142
market segmentation, 147, 150
Martí, José, 95, 97, 116, 122, 130

Matanzas, 9, 118, 151
Matusalem Rum, 17, 28, 122, 129
Mialhe, Frédéric, 118–19
Miami, 21, 69, 83, 86, 89–90, 92, 148–49
Miller, Anastatia, 109–10
Mistral Productions, 2, 4
modernity, 2, 16, 123–24, 138
mojito, 8, 40, 42, 58
Morales, Asbel, 41–42, 93, 110, 132
Morales Rum, 13, 28
Moreau, Lucia Victoria Amalia, 73–74, 104, 106
Moreau, Pedro Benjamin, 73, 106
Munne, John, 107
museums: corporate museums, 98, 100, 102, 104, 112; economic importance to Cuba, 94–95, 97; as ideological state apparatuses, 94–97; and power, 95
Myers's Rum, 32
mystification, 111

Napoleon, 95, 97
nationalization, 72, 81, 85, 87, 109
neocolonialism, 151
"New Man," the, 41, 96
New Yorker, 30–31, 76–77, 126
New York Times, 30, 32, 76, 126–27
"Nothing Compares to Havana" (advertising campaign): creative execution, 37–39, 42, 131–32, 142; socialist implications, 37, 45–46, 134, 142

Obama, Barack, 93, 145, 157
O'Brien, Conan, 92–93
Oficina del Historiador de La Habana Vieja (OHCH), 97
Orientalism, 15, 122
Ortíz, Fernando, 7, 133

Pernod-Ricard: corporate history, 33; partnership with Cuban state, 3, 13, 70, 81, 91, 152, 155; partnership with M&C Saatchi, 4, 34; product portfolio, 34; public statements, 36, 40, 47, 56, 93, 109
Peterson, Gilles: as brand ambassador, 1–2, 21, 56, 58, 63, 65; early life and career, 56–57; global ethos, 66–67; work with third-world musicians, 54, 57–60, 67
Phillips, Courtney, 43–45, 132
post-Special Period aesthetic, 3, 39, 139
professional habitus, 53
Promise of Cuba, The, 146–50

INDEX

public diplomacy, 92, 142–43
Puerto Rico, 21–22, 70, 72, 90, 94, 102–5, 111

racelessness, 116, 122, 130
racism: in advertising, 113–14; in Cuban society, 49, 51, 116–18, 134; in rum production, 111–12
Ramírez, Paul, 69–70, 89
Renié, François, 47, 56
Republican Era: and advertising, 23, 38, 79, 83–84, 122–26, 139; and the arts, 49; and consumerism, 123, 138; and racism, 3, 116, 133
rhum agricole, 27
Rhum Clement, 15
rhum industriel, 27
Rhum Vieux, 122
Ron Añejo, 27, 87
Ron Castillo, 122
Ron de las Tres Negritas, 122
Ron Diplomático, 13
Ron La Progresiva, 135
Ron Legendario, 134, 136–37
Ron Marno, 32, 129
Ron Mulatta, 134, 136
Ron Perla del Norte, 153
Ron Tutankamen, 122
Ron Viejo Palau, 122
Ron Vigía, S.A., 135
Ron Zapaca, 61
Rum: distillation, 27, 99, 110, 136; division of labor, 40–42, 132; early consumption, 8, 26–27; legitimization, 27, 122; regulation of, 7–8, 16, 75, 121; symbolic consumption, 26–28, 101
rum collins, 28
Rum Negrita, 30, 129
Rutter, Nick, 40–41, 137

Saatchi, Charles, 62, 100, 113, 137
Saatchi, Maurice, 62, 137
Saco, José Antonio, 116, 133
Sánchez, Cecilia, 96
Sanger, J. W., 14–15
Santero Rum, 134, 136–37
Santiago de Cuba, 7, 17, 73–74, 80, 104–7, 115, 118, 122
scarcity, 13, 26, 32, 100
Schenley Import Corporation, 76
semiotics, 16, 82, 141
sherry, 26–27, 120
sign wars, 71

Sitges, 73, 95, 105
Skepta (Joseph Junior Adenuga), 67
slavery: abolition, 119; representation of, 111–12, 119, 134; and sugar production, 5, 7–9, 117, 151; and violence, 7–8, 22, 117–18
Socialism and Man in Cuba, 144
Socialist realism, 45, 50
Soviet Union, 13, 15, 33, 45, 50, 62, 134, 145, 148, 155
Special Period in a Time of Peace: and the arts, 51, 97, 143; austerity and disillusionment, 51, 62, 134, 145, 148; economic reforms, 3, 13, 52–53, 97, 148
Suárez, Danay, 58–59, 65–66
sugar production: impact on Cuban culture, 5–6, 130, 133; representation in art and advertising, 6, 40–41, 117–20; under Spanish colonization, 6–7, 17–18, 109; under U.S. occupation, 6, 8, 49; use of slave labor, 117–18, 121 (*see also* slavery)

Taínos, 7, 28, 74, 125–26
tarnishment, 80
Team Enterprises, 18, 70, 89
Telegraph, The (UK), 55, 64
Ten Years' War, 119–20
tequila, 16, 18, 26, 34, 61
therapeutic ethos, 124
therealhavanaclub.com, 87–89
tourism: and the arts, 5, 55, 58, 61; economic importance to Cuba, 15, 64, 93, 97, 102, 139, 143; foreign investment in, 33, 155; and race, 134; during Republican era, 8, 55, 76
tourist gaze, 99
trademarks, 79–80
travel industry, 15, 138
"Traves de Los Años" (advertisement), 29–30
Triangle Trade, 7
Trinidad, 21, 118, 139, 154

UNESCO: list of intangible heritages, 110; world heritage site, 97
"Un Olor Que Entra Por Mi Ventana" exhibit, 47–48
urban cultural explorers, 35
U.S. military occupation: impact on rum industry, 71, 74, 121, 151; and North American interests, 6, 8, 14; representation in advertising, 78

Vizcaya, La (coat of arms), 10, 33, 82, 152
Vizcaya, La (distillery), 9, 107, 152–53

wars for independence: impact on rum industry, 4, 10, 75, 121; promise of racial equality, 112, 115–16, 121–22; role of Bacardí family, 95, 106–7; US intervention, 6, 8, 78–79, 143
W. A. Taylor and Co., 30, 126

Wenders, Wim, 55, 65
wine industry, 8, 15–16, 26–27, 82, 99, 120
World music, 52, 55, 60, 65, 67

X Alfonso, 59

Yoruban culture, 67, 134, 154

Zafras de Antaño, 117

About the Author

Christopher Chávez is the Carolyne S. Chambers Distinguished Professor of Advertising and director of the Center for Latina/o and Latin American Studies (CLLAS) in the School of Journalism and Communication at the University of Oregon. He is the author of *The Sound of Exclusion: NPR and the Latinx Public* and *Reinventing the Latino Television Viewer: Language, Ideology, and Practice*.

Isle of Rum